HISTORIC GARDENS
of WORCESTERSHIRE

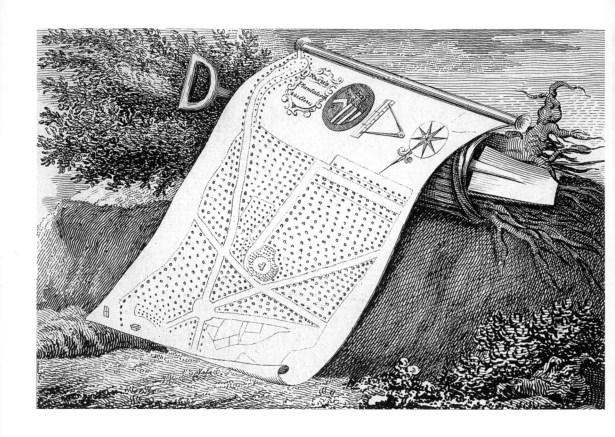

HISTORIC GARDENS
of WORCESTERSHIRE

Timothy Mowl

TEMPUS

For Jeffrey Haworth

The publication of this volume has been made possible by a grant from

THE LEVERHULME TRUST

to cover all the necessary research work

Frontispiece: 'Nash's Plantation' *from T R Nash's* Collections for
the History of Worcestershire *of 1799 Bristol University Special Collections*

First published 2006

Tempus Publishing Limited
The Mill, Brimscombe Port,
Stroud, Gloucestershire, GL5 2QG
www.tempus-publishing.com

© Timothy Mowl, 2006

British Library Cataloguing in Publication Data.
A catalogue record for this book is available from the British Library.

ISBN 0 7524 3654 6

Typesetting and origination by Tempus Publishing Limited
Printed in Great Britain

Contents

The Leasowes (detached)

Arley Castle

Hagley
Field House • Clent Grove
Broome

Bewdley

Winterdyne
Castle Bourne
Church House

Kidderminster

Blackstone Hermitage

Stone • Harvington

Stourport-on-Severn

Bromsgrove • Alvechurch

Areley Kings • Redstone Hermitage

Hewell
Grange

Redditch

Tenbury Wells

Dunley • Hartlebury

Brick House Farm

Webbs of Wychbold

Kyre

Pool House Astley • Astley Towne House

Hanbury

Abberley

Chateau Impney

Shurnock

Ombersley

Droitwich Spa

Holt • Westwood • Hadzor

Mere

Witley Court • Cockshutt Farm

Thorngrove

Inkberrow

Bevere

Huddington

Worcester

Rous Lench

Leigh Court

Spetchley Park

Pershore

Cleeve Prior

Madresfield

Holland House
Croome Park • Cropthorne

Great Malvern

Old Rectory
Birlingham •

Evesham

Elmley
Castle

Little Malvern

Strensham • Bredons
Norton Manor

Abbey House

Broadway
Russell House
Luggers Hill
Court Farm

Castlemorton
Bannut Tree
House

Bell's Castle

Bredon

Conderton

Birtsmorton

Overbury

Pull Court

Kemerton Priory & Court

Acknowledgements

My first thanks go to Professor Sir Richard Brook and his Trustees at the Leverhulme Trust whose generous funding of the research for this study, the last one on Cornwall and the next one on Oxfordshire has made the present Worcestershire travelling and garden visiting a positive delight rather than a financial worry. I am most indebted to Jeffrey Haworth of the National Trust who has shared with me his extensive knowledge of the county's houses and their owners and to whom this book is dedicated. Thanks also to Paul Stamper of English Heritage who made all the Historic Register of Parks and Gardens entries available and who has offered his perceptive insights into the landscapes and gardens. John Comins of the Hereford and Worcester Gardens Trust has also supported the venture and been most informative on Hewell Grange. I must acknowledge my debt to Richard Lockett's *Survey of Historic Parks and Gardens in Worcestershire*, without which I would have missed many important historic sites; also to Catherine Gordon's invaluable study *The Coventrys of Croome*.

Other owners, friends, colleagues and Bristol University MA Garden History students who have been particularly helpful include: Lord Sandys, Professor Hugh Edmondson, Lord Cobham, Nicholas Kingsley, Dianne Barre, Tom Oliver, Kate Felus, Marion Mako, Clare Hickman, David Lambert, Tom Williamson, Jennifer Meir, Elizabeth Owen, Rosemary Lauder, André Rogger, Sue Grice, Stuart Prior, Paul Underwood, Angie Sheasby, Lady Morrison, Peter Hughes, Tim West, Peter Cook, Brian Thorp, Graham Banner, Joyce Purnell, Rosalie Dawes, Tim & Lesley Smith, Tony & Linda Tidmarsh, Sheila Harris, Timothy Gwyn-Jones, Mrs Lane, Brian Powell, Sophie Webster, Dean Butler, Brian Bolam, Jane Carr, Penelope Bossom, Mike Pengelly, Ben Holland-Martin, Jim & Janet Sheridan, Noel Sinclair, Kay & Red Haslem, Michael & Jill de Navarro, Lord Birdwood, Josephine Elwes, Annette Smith, Mr & Mrs Dick Hickton, Pip Webster, Elizabeth Atkins, Pat Summers, Paddy Parsons, Peter Cooper, Matt Darby, Adrian & Meriel Darby, Steve Worrallo, Victoria Trevelyan, Nigel Goodman, Michael Darvill, Louisa & James Arbuthnott, Peter & Jean Reynolds, Laura Valentine, Camilla Costello, Louise & David Needham and Michael Cousins.

I would like to make special mention of the Croome archivist, Jill Tovey, who was so helpful in disentangling the complex landscape at Croome and Robin Whittaker and Lisa Snook for their help with archival documents at Worcestershire Record Office.

Ann Pethers of the Bristol University Arts Photographic Unit has photographed and developed the archival images from my own university's Special Collections. I must thank Michael Richardson once again for bringing many important texts to my notice. Peter Kemmis Betty, Fran Gannon, Laura Perehinec and Tom Sunley have been an efficient and enthusiastic team at Tempus, and Douglas Matthews has compiled another thorough index. My agent, Sara Menguc, has been a constant support and encouragement as I have endeavoured to keep to my annual schedule with the series in tandem with researching and writing a major biography on William Kent.

As with all the books in this series, *Historic Gardens of Worcestershire* has been researched alongside my teaching of Bristol's University's MA in Garden History, so I must thank my Co-Director, Michael Liversidge, for his advice on matters art historical and Mark Horton in my new department of Archaeology and Anthropology on matters archaeological. My friend and collaborator on architectural studies, Brian Earnshaw, has accompanied me on all the garden visits, undertaken several areas of the research and done his usual intellectually combative job of editing the text at manuscript stage. My wife, Sarah, and daughter, Olivia, joined me on two early visits to Stourport and Bewdley where we all enjoyed Black Country hospitality. My son, Adam, was too busy settling into Corpus Christi, Oxford, but as Oxfordshire is my next county I hope to see more of him in his university city.

Timothy Mowl, Bristol, Winter 2006

Introduction

A county of elusive character

Worcestershire has come as a salutary but stimulating shock to my garden expectations. This series was planned on the premise that each of England's ancient counties, even Rutland and Bedfordshire, was a distinct horticultural kingdom where an interaction of forces – social, historical, climatic and geological – had developed a unique and valuable garden history, which deserved to be celebrated separately, away from stale generalisations about 'English Garden History'. It was unfortunate that the first four counties covered by the series – Gloucestershire, Dorset, Wiltshire and Cornwall – had, despite their rich individuality and many differences, a certain sameness of hard geological bones: limestone, chalk and granite, and the same tame, even grudging, river systems. The result was that each of the four county books was trapped into following roughly the same sequence of stylistic chapters, from a remote, in the case of Cornwall a prehistoric, past through the predictable garden periods: Tudor, Formal, Arcadian, Picturesque and the rest, to the twentieth-century contemporary.

Worcestershire has been refreshingly different. No one would ever describe it as a hard county. The sun seemed to shine generously while I was walking its gardens, yet the county came across as wet, littered with ponds and a profusion of wide, water-filled moats, a shire divided by three rivers – the Severn, the Teme and the Avon – all inclined to flood incontinently. Lowland Worcestershire, and most of Worcestershire is lowland, is a place of soft red soils and mud, its fields are studded with the disused marl pits which have produced the salmon pink bricks of its towns and farmhouses. Those parts of the county, however, which are not moist and low-lying have gardens of quite different character and development. This meant that certain chapters have had to be devoted to a single important garden like Croome Park, or a single influential garden designer like Alfred Parsons, while others concentrate on mini-regions; which has quite broken up the usual march through chronological periods. Those mini-regions include that long belvedere of hills running north from cool, intellectual Malvern to Abberley; the gnome-land of hermitages, cliff walks and cave houses hollowed out from sandstone around Wolverley and Bewdley; that limestone region of upper class retirees around Bredon Hill; the moats and intricate half-timbered farms of de-forested Feckenham, near Redditch; and lastly, the exciting southern fringe of the industrial Black Country where the natives talk as if they were reciting the *Anglo-Saxon Chronicle*.

That makes five atypical regions in one small county. So is Worcestershire raw, direct north-country in character, or superior, reserved southern? Neither cap quite fits; even a Midland Mercian identity is suspect. It should really be a Welsh Marcher county like Shropshire and Herefordshire. Worcester city was the usual base camp for a royal army out to subdue the Welsh; and Ludlow, seat of the Council of the Marches, lies a mere 6 miles from one of Worcestershire's battered arms of land around Kyre Park. The trouble is that the county does not have one inch of Welsh border. That battered look is another Worcestershire characteristic. If it had defended itself resolutely it would be a much bigger shire than it is. On a map, especially a pre-1850 map, the county resembles an exploding pudding with island pieces flying off into other counties like Warwickshire and Staffordshire, while other parishes have been grabbed from Gloucestershire to compensate and a long arm reaches out to snatch the loveliest of Cotswold towns, Broadway, from the county to which it should really belong.

It is as if Worcestershire never had a strongly entrenched, landowning family of aristocrats like the Beauforts and the Berkeleys in Gloucestershire or the Brydges in Herefordshire to protect its boundaries when parliamentary committees began interfering, which is largely true. Worcestershire, like County Durham, was a bishop's county, though not a sturdy prince bishop's as Durham was. The Bishop of Worcester was easily the biggest landowner in the county. John Doharty's 1745 map of Worcestershire in the County Record Office is enormous, because it has to survey all the manors that the county gentry held on lease from the bishop.[1] Ruling from at least three palaces, though usually a mild old gentleman in the evening of his days, the bishop was the county's leading feudal lord. He had a diocese that extended, before Henry VIII shook the boundaries up, right down the Severn to include Gloucester and Bristol. He was seriously rich.

When Queen Elizabeth came on one of her slow, splendid and expensive progresses to the county in 1575 she automatically stayed first with the bishop for several days at his Hartlebury Castle. Then, after a week in Worcester with church services, speeches and hunting, she went, still escorted by the bishop, to gratify the Savages, Worcestershire's leading lay aristocracy, in their new, not very impressive house, Elmley Castle, down on the Gloucestershire border below Bredon Hill. The Savages managed to put up an impressively complex sundial (*1*) in the gardens to mark her visit. Stone balls pivoted on the top of a slotted column, which looks as if it could tell the time in Tokyo and Valparaiso; the mansion has been demolished and the sundial stands now in Elmley Castle churchyard. The bishop remained in attendance to escort the queen to her next stop in Gloucestershire at Sudeley Castle. On the county border, in the presence of the gentry of both shires, 'there receiving her Majestie', she said to the Lord Bishop of Worcester:

'My lord, I wold talk with you', Who alighted from his horse: to whom, after some private talk had by her Majestie unto him, she sayd, 'My lord, I pray you commend me

1 *This sundial, now in the churchyard of Elmley Castle, was first set up to look scientific in the gardens of the Castle when Queen Elizabeth stayed a night with the Savages in 1575 on her progress into Worcestershire*

hartelie to the bailiffs of Worcester, and to the brethren and to the whole citie…I like as well them as I ham liked of any people in all my progressive tyme in all my lyff'.[2]

Which 'comfortable commendations and sayings of her Majestie towards the citie',[3] the bishop faithfully reported to the bailiffs and brethren on his return. To their gratification, Elizabeth had even managed to squeeze out a few genuine tears as she left the gates of her loyal city. So the bond was real and the bishop had tied the knot. It would be in the next century that the Earls of Coventry at Croome rose to foremost county ranking and the century after that, the nineteenth, before the brilliant and artistic seventh Earl Beauchamp brought Madresfield to the same.

So Worcestershire is a quiet county, singularly lacking in aggressively fortified castles, a little indeterminate perhaps, but all the more rewarding to explore because of that multiplicity of parts. Certain star gardens, of the 80-odd visited, remain especially bright in the memory, often for their guarded privacy and difficulty of access. Scrambling over the churchyard wall at Leigh, a few miles south-east of Worcester, to find two Jacobean banquet houses, axial to their house and now fronting an empty lawn, was like stumbling into one of Kip and Knyff's engraved parkscapes of 1707. Then there were the gloomily haunted gardens of Huddington, haunted not by the ghosts of the tortured Gunpowder plotters, but by the ghosts of so many other county gardens from which the Edmondsons have rescued valuable fragments and even whole buildings. The fifth of November would be the perfect day to enjoy Huddington as the short afternoon was closing in. That oddly pagan grove of plane trees around the serpentine water at Overbury Court, near Bredon, was a more wholesome pleasure. Why were plane trees planted so often on city streets, but so rarely in gardens when they have the most beautiful trunks, grow to a giant size and are very long lived?

On the theme of trees, two more gardens deserve a special mention. Ombersley has an arboretum so widely spaced and gentlemanly that every great tree remains a memory with that 120ft Wellingtonia in front of the house most memorable of all. It has an inside canopy of sweeping branches as well as a cathedral-like outer spire. In contrast, Rous Lench's trees are dark and restrained, but among the many gardens of yew hedges visited in this or any county Rous Lench is the most various with its three avenues of funereal hedges climbing a steep hill and three terraces of the same criss-crossing them to make garden room after garden room.

Just two more gardens deserve special mention. First that maze of whimsical poetry which Veronica Adams and Mike Roberts have devised to fill the walled garden at Birtsmorton. While the modern gardens of other counties carry abstract or sexually explicit sculpture, Birtsmorton, in a gentle, unassuming Worcestershire way, has peopled its grounds with shepherds, shepherdesses and naughty children, laughing and smiling. The last star garden of the eight, and a personal favourite of mine, is Witley Court, simply for the astonishing beauty of its restored Perseus fountain (*2*). Chatsworth has nothing to equal it and nothing in Versailles is superior. When English Heritage can have the patience, the funding and the skill to restore Perseus to life there cannot be much amiss with the nation's care for its gardens.

The restored Perseus leads naturally to the subject of restoration and the National Trust's courageous restoration or recreation, it is hard to choose the most appropriate word, of two of the county's most historically important, but almost lost, gardens: the formal seventeenth-century layout at Hanbury Hall, near Droitwich, and the Lancelot Brown and Robert Adam Picturesque Arcadia at Croome Park, near Great Malvern.

It was easy in the past, if not to despair of the National Trust, then merely to salute its middle class *bien pensant* airs and herbal soap containers. But in this county, under the thoughtful and imaginative direction of its local Historic Buildings Representative (as he was originally styled), Jeffrey Haworth, the Trust has saved, and more than saved, it has recreated gardens of two sharply contrasted periods from the scantiest of remains: muddy pools and broken buildings. The result has been educational in the best sense. In restored Hanbury (*3*) it is now possible to understand the limitations as well as the delights of those vast formal layouts captured in the pages of Kip and Knyff's *Britannia Illustrata*. In restored Croome the whole process, artistic and engineering, of making something out of a tract of land that was previously nothing, can be traced, enjoyed and criticised. The old illustrations have come to life and the National Trust deserves

2 *James Forsyth's Perseus and Andromeda Fountain was constructed for the Earl of Dudley in the Nesfield garden that fronted Samuel Daukes' south elevation of Witley Court, challenging pomp with complexity*

3 *The National Trust's restoration of the Sunken Parterre at Hanbury Hall has brought to life the engravings of Kip and Knyff's* Britannia Illustrata

the warmest congratulations for taking the risk. Criticism was not only inevitable, but has also been positive. In the first of these two gardens can now be experienced what the young Lancelot Brown was fighting against, and in the second what his first, gallant, but imperfect solution was. Walking them is better than reading any number of garden books; the Trust can afford to rethink most of its garden properties.

1

An inland county curiously obsessed by water

Worcestershire is, by English standards, very moderate in size, yet it has 111 moated medieval sites recorded by the *Victoria County History*.[1] Even that turns out to be a conservative estimate as, according to David Wilson's *Moated Sites*, the county has 146.[2] Perversely, one of the county's few inhabited castles and the most aggressive looking one, Holt Castle north of Worcester, has no trace of a moat, which casts some doubt on the usual theory that a moat was a defensive feature. Holt stands proudly above a broad terrace in the middle of its garden (4), and that was where King Richard II presided, on a visit in the 1380s, over a jousting tournament while staying at the castle home of his friend, Sir John de Beauchamp.[3] The steep little cliff below the terrace was presumably considered an adequate protection.

The John Doharty map of 1745 illustrates a timbered gatehouse in the forecourt of the castle.[4] This has gone, but for an authentic frisson of a genuine medieval garden feature there is, up on raised ground to the right of the entrance forecourt, a narrow doorway in a crumbling stone wall. This leads to a short terraced walk, now planted with tree peonies, that runs at right-angles to the tilt-yard terrace and is backed now, as it was perhaps then, by an orchard. The tilting terrace is clearly shown on a sketch in the Gough collection in the Bodleian Library, Oxford (5), of the 'South-East View' of the Castle taken on 9 September 1721.[5] By then its southern edge had been dramatised by pyramidal conifers and there was a pyramidal-roofed garden house sited on the orchard wall. Otherwise Holt Castle's gardens are Edwardian in date.

Many Worcestershire moats surround a house so closely that the house walls rise out of the water; others are dug around substantial island areas with a house set in the middle on dry land. Others again lie in the fields or amongst trees with no sign that they ever contained anything but perhaps a garden that has now returned to brushwood and trees. Many of these moats still brim with water, varying in depth, often as wide as 15-20ft, their banks, though overgrown, supported by stone or brickwork. These moats can, particularly in autumn, be mildly beautiful in themselves, overshadowed by trees, rich with water lilies and water plants, and a notable resource for wildlife. It needs to be stressed that 146 is a remarkable number of such features in such a limited area. Coming to Worcestershire from counties with harder geological bones of limestone, chalk or granite − Gloucestershire, Wiltshire and Cornwall − has been a topographical culture shock. Ten, or at the most twenty, such broad, roughly square moated enclosures was the previous county average; so from the medieval to the Tudor period these multiple moats must be at the heart of any survey of Worcestershire's first garden layouts. They are a peculiarly Midlands phenomenon, and certainly another clear proof that no generalisations can usefully be made about English garden history, which needs, if it is to be accurate, to be county based.

By a happy accident the first Worcestershire house and garden visited on this county survey was Birtsmorton Court (*colour plate 1*) down in the south of the county a few miles west of Tewkesbury.[6] At the time it seemed an absolute prodigy of picturesque beauty, a house in a hundred. Since then there have been so many more that it has come to seem just another outrageously romantic moated house among dozens: a typical example of the county's complex of house, moat and garden. Because it is so typical in its arrangement of parts it is worth examining Birtsmorton Court and grounds in some detail before custom stales novelty, as many of its features will be found again in gardens all over the county. There are also some clues at Birtsmorton as to the mystery around this moated profusion; but there will inevitably be distractions from the brilliant modern garden which has been laid out by Veronica Adams, with ironwork by Mike

4 *The lower terrace of the garden at Holt Castle is assumed to have been the tilt-yard where Richard II presided over a joust. It is now laid to lawn and planted with formal yew hedges*

5 *A 1721 sketch of Holt Castle showing the former tilt-yard dramatised by conical bushes.* Bodleian Library, Oxford, Gough Maps 33, fol.73v

Roberts, within the original confines of the fortified fourteenth-century manorial complex. A garden is an organic creation, one like Birtsmorton grows over a period of several centuries, and while the Adams-Roberts layout may sometimes distract from consideration of Birtsmorton's original medieval grounds, it would be wrong to cut modern planting out, leaving it for discussion in a later chapter. So loggias and herbaceous borders will be presented alongside the fourteenth-century features, even though Birtsmorton has one of the most impressive modern gardens in a county not as well endowed with experimental planting as might be expected, given the wealth of retirees from neighbouring Birmingham.

The Court lies behind Birtsmorton church, up a short drive and among trees that hide it until the very last moment when it is revealed like some improbable film set for a cloak and dagger romance. This is only the first of the Court's four ranges, all of which rise directly out of the water of the moat, with just one a narrow ledge of garden on the far western side where the moat becomes so wide as to be described as a lake. It is full of fish and that is something to be remembered in relation to all these early grounds. They were never simply gardens, but larders for a largely self-sufficient community. Latrines, like the charmingly ornamental half-timbered pavilion at Huddington Court, emptied straight into the moat to feed the fish, which then fed the house. These earthy realities need to be accepted. People in the fourteenth century had as much appreciation of the beauty of foliage and flowers as we have, but their gardens and grounds still had to keep them alive.

One narrow bridge leads across the water to the four-gabled range of brick and timbers on a stone foundation,[7] but the principal entrance is on the north side over a second single-arched bridge under a battlemented gatehouse. This gives on to a courtyard with a garden device, entirely modern, of embarrassingly effective drama. The lead statue of a sixteenth-century pageboy (6) is set in the centre of a paved area to welcome any visitor with the gift of a lead rose in the broad lead salver that he holds out. It is the first and most poetic of many such garden statues in the grounds. Behind the pageboy is the screens passage of the house which leads through to the ledge of garden mentioned earlier. Ten feet wide, a lawn paved with millstones widening at the south-western corner and smudged with pink hydrangeas, it is the perfect belvedere for afternoon tea or after-dinner drinks. From it the principal features of the medieval and Tudor grounds can be absorbed.

Across the lake-like extension of the moat on this west side is an equally generous sweep of lawn set casually with whimsical lead figures, a truculent boar and a naked child teasing a swan. Mature trees close in the view, but what cannot be seen is the first of Worcestershire's mysterious double moats. Much smaller than the lake-moat around the house and largely dry, it has been dug some 20 yards further out, encompassing, therefore, a wide area. But did it enclose a garden or an orchard, was its purpose

6 *This statue of a pageboy offering a rose greets visitors in the courtyard of Birtsmorton Court and is one of many whimsical modern gestures in the grounds*

defensive or was it simply to keep livestock in or perhaps out as in Chaucer's 'Nun's Priest's Tale' where the poor old widow had 'A yerd…, enclosed al aboute/With stikkes, and a drye dich withoute'? Some of the evidence is conflicting, but these are the questions this chapter must try to resolve because they are fundamental to Worcestershire's early garden experiments.

Returning again to the view from the garden belvedere: the lawns run south, due west the trees gather around the Westminster Pool, a long, broad rectangle of dark water, so called because it was dug out in the same year, or so legend has it, that Henry Yvele finished the nave of Westminster Abbey and to the same dimensions. The nave was built for Richard II in the style of the choir of Henry III's reign, so that would date the Pool and probably the whole layout to around 1390. What is so impressive about these Worcestershire moats is that their waters are usually alive; they are flowing. From this narrow garden belvedere it is possible to hear the sound of water tumbling down into the moat from the Westminster Pool, which is some 4ft higher, up a bank of brooding gunnera. On the far, east side of the Court the water flows out to a second moat, much smaller, around what may have been a pleasaunce for the ladies, tangled now with a few white roses, but also alive with the sound of running water and easily accessed from the east range by that first bridge.

That is only the half of Birtsmorton's garden offerings. Rising above the gunnera on the far north side of the moat, is the real garden (7). This is a great square enclosed, not just by a high brick wall, in places of Tudor date, but by one of those almost defensively solid evergreen hedges that give an historic resonance to any garden with their many rounded towers of yew. These hedges take two men a week to clip. Inside the double boundaries is a marvellously complex Adams and Roberts garden crammed with the whimsical inventions that are such a feature of modern Birtsmorton. But to recreate the functional realities of the fourteenth-, fifteenth-, and sixteenth-century layout, that brick enclosed rectangle with its ornamental four-centred arched entrance has to be seen as a vegetable garden with espaliered fruit trees along its warm walls.

By the fourteenth century broad beans had ceased to be a field crop and were being eaten fresh and green. White and green peas had been introduced, lettuce came in the sixteenth century as did parsnips, barely in time to be ousted by potatoes from America.[8] Cabbages were another fifteenth-century introduction as were cauliflowers; but carrots of multiple colours, white, black and red, seem to have been around for a long time. Spinach is a vegetable that garden historians wrangle over;[9] but, as some species of kale, it could, like celery and chives, have been around in time to be cultivated in Birtsmorton's walled larder. What is intriguing about all these lists of imports and introductions is the implication that, until the fifteenth century, there could have been little or no call for the large walled gardens that are now commonplace accompaniments to any big English country house because there would have been little to grow in them except fruit and pot herbs.

Leaping ahead from fifteenth-century vegetables to late twentieth-century inspired whimsicalities, the garden which Veronica Adams has created within these brick and

7 *Veronica Adams was the designer of the modern garden laid out within and without the seventeenth-century Walled Garden outside the moat at Birtsmorton*

yew dual walls achieves everything that she only half achieved inside similar walling at Spetchley Park in the middle of the county. That great yew hedge encloses two inner gardens, a White Garden and a Garden of the Four Quarters, both laid out to celebrate the Millennium: the former an enriched Sissinghurst, the latter far more appropriate to a medieval garden as Europe was at that period inclined to copy the four-quartered gardens of Persia.

Adams' White Garden is centred upon a large octagonal Tudor-style lead tank with a fountain where a naked small boy is grappling, this time with a big fish: very Italian. Peonies, daisies and arches of jasmine preserve a token whiteness and statues of eighteenth-century shepherds and shepherdesses hold court (*8*), one in each corner. Some play musical instruments: a tambourine, a fiddle, a flute; one carries a lamb. Adams likes to quarter her spaces decisively with each statue backed by the silvery foliage of a weeping pear. The lamb carrier has a backdrop of contrasting giant thistle and small pink roses. What is so pleasing is the way that the statues literally people this garden and create, with the octagonal basin, diagonal vistas from any number of points. Mike Roberts has terminated one of these vistas with an ironwork Loggia and seats in his distinctive smith-work, half-Art Nouveau, half-Gaudi in his Catalan historicist phase.

It is a garden of the most complicated features, as anyone will discover when attempting to move through that yew barrier from White or Four Quarters to the giant herbaceous borders that triumph between the yews and the original brick walls. Mike Roberts has forged an emotive tangle of iron around one of the arched doorways; there is something to discover at every turn in what should be a logical quartering, but which develops into a satisfying bewilderment of mazes. The Four Quarters of the second garden are dedicated to Medlar, Quince, Armillary Sphere and, in the true Birtsmorton spirit, to The Little People. The first three speak for themselves, though the Medlar Quarter has an earthy potager with Indian corn. The Little People are clipped out of box bushes, all very child-friendly. There is a rabbit, a chicken and a pig, but the scarecrow is literally scary, a dark note in a sunny garden; he looks like a real dead person propped up amid lavender bushes!

So often in this garden there is the sound of water falling, but the source is hidden. It is hard to convey the delicious claustrophobia of these grounds. One keeps trying for a way out, but when one is offered it leads only to yet another enchanting incident so there is none of the tedium of a true maze. The Court is so textured, patched and various in its leaning angles that it ought to out-point its gardens quite comfortably. In fact it does not. They are equally memorable and work separately yet in medieval-style accord. While there are no grand contrived effects this garden is great, homely, tactful and, lastly, a perfect demonstration of the mysterious Worcestershire moat in its most

8 *Worcestershire's modern gardens tend to play safe with sculpture as here with the Mozartian characters inhabiting Birtsmorton's White Garden*

complex double form. That long sinister Westminster Pool has its relaxed equivalents in fish ponds tacked on to one corner of many other moated sites. Apparently those wide moats did not produce enough fish for a hungry household and an extra fish larder was usually created at the point where the feeder stream was led in. It would be interesting to know if that small moated but un-walled area on the east side really was intended as a flowery ladies' pleasaunce, not just another vegetable garden.

The pleasurable therapeutic side to a medieval garden should not be forgotten. At Evesham, Abbot William Chiriton, who ruled from 1317 to 1344, enclosed Shrawnell Park in Badsey, a few miles to the south-east of his abbey, and had it planted with oak and ash trees, building an infirmary there for his monks when they were sick or weak from their annual blood purging.[10] He planted more trees at Evesham in his own lower orchard towards Hampton. The next Abbot, his successor, William Boys (1345–67), laid out another garden next to the Avon, curiously called 'Sturdy', and planted it with herbs and trees around fish ponds, '*pro recreatione et solatio*', for the exercise and peace of the monks.[11] Next in this sequence of holy gardeners was Abbot John Ombresley (1367–79) who enclosed 300 acres of land and water in 1376 to create a park at his native Ombersley; though whether that was for the peace of his brethren or his own delight in killing deer is less certain.[12]

Birtsmorton was only the first in the eye-catching sequence of Worcestershire moats. As double moats seem more inclined than single moats to direct the design of a garden it is worth listing a few of the county's doubles. Madresfield, Huddington, Hartlebury, Alvechurch and Strensham can be added to Birtsmorton. Whether all these doubles served the same purpose as the pair at Birstmorton: enclosing a large, cattle-free garden for one purpose or another remains to be decided. They could have been an enclosure for ducks and chickens, a shady place for dry walking after wet weather or for defence.

Moat Farm, for instance, at Lower Strensham, has the most aggressive double 'Homestead Moat' in the county.[13] The farmhouse is a quietly elegant William and Mary-style house, a favourite form in the area, lying back from the road behind tall yew hedges. The farmyard is tucked away out of sight and it controls the causeway leading across the wide, deep outer moat onto the high wooded bank that runs in a kind of raised open-air cloister 6ft high in a square between this outer and the equally wide and deep inner moat (9). This means that there is only a bank between the two moats with no space for any garden, just enough for a walk. The place is a delight for the farmer's children who boat on the two moats, but something of a worry for their mother as the moats are quite deep enough to drown in. That causeway, which was originally two bridges, continues across the second moat to the inner island or keep, and keep is what apparently it once was.

The Strensham double moats are the remains of a small but seriously fortified concentric castle-house which Sir John Russell was licensed to crenellate (and apparently to moat about) in 1388. Its inner rampart walk is 300ft by 250ft and rises to 14ft above the water level. A stream feeds a large marshy fish pond or reservoir on the

9 *Only the great double earthworks and twin moats of Strensham Castle survive, densely wooded, behind Moat Farm. Was the causeway between them a garden walk?*

south side, Strensham's equivalent of Birtsmorton's Westminster Pool. But Strensham's moats are quite unlike Birtsmorton's double moats in the contour and extent of land between the two separate waters, and Cromwell considered Strensham dangerous enough to order it to be slighted.[14] A castle-house like Birtsmorton Court will have occupied the inner island, rising directly out of the water, but was there an outer wall on the rampart or was it a pleasure walk? Memories of the equally well-preserved water courses at Bindon Abbey in Dorset suggest the latter.[15] Bindon, where Thomas Howard inherited in 1544 a monastic property, a Cistercian abbey with the monks' gardens and a system of water sluices, has two double moats, the larger square enclosing an island with a high viewing mount. If the monks created such raised walks, '*pro recreatione et solacio*', was Sir John Russell doing the same? There is, as the monks and the farmer's children prove, a fascination to water courses in a garden area, and then of course there would be fish. But would Cromwell have troubled to slight a pleasure garden?

As was stressed in the introduction, Worcestershire was very much the bishop's county and the bishop had his own version of Bindon: his complex of buildings and moats at Alvechurch in the north of the shire.[16] This site has not been fortunate; a modern house stands on one of the two original square islands, trees have largely taken over and a new housing estate for Persimmon Homes is being built (October 2005) right up against the north moat, a very steep ditch still with running water. Alvechurch is always described as the Bishop's Palace. But was it really that? It has two moated enclosures, one supposedly an outer court, the other for the bishop's lodgings. Documentary evidence suggests something much simpler:

> The parcke was yeerley wourthe 49s. 8d., and had within it towe pondes with Ilandes in the myddest of eyther, whose fyshinge was yeerely valewed at 5s., and the pasture of the Ilandes at towe shillings per annum. And in his demeane landes hee had Charter Warren graunted by the Kinge, 39 Hen. 3.[17]

From this description it seems more likely that this 'palace' was, in fact, a hunting lodge set amongst two rich moated meadows with the deer park extending all around them. The man in charge of the park in Henry II's reign was 'Reynold', no surname given.[18] There was the usual large fish pond to the west, which is now a series of mounds and the River Arrow fed the channels of the moats.

Earthworks of gardens can often be very informative, but for a modern reader and investigator it is irritatingly vague precisely what the two island enclosures were used for. Back in 1246-7 one of the bishops had bought from a nursery or 'impgarth', 300 willows to plant on his park at Fladbury.[19] What could he have done with them? Might the trees have supported the banks of a fish pond, or even created an arched willow walk or maze? We have no definitive answers. In another accounting for the bishop the pasture on those two Alvechurch islands was not valued because animals from the park – deer, sheep, cows – had been getting in and feeding on it,[20] which hardly sounds like a carefully cultivated garden area. On another of his many estates the bishop had a vineyard in a large 7.5 acre garden at White Ladies Aston, south-east of Worcester. In 1282 its 'herbage' and fruit were worth 10 shillings a year, by 1299 the garden had been doubled and was worth £1.6s.8d.[21] But what had been done? Were there more grapevines? The only elements surviving today on the site are two arms of a moat around yet another Moat Farm.

Where double moats are concerned there is a puzzling but undeniable similarity between the double moats at Strensham and Abbot Godfrey's 1302 Herber (*Herbarium*) next to the Derby Yard at Peterborough Abbey.[22] A plan drawn of the Herber shows it with exactly Strensham's pattern of square moat within square moat with bridges to reach a central island which was planted with 'pear-trees and very lovely plants (*herbis dellicatissimis*)'.[23] Could the Russell house always have stood where Moat Farm stands today, and are the Strensham moats the remains of a medieval herber and not a concentric castle at all? That high raised walk between the two moats with its surviving stone foundations of viewing bastions at each angle does look very like an open air cloister, the natural form for outdoor recreation and the enjoyment of views.[24]

What seems to have interested the bishops of Worcester more than their herbers were the deer in their parks outside these moats. As late as 1699 Bishop Lloyd was appointing gamekeepers to 'take from any person or persons prohibited....any guns, bows, greyhounds, setting dogs, ferrets, cony dogs, or other dogs to destroy hares or coneys, and also hare's tra'mells and other nets, hare pipes, snares, or other engines';[25] in a word, poachers of the bishop's game. That year 'my Ld' personally killed four brace and a half of bucks out of the herd of 125 deer in his park at another of his palaces, Hartlebury.[26]

Hartlebury, the most prestigious of the bishop's seats, is surrounded on three sides (four originally) by a very wide, deep moat (*10*), one that rivals even the moat about Madresfield, seat of the Beauchamp earls, the county's leading aristocratic family.[27] It is possible, even probable, though outside the range of proof, that because their bishop, who was the most potent landowner in the county, lived within the confines of a most dramatic moat, Worcestershire gentry, from small yeomen farmers upwards, considered it a badge of rank to live likewise behind watery ditches. This theory does not, however, solve the double moat problem.

Despite its unhappy Victorian additions in pale brick and yellow stone, Madresfield rises as operatically from the waters of its formidable moat as does Birtsmorton, and Madresfield does have, like Birtsmorton, a much shallower, dry outer moat which contains most of the formal gardening around the house.[28] That formality appears to be largely of the early twentieth century and could well have been devised by the seventh Earl Beauchamp simply to fill the gap which at Birtsmorton is largely a lawn. So, though Madresfield's deployment of the double moat could be a pointer, it does not solve the mystery.

Huddington Court's double moats are a little more helpful.[29] There is an average gap of 10-15 yards between the lovely, lily-choked inner moat and the moist outer moat of that rakishly elegant half-timbered house. Most of this fluctuating band of space has been filled over the last two generations of Edmondson owners with inspired salvage from Strensham Court when it was demolished in the 1960s. But what is original and

10 *This eighteenth-century view of Hartlebury Castle shows the vast moat, almost a lake, at the rear to the west, which survives today.* Bodleian Library, Oxford, Gough Maps 33, fol.74r

of sixteenth-century date between the moats is the quaintly half-timbered privy, a place to linger in during warm weather, but a purgatory in every sense during the winter. If the 'intermoat' at Huddington was, as the privy suggests, more a service area than a garden, was the intermoat used as a safe refuge at night for ducks and hens, no more in fact than a farmyard? The Court and the stables were also within the intermoat supporting the farmyard theory, but everything else, including the twin pigeon houses, is a recent importation.

Harvington is another romantic piece of moated evidence. There the 1576 brick ranges on a fifteenth-century stone foundation rise again in true Worcestershire fashion, straight out of murky water, with just one little corner of modern garden bright with knots and flowering bushes to the left of the main entrance bridge. There is an orchard area to the back of the house which may have worked as a secondary moated area such as Alvechurch once had. Of the county's other notable early houses, Mere Hall near Hanbury has the relic of a moat to one side of the house at a fair distance from its walls and there is a deep-delved lily pool behind Hanbury Hall's detached Long Gallery. This is a likely relic from the earlier house on the site, scorned and filled in when the Vernons removed such medieval features in their post-1680 rebuilding.

The most promising way to solve the garden functioning of moats, single and double, is to concentrate, not on the great country seats where wealth has obscured the evidence, but on yeomen areas, where farmers have not been much inclined to change and the only threat to moats has come from prosperous business men moving out from town to renovate half-timbered farmhouses that were already perfectly textured. Moats are generally distributed over most of lowland Worcestershire, but they concentrate heavily in the parishes of Inkberrow and Feckenham, in the north-east of the county, eight in the former and six in the latter. This is a time-patterned and engaging part of the county, once covered by the royal forest of Feckenham, where King John, the Plantagenets' most committed hunter, had a lodge, now Tookeys Farm, below the Ridgeway at Astwood Bank. Tookeys has a moat and a chain of small ponds trailing down the hillside below it, so it follows the usual Worcestershire moat design. What must make any alert topographical detective suspicious is, however, the presence in fields nearby, and indeed over all these two parishes, of disused marl pits where the underlying clay has been dug out to make the bricks that, virtually universally in this area of splendid half-timbered yeomen houses, have been used to infill the gaps in the timber framing.

What happened when a prosperous yeoman came to build a new timber-framed house was that, while the joiners and carpenters were busy with the frame, a small brick kiln was set up, a marl pit was dug and the brick infilling was created cheaply and locally. Might that explain the fish ponds or even the moats themselves? This underlying Worcestershire marl raises another pointer to the moat mystery. Visiting these houses with their feet in the water, it was natural to commiserate with the owners on the problem of rising damp. In every case the response was a cheerful denial that any such problem existed. The moats do not cause damp, they cure it, providing essential drainage for the house and for the garden. Without a moat and with impenetrable clay below it the building would become damp. It is striking to observe in all these many moats how alive the waters are. As at Birtsmorton there is a flow through the area; they are not foul smelling pools, but wholesome fish-full waters. As Ben Jonson wrote in his poem praising Penshurst Place in Kent: 'And if the high swollen Medway fail thy dish,/Thou hast thy ponds, that pay thee tribute fish'.

Ditches and moats were on most soils essential drainage features. The sophistication of medieval garden and field drainage systems should never be underestimated. The Agricultural Revolution goes a long way further back than the eighteenth century, and it seems likely that this profusion of moats in certain areas of Worcestershire was a shrewd practical response to water-logged ground that could have made houses damp and gardens unproductive. Clearly, therefore, two moats were better than one: a deep one around the house and a shallow outer one around the garden area of intensive cultivation. Moats are likely to have been Feckenham Forest's local variant. Where de-forestation took place anywhere in the country, it was an opportunity for an enterprising yeoman to clear the trees and create, as a status symbol and sign of ownership in an area where legal regulations had slackened, a broad moat to contain his new farm complex. This accounts for Worcestershire's unusual proportion of isolated moated sites; 83 out of 146 are sited away from villages. It was England's equivalent of America's Wild West where frontiersmen were turning rough forest land into prosperous pasture. Feckenham Forest was not de-forested (the process known as assarting) until the late Tudor and early Jacobean period, hence the date of around 1600 for most of these farmhouses.

One exploration of this area, still rich in hedgerow oaks, with narrow lanes, strikingly handsome farmhouses and an irregular terrain, will offer telling and readily accessible evidence on these moated grounds. Inkberrow church and the Old Vicarage lie up on the same level as the main village street, but immediately behind the Old Vicarage the land dips steeply down and there, in what was the church glebe land, is a perfect square, water-filled moat (*11*) about 15ft across enclosing an island of about an acre. There are traces of stonework supporting the island's banks, but it has no building, only trees and undergrowth. At one corner the usual small fish ponds trail away. A stile leads invitingly to it and a Millennium boardwalk has been laid all the way round the outside of the moat, but there is no bridge to the island. It is idyllic. But what was its purpose? The *VCH* speculates on Inkberrow's Vicarage House: 'This stood, in all probability, at the foot of the Church Hill within the moat which still remains…apple trees and nut bushes flourish in the enclosure'.[30] It adds the story of Frederick Edwin, aged 30, who accidentally drowned in it and was buried on 6 August 1839. The Parish Register records that when a new vicar, Mr Hemington, was inducted in 1747:

> The Vicarage House was in so ruinous a condition that the workmen who repair'd it ran the hazard of their lives, all the floors and ceilings and a great part of the outward and inward walls being ready to fall, some part actually fallen. The barn and all the outhouses Stables & etc were so far gone to ruin, that they were past repair and were rebuilt between 1747 and 1752.[31]

There is no mention of a bridge or a moat and the Old Vicarage still stands high up above, opposite the church where it would be expected to stand. But one of the perks that came with the post of vicar of Inkberrow was that the incumbent was also Lord of the Manor, so the moat and island down in the valley must be the site of the old Manor which the vicar used as his vicarage.

A useful follow-up from Elysian Inkberrow would be to Brick House Farm, a mile to the north of Feckenham. In attempting to recreate the typical late Tudor farm complex of Worcestershire, Brick House (the name itself suggests a marl pit) is an untouched specimen of much charm and great value in an area of over-restored houses. The L-shaped farmhouse, the stables, the chicken house, even the privy, are all of 1601, and until recently there was an octagonal pigeon house. A stream runs down across the front of the house, but its garden with apple trees and a semicircular garden seat lies on higher land behind the house; the farmyard lies to the left, the privy, a single-seater, to the right. This is how a Worcestershire yeoman's farm and garden were laid out before gentrification set in; the textures are a revelation. Lower Grinsty Farm, in the middle of Redditch golf course, has the same cluster of farm buildings but all in perfect order with the small garden area set behind the original hall-type farmhouse, a single cell structure set within its moat, in marked contrast to the handsome yeoman house of late sixteenth-century date built next to it.[32] At Brick House and Lower Grinsty there are now only traces of a dry ditch without.

11 *The medieval vicars of Inkberrow had the perk of a manorial lordship, which may explain the moated garden lying in the valley below the present Old Vicarage*

In absolute moat-contrast, a Rolls Royce to a Morris Minor, are the moats around Shurnock Court and Astwood Court.[33] These are as broad and as living-watered as that houseless moat at Inkberrow. Their moats enclose large areas, perhaps 2 acres with the houses, timber-framed at Shurnock, brick-built and later in date at Astwood, both well away from the water's edge. Shurnock is a postcard picture with wrought iron gates, velvet lawns, a spouting fountain and an elegant iron bridge to cross the water. These are further clues. Is 'Court' the key to the type of moat? Were broad handsome moats like these two, and that at Inkberrow, status symbols? Is the drainage theory still relevant? The answer is probably affirmative; that underlying marl is widespread. But were these two attractive and sizeable moated islands ornamental gardens or domestic animal refuges from foxes or deer?

An un-wrecked jewel among these lovely but variably treated yeoman houses is the White House, one of several attractive half-timbered farms along Callow Hill Lane immediately below the impending wave of Redditch's new housing. That retains one arm of its moat, the rest was filled in by a previous owner. It would be interesting to learn whether dampness followed the filling in. Conclusions to this moat investigation must be broad. Most moats were status symbols, they had functional advantages in drainage, outer moats could protect domestic fowl, inner moats and attendant fish ponds fed the household. A small dry ditch, as in Chaucer and as at Brick House Farm and Lower Grinsty Farm, was the equivalent of a hedge. Some moats may have been created in part when bricks were being made for the house itself.

While such archaeological evidence is valuable it is wise sometimes to pull back from the gardens of a time as remote as the fourteenth, fifteenth and sixteenth centuries and try to understand how they would have worked for their contemporary creators. We see gardens as symphonies of flower colour or as collections of exotic rarities, but even Tudor monarchs lived in a rather stinking England. For them a garden was primarily a release into fresh air with the bonus of scented leaves rather than colourful flowers. It is no accident that the medieval word for a garden was usually 'herber', a place where leaves could be crushed and enjoyed, as in our modern sensory gardens for the blind.

It would be a mistake, though a natural one after seeing so many modern recreations of Tudor gardens, to think that Tudor garden aesthetics were limited to small board-lined beds of herbs. From the following passage it is apparent that Tudor gardens and parks were valued just as we would value them for their natural vistas; the Tudors had no need of Wordsworth to make them appreciate hill scenery, natural fruitfulness and hypercharged, preferably perfumed, fresh air. On her August 1575 visit to Worcester, Queen Elizabeth had bad luck with her hunting at Hallow. For some reason the bucks did not run past her stand for her to shoot at them. But she did enjoy other and more subtle park and garden pleasures, and Thomas Habington's account of them will take a reader further into the aesthetics of the period than any amount of moat hunting:

The syte of Hallowe, lyinge a myle and a halfe from Worcester on the westerne bancke of Seuerne, is so raysed on a small hyll with that distance from the river as receavinge onely the commodityes thereof is nowaye annoyed with the contagion vaporinge from the water, the house hathe a most pleasant prospect over Seurne, and all Worcester, eaven to Breodon's hylles, placed in a lyttel but most delicate parcke, whose higher ground aboundinge in mynte yeeldethe a sweete savor, and whose sandy pathes are eaver drye, in so much as Queene Elizabethe huntinge theare (whylest the abundance of hortes beatinge the mynt dyd bruse but a naturall perfume) gave it an extraordinary commendation, a deynty situation scarce secound to any in England. Thys was to the Religious of Worcester's churche a retyred place of recreation, least the yre bowe beeinge eaver bent in devotion might otherwise breake or bee weakened. Hallowe is not onely a spatious but a commodious Lordshyp to the Byshoppes of our dioces, respect you eyther the leasehoulders or Customary tenauntes, ffor southe from the parcke and waren by Seuerne's bancke lyethe the manor of Hynewyke, as ryche in medowes and pastures as that river can afforde, and thoughe inferior in pleasure, yet surmounting the parcke in profytt. And next adioyninge was Hynewyke's were, a gulfe commodious for provision of fyshe....Theyre belounged to it a Neyt, or river iland, and a fyshinge in Seuerne, together with a medowe betweene Seuerne and the Kinges Highe waye leading to Hynewyke.[34]

There is still a 'Hunting Grove' in the grounds of Hallow Park on the west bank of the Severn above Worcester. The queen was hunting in a park which the Prior of Worcester had set up in 1312, possibly as another of those hospitals for infirm monks as there was a chalybeate spring there in otherwise well-drained ground.[35]

It may strain a modern sensibility to appreciate that the scent of mint leaves crushed by frightened animals trying to escape slaughter from the arrows of a queen could be a true garden pleasure. But it was, just as was the view of Bredon Hill, the view of the city's spires and towers, and the luxury of dry, sanded paths. When we can empathise with these alien pleasures and appreciate an earthy relish in the promise of abundant fish suppers from a well-sited weir, we are on the way to a true understanding of medieval and Tudor garden aesthetics; but only then.

2

The lure of dazzling example –
the aftershock of Westwood Park

Renaissance influences shaped the gardens in the various English counties at different times and often in distinctly different ways, with Italian, French or Dutch versions according to the foreign models with which their patrons or designers had been familiar. Cornish gardens, for instance, made a late and reluctant move towards formal gardens with severe Doric loggias that cautiously linked houses like Godolphin and Penheale with a forecourt garden and vernacular pavilions.[1] Dorset, in contrast, had achieved a sensationally grand, three-part, axial Franco-Italian garden at Lulworth Castle as early as the reign of James I.[2] This was because the Howards wanted to attract the favours of a monarch devoted to hunting and that formal, axial layout at Lulworth ended in a deer park and a deer pavilion. The device worked.

In Wiltshire it was the same story. With two rival courtier fanatics, the Herbert earls of Pembroke at Wilton and Sir Thomas Gorges and his wife, a Swedish aristocrat who was Queen Elizabeth's favourite lady-in-waiting, at Longford Castle, the county had two formal, axially-planned gardens as patterns for the lesser county gentry to follow.[3] By Charles I's reign Wilton had a nationally admired, axial, three-part garden with all the prestige of Inigo Jones's name as its designer working on French models. The result of these precedents was that, when the Thynnes of Longleat came, in Charles II's reign, to spend a fortune on their grounds, they unhesitatingly laid out an ambitious axial garden of multiple divisions in completely the wrong place: up a steep hill.[4] There is little doubt that once a grand example has been set later county gardens tend to follow it, and most grand examples, like Lulworth, Longford and Wilton were long, axial formal sequences, joyful escapes from the confines of medieval moats.

Worcestershire was different; it had Westwood Park for its model, more a romantic palace than a house, and Westwood's garden and park were not axial at all, but laid out in a tremendous starburst, dramatised by four three-storey garden towers and set about with a cobweb pattern of forest rides. Consequently neither of Worcestershire's other two grand formal gardens, laid out well after Westwood at Hanbury Hall, in 1700, and Croome Court, in 1712, were conventionally axial. But that is to anticipate. Westwood's garden was not Elizabethan, it was a concept of the Commonwealth, devised by a symposium or house party of defiant, persecuted High Anglican divines, to be realised after the Restoration of the monarchy in 1660, in the sunshine of a triumphant restored Anglican Church. The description may seem an oxymoron, but Westwood's was a religious hunting garden.

The county had, however, been making modest gestures towards formal garden design long before Westwood's great shadow fell upon it. Bredons Norton is a pleasant but insignificant little manor house with a small garden tucked away at the side, yet it has a high-spirited and convincingly classical gateway arch of golden stone with grilles of crescent-shaped ironwork. The date carved on it, of 1585, proves that the formal garden spirit was stirring early even if the layout was weak; but the garden gateway is more sophisticated than the house it serves.

The Doharty family's illustrated maps and surveys of the county's seats reveal a number of orderly small gardens.[5] John Doharty junior's beautiful map of Feckenham is dated 1744, but it is based on John Blagrave's survey of 1591 and it proves that Feckenham Lodge had a garden neatly quartered into four equal lawns around a circular space centred on a feature, either a sundial or a small pool. A wooden paled fence contains the formal area and there are two rectangular beds for flowers or vegetables at the side. Another Doharty map, prepared between 1751 and 1753 for the Dean and Chapter of Worcester,[6] shows Bevere Manor with an oval lawn to its entrance front and another quadripartite garden on its south front with an exedra to the house and another exedra to the east. More typical of the period, though still gestures towards order, are the ornate twin banqueting houses in the forecourt of Leigh Manor. Again, as at Bredon's Norton, the garden buildings are leading the way stylistically, being far more considered and fashionable than the house which they serve. This is a mark of lodges generally: owners could afford to be modish when they were building on a small scale.

Before closing in upon the grandiose complexities of Westwood it is worth supporting that last point by reference to the garden activities at Sir Nicholas Lechmere's house of Severn End on the water meadows near Tewkesbury. The house is for the most part a picturesque huddle of gabled and half-timbered vernacular ranges,[7] but Sir Nicholas' garden house is a neat, two-storey classical structure raised on a loggia of two round arches. It presides over a garden begun, according to Sir Nicholas' diary, in 1657 and 'In ye yeare 1662 I finished ye mount-walke, ye stone-work was done by Goddard...at ye rate of six pence a foot for ye coping & 4d ye foot for ye steppes'.[8] This 'mount-walke' survives unchanged today on the east side of Severn End's attractive south garden. It is a raised terrace accessed by two 'forthright', flights of eight steps, and gives views out to the water meadows, inwards to the knots of the flower garden, now lawn. The garden house was Sir Nicholas' study (*colour plate 3*) where he kept his will and escaped from his ten children and host of dependents. 'In the year 1661', he wrote, 'I built the floodgate and ye same yeare I built my study at the south-west end of ye garden'.[9] These garden pavilions were a functional necessity for a house where privacy was impossible, with servants everywhere and few corridors.

What is so useful about Severn End and Sir Nicholas' precise records is that here we have a simple, plain garden and surrounding parkland which was the exact contemporary of the ostentatious garden and park being laid out at Westwood. By the detailed recollections which Sir Edmund Lechmere wrote, of life back in his grandfather's time, we have a record of Sir Nicholas' library. It was limited to five books: Burns' *Justice*, *The Newgate Calendar*, the Bible, the Prayer Book and that book of devotions which was written by the pious committee living together at Westwood in the grim days of the Commonwealth: *The Whole Duty of Man*, a volume which would find a place in most country house libraries for the next hundred years. The three avenues of trees which radiate out from Severn End's west front are another relic, planted in 1640, of Sir Nicholas' time, and offer a further contrast with the wide mesh of hunting rides that surrounded Westwood, remembered today by that most dramatic of all Kip and Knyff engraved views of country house estates in their *Britannia Illustrata* of 1707.

There was another, modest, inexpensive starburst of straight, formal avenues laid out on the Westwood pattern around Cockshutt Farm in Wichenford parish (*12*). Carefully recorded in a slim notebook of maps and diary jottings: 'rain'd all night, fair in the morning: a few showers'; 'fair night an Aurora Borealis',[10] it seems to have been the work of an educated, under-funded and conservative gentleman who was still, on 23 September 1729, thinking in Westwood and Carolean formal terms. Cockshutt was

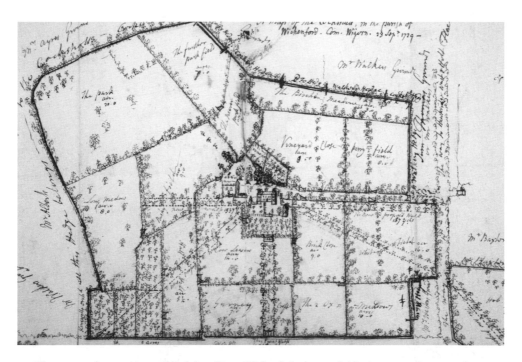

12 *The pattern of avenues around Cockshutt Farm, Wichenford, was recorded by its conservative owner in 1729 and seems more influenced by Westwood's radial layout than by the usual axial treatment.* Reproduced by permission of Wychavon District Council

rather a small manor house than a farm, with twin parlours in wings, one on either side of a central block of hall, screens passage and kitchen. Its owner-designer had laid out around the house as the central focus that starburst of five avenues, one of elms, one of limes, one of chestnuts and one, 'the back front Walk or Apple Walk to ye Vinery'. Only the fifth avenue had a drive to Worcester laid along it. No sign of informal planting is indicated and there is no long axial garden to this bucolic curiosity.

But then dates in a rural county like Worcestershire are no accurate guide to garden fashions. That Doharty map of 1751, mentioned earlier in this chapter, illustrates a whole cross-section of the kind of gardens that were being laid out in the mid-century on the north-western residential suburbs of Worcester. While the two Bevere houses are both limited to simple quadripartite layouts, which could have been planted at any time in the past 90 years, one of their neighbours, Mr Cooke, was moving forwards. Cooke's house, winged and Carolean if Doharty's sketch is a true guide, was sited on a lane off the Bewdley turnpike by Barbone Bridge at North Claines (*13*). West of his house, beyond a conventional exedral recess, Cooke's grounds were laid out with a formal avenue, but his gardens facing east and the Barbone Brook had, beyond a pigeon house and 13 rectangular beds, a fashionably sinuous serpentine water with walks along its banks. Though it had been dammed originally to create a millpond, like the lakes at Ombersley, it was a clear case of a garden on the cusp edging from formalism towards Rococo manners.

Cooke's serpentine has survived and even gained an islet, but not one of Worcestershire's three major formal gardens has been kindly treated by time. Hanbury Hall suffered the

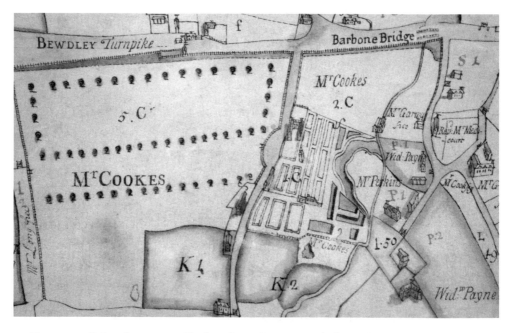

13 *The younger Doharty's 1751 map of lands in the north Worcester suburbs reveals a garden on the cusp from formal to serpentine Rococo, the property of a Mr Cooke.* Worcestershire Record Office

Capability Brown fashion for open, lawn-like parks. The post-1712 formal layout which Gilbert, the fourth Earl of Coventry, set up at Croome Court was swept away within 40 years by the innovative garden programme of George William, the sixth Earl. Westwood has suffered a more subtle indignity. Its buildings survive (*colour plate 2*), admirably cared for by the condominium which has taken them over but, where the great wood with all its intricate web of hunting alleys once surrounded those extraordinary towers is now an enormous open field of wheat, an incongruous bare prairie. 'Lusty' Sir John Pakington's Great Pool, the biggest fish pond in the county, is all that remains of the hunting park.

Anyone taking the private road that leads up from the handsome cottage-style Droitwich Lodge to the house will begin optimistically, passing through a fine belt of trees; but then the wheat field opens up and any sense of surprise, of Camelot suddenly revealed behind great trees and what must have seemed like a town wall, is lost. Even so, stripped and bare, with only the Gatehouse and two of its original four garden towers left, the buildings have a memorable presence (*14*). To understand the origins of the garden illustrated by Kip and Knyff it is essential to follow the sequence of construction on the site.[11]

Lusty Sir John Pakington was the third in a line of Pakingtons who had gathered 32 manors in the free-for-all of property acquisition that followed the Dissolution of the Monasteries. They appear to have profited by exercising their bluff charms on susceptible monarchs; the first Pakington having been given the exclusive right to wear his cap in Henry VIII's presence. Queen Elizabeth was clearly taken by Lusty Sir John's hearty physicality, but when he proposed swimming from Westminster to Greenwich

14 *The bristling gables, gatehouse and sentinel towers of Westwood Park, once set within a hunting park of starburst avenues and woods, are now stranded in a landscape of wheat*

for a wager she forbade the test. There was a frisson to being a woman in complete control of muscular young men; and if one painting is any guide Sir John had good legs and a handsome face with a moustache and a short beard.

The Pakingtons' principal seat was at neighbouring Hampton Lovett and Sir John built no more than the middle, three-bay, three-storey central section of the existing house to serve as a hunting lodge, though a very grand one with a Roman triumphal arch serving as its porch and a great hall-dining chamber immediately inside for rowdy hunt suppers. That block would have stood perfectly well alone without the four wings added diagonally by Sir John's grandson, the third Baronet, after 1660. The money for that first multi-windowed three-bay tower came from Lusty Sir John's marriage to a rich widow of a silk merchant. He parted from her nine years later 'on foul terms'; Christopher Hussey, to whom we owe this anecdote, claimed when writing of the third Baronet, who was certainly the author of the wings, that 'it is difficult not to suppose that he took the idea of them from something in the original design which made rectangular additions unreliable'.[12] However, Hussey offered not a shred of proof for the theory. The real story behind the conception of the diagonal wings and the four garden towers is much more interesting and implicit in Hussey's otherwise scholarly account.

Sir John's son died one year before his father,[13] leaving a four-year-old child, the third Baronet, as his heir and a ward of the powerful Lord Keeper, the first Baron Coventry of Croome.[14] As was usual in such circumstances, the Lord Keeper took advantage of his role as guardian to marry the boy off to his daughter, Dorothy, a girl both learned and pious. There followed the harrowing years of the Civil War which saw the young third Baronet, who was an ardent Royalist, heavily fined and often threatened by Parliamentarian forces, Worcestershire being a favourite battleground in the wars. It was after the third Baronet had unwisely shown his loyalty yet again at the time of Charles II's defeat at Worcester in 1651, that he and his godly wife, Dorothy, seem to have retreated into a pious huddle with a group of like-minded Royalist divines. His principal seat at Hampton Lovett had been wrecked during the wars, so they retired to their handsome haunting tower of Westwood, possibly taking comfort from the figure of Justice over their porch.

Thanks to his wife's reputation for piety and his own proven Royalist sympathies, Westwood became a refuge for a whole group of Royalist clergymen who had lost their livings to Puritan ministers.[15] It is difficult to appreciate the mind-set of this group. They were not the Royalists of convention: hard drinking, cheerful gallants, but a group of priests who had seen their Church of England, half-Catholic, half-Protestant, collapse before the certainties of Puritanism. Their response seems to have been a determination to strengthen their own church, in preparation for the return of a rightful king, by a pattern of devotions slanted more towards a devout Protestantism of prayer and Bible study rather than to that High Church emphasis on the sacraments, which had been at least partly responsible for the split between the king and the Church on one side, with the people on the other.

Virtually every one of the group: Hammond, Fell, Henchman, Morley, Allestree, Pearson, Gunning and Fulman would become bishops or deans after the Restoration. They represented the future, and their manifesto, published anonymously in 1658, and apparently written by a committee over which Dorothy presided, was that fifth book in Sir Nicholas Lechmere's small library: *The Whole Duty of Man*, 'laid down in a Plain and Familiar Way for the Use of All, but especially the *Meanest Reader*. Divided into XVII Chapters One whereof being read every Lords Day the Whole may be read over Thrice in a Year Necessary for All Families with Private Devotions for several Occasions'. It may be difficult now to appreciate its appeal, but in those years of intense religious argument it was a wildfire success, a best seller for the rest of the century, one subject to frequent speculation as to whom, Dorothy, Hammond or Allestree, was its author. Whatever the answer the Pakingtons had been at the spirited heart of it. The book made their reputation and King Charles, returned to the throne, awarded them a massive £4,000 compensation; which would have gone a long way to finance those four diagonal wings and their four guardian towers that went up after 1660.

That first decade after the Restoration was a time for historicist gestures and affirmations of defiant conservative Christianity. The newly restored King Charles commissioned Hugh May, essentially a classical architect, to reshape Windsor Castle with token round-arched neo-Norman towers as a backdrop to the revived pageantry of the Garter ceremonies.[16] Was the greatly extended new Westwood a part of this movement: an historicist project, an allegorical citadel of the faith, one brooded over and conceived in those 11 years of the devout house party? It seems most probable as it was quite unlike the normal, plain classical houses of the Carolean period: four towers for the Four Evangelists and ten avenues radiating out into the woods for the Ten Commandments? Again it seems most probable. It was Worcestershire's strangest garden, a formal starburst not a formal axial line, and a starburst animated by the vertical accents of tall garden buildings: this was to be the unusual pattern for the county's next two formal gardens, though not, in strict critical honesty, an entirely successful one.

The Kip-Knyff engraving enables us to study it in detail (*15*). At the centre, not just of its garden hexagon, but of the entire forest park, was the house, rising like the new Jerusalem with the intense verticality of its own four pyramidally-capped towers, the outer four garden towers and the cupola over the gatehouse. The garden was in four divisions, each segment divided by walls that served, like those at Severn End, as viewing terrace walks. Outside that hexagonal circuit was a fence, and this enclosed on the eastern, Droitwich, side a large orchard and a small pleasaunce of twin plots bordered by alternate round and pointed yew bushes. On the opposite, western, side was a large Kitchen Garden. At the back were the stables and an exercise yard; at the front between the gatehouse and the entrance porch, there were two plain lawns. The gardens were as functional and unassuming as the house was vainglorious and allegorical; and that would be Worcestershire's template for the next few decades.

Anyone who, quite reasonably, doubts whether a great house and an unusual garden could influence the garden decisions 40 years later of a successful lawyer, Thomas Vernon, or 52 years later, those of the fourth Earl of Coventry, should study the architectural influence which Westwood exercised in Worcestershire for at least that long, and quite contrary to the national fashion for simple, inexpensive Palladian façades. Such was the

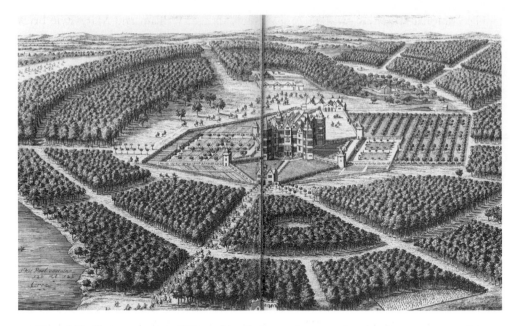

15 *Kip and Knyff's 1707 engraving of Westwood records the great hunting park and garden in its prime with its four garden towers and its ten outer avenues, a deliberately old-fashioned project of the 1660s*

aura of Westwood and the seductive ornamental charm of its many shaped gables and Jacobean detail, which was already out of date when it was first put up in the early 1660s, that a cheerful minor galaxy of 'King James' Gothick'[17] houses sprang up in north Worcestershire, where unsophisticated patrons paid their builders to add shaped gables, ogee-arched windows and haphazard colonettes to their small manor houses. There is nothing else in the country of that date quite like Pool House, Astley, south of Stourport, where the mid-eighteenth-century garden front has been applied to a seventeenth-century house whose bones sometimes show through. Broome House, east of Kidderminster, has another ogee-gabled façade: an inventive delight of illiterate details picked up from Westwood and applied with a brave indifference to correct forms, which can only have come from admiration of Westwood's equally courageous indifference.[18]

The appraisal and criticism of historic gardens, like that of historic houses, tends to be biased towards admiration and praise. This is natural enough as one is so pleased that a garden has survived at all, and so grateful to the owners who have kept them going and allowed an outsider to enjoy them. It does, however, lead to a mild dishonesty, to over-enthusiasm, and this is the problem with any consideration of the first major formal garden in the county to have been influenced by Westwood's curious centralism. This, of course, is Hanbury, where there is the added difficulty that the National Trust has spent a fortune on its restoration and the Trust needs all the encouragement it can get. With that disclaimer it is now only fair to readers to offer a frank personal view on what has happened to the gardens at Hanbury in the past and in the present.

The National Trust was given in 1953 a mildly elegant William and Mary-style brick house with the usual long, weary windows, but with surprisingly sensuous, even sexy Baroque murals inside by Sir James Thornhill at his least inhibited. Unluckily the grounds had, by 1780, been Brownified as an economy measure, destroying the complex formal gardens recorded in Joseph Doharty's brilliantly detailed 1732 view (*16*), loose-leafed in his 'Terrier to a Book of Maps'.[19] This left the Trust with a dull Brown-type park around a pleasing but retiring brick house, so a brave decision, a very brave decision, was made to reinstate large portions of that formal layout with grants from the European Union and a generous bequest from Dinah Albright.[20] It has resulted in a far more visitor-friendly garden full of features to interest even the most casual visitor. Only the pond next to and below the strangely sited Long Gallery and the Long Walk which, with some broken cedars, stretched beyond this, had survived as genuine relics of what, on the present evidence, must have been a pedestrian and ill-thought out scheme from the great George London of the Brompton Park Nurseries. One of the most valuable results of the Trust's reconstruction has been the chance it gives visitors to judge London's skills. He was easily the most influential gardener of his time and judging by his draught for Hanbury and the uncoordinated shower of enclosures which, as already mentioned, he inflicted upon Longleat in Wiltshire, he was uninspired. There was, however, the possibility that his patron, Thomas Vernon, asked him in 1700 to devise something like Westwood with the gardens clustered all around the house, with occasional outward arms and a lavish show of twinned garden pavilions. That certainly is what Vernon got.

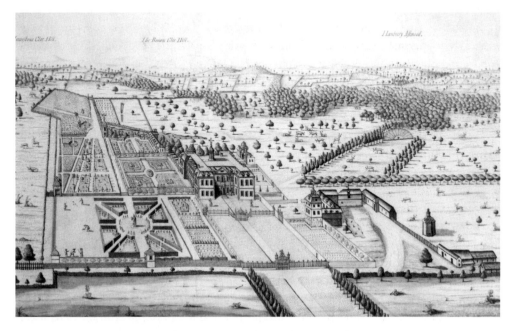

16 *This 1732 Joseph Doharty view of Hanbury with all its formal enclosures has been the basis of the National Trust's ambitious reconstruction of the late seventeenth-century grounds.* Worcestershire Record Office

The Trust has restored most of what the Doharty view records; that handsome brick Orangery which looks to be coeval with the house is surprisingly much later, an old-fashioned design of about 1750, not shown therefore on the Doharty view. So we have to explore a partial but brave and satisfying reconstruction. On the first approach to the house, however, almost everything is changed from Doharty. To the right before the forecourt was the onetime administrative centre of the estate, a tall, three-and-a-half storey block of stables. This has long since gone, but for the garden recreation it was the focus to a long, wide double avenue of trees leading out north-east to an unusual feature, partially re-instated, called the 'Semicircle', a green platform planted with trees, apparently for the leisured observation of sports associated with the deer park and for the enjoyment of views.[21] The amphitheatre, probably the most unusual feature of the grounds, is not readily accessible as woodland has grown over it. Even the entrance forecourt to the house has been changed. Originally it was divided into two areas by ironwork screens, one possibly for coaches, the other for pedestrians. Now there is only one court with two vividly tiled and Moorish-roofed pavilions of 1856 by R.W. Billings. They do not accord in style with the house, but they are enjoyably Victorian in their self-confidence.

The Trust decided to concentrate its efforts on four formal areas as Doharty recorded them, with additions from several later views. Reluctant to erect solid brick buildings, which would be extremely costly and might outface the main house, a pragmatic decision was made to build wooden pavilions and even a wooden obelisk. While this partial reconstruction is informative it needs time to mature, so any adverse criticisms are responses to a very young garden. The point can, however, be made, albeit tentatively, that Hanbury explains why, around 1720, landowners began to move from these disconnected formal areas where a visitor has to walk from one rectangle to another. They were found to be aesthetically inferior to the Arcadian or 'Rococo' gardens which supplanted them, where visitors could pass easily, without complete breaks of mood, through naturally-seeming groves and waters to enjoy atmospheric pavilions of eclectic pleasure – Gothick, classical, Turkish or Chinese. Those Arcadias were, at heart, rejections of gardens for plants and a move towards gardens as cultural encyclopaedias. They were, in addition to being more romantic, much cheaper to run, far less labour intensive.

First and most immediately impressive of the Trust's restorations was the Sunken Parterre (*colour plate 4*) with its flower compartments under the skirts of the house to the west, laid out in 1995. The Grove was reinstated to George London's layout in 1999. The Wilderness with its wooden obelisk followed in 2000 and the Bowling Green (*17*) was re-laid with two wooden pavilions in 2002. Add to these the twin trellised pavilions in the Fruit Garden outside the Long Gallery and a pavilion at each end of the axis that ran through Britannia's statue in the Grove, that totals up eight pavilions and the Long Gallery in one quite limited area of basically unrelated enclosures. The gardens do seem to be straining towards some kind of axis; and after the Doharty view had been drawn, that small axis through the Britannia Grove to a tall, spired pavilion, which has yet to be replaced, was generously extended to reach, in an afterthought of planning, the Orangery with its sumptuous pedimental carvings of baskets of plants and fruit with side wreaths.

17 *The pavilions on Hanbury's recreated Bowling Green are wooden replicas of the stone originals shown on the Doharty view*

It is around the Orangery that the formal George London layout began to turn half axial, as it picks up the old Terrace and stone ha-ha with shattered cedars, half-Arcadian with the Orangery acting as an isolated temple on a clearing in a grove. The intellectual pleasure of walking Hanbury's grounds is this sense they give of one garden period straining to turn into another after a false start that could be blamed in part upon London in a hurry, and in part on Thomas Vernon trying for the Westwood effect of concentrated clutter, but without Westwood's allegorical geometry.

Westwood's links with the Croome of the Tory first, second, third and fourth Earls of Coventry was much more familiar and close than its links with a successful, but not very discerning, Vernon lawyer at Hanbury. Dorothy, it will be remembered, had been a Coventry, the daughter of the Lord Keeper, Thomas Coventry, who founded the family fortunes in James I's reign. That lost 1712 formal garden south of Croome Court was of its time, but it still had geometrical hankerings after the starburst effect of Carolean Westwood.

The Croome earls of Coventry, like the gardens at Croome Court, were sharply divided politically and, though genealogical claims of succession are often complex and dull, a brief study of the family's history is essential to make sense of their garden's history.[22] For a start, not only was 'Coventry' the title, first of their barony, which lasted from 1628 to 1697, and their earldom, which was awarded for a gift of £500 to William of Orange in that year, but it had been from the very beginning their surname, rather as if Mr Jones had become the Earl of Jones.

The fifth Baron Coventry, who bought his way to becoming the first Earl of Coventry, was Thomas and, despite his bribe to a king, who was the hero of the Whig party, he was himself a Tory and a supporter of the Stuarts, as were his successors the second Earl, and his brother, the fourth Earl. The third Earl hardly counts as he died aged ten at Eton a mere two years after succeeding to the title; the fourth Earl was, of course his uncle, and it was he who began a formal garden of distinctly Westwood association on the south side of Croome Court as soon as he succeeded to the title. To complicate the genealogy he died aged 51 in 1719 after only seven years enjoyment of the title, but in that short space he had laid out the formal garden and built lavish stables and kennels on the east side of the house. He died, consequently leaving the estate £2,172 in debt, much of which had been spent on the garden, for which we have full records.

Then came one of those serendipitous leaps of inheritance which come up occasionally. For the fifth Earl William to succeed the fourth Earl Gilbert, it has been calculated that, between his birth in 1678 and his succession in 1712, 38 people died who would have succeeded the fourth Earl if only they had lived longer. The fifth Earl was, in fact, a remote descendant of the first Baron, the Lord Keeper's brother. That wide genealogical leap was important because the new fifth Earl was a true Whig supporter. He had travelled to Hanover in the train of George I in 1718 and he was, before succeeding to the title, a Whig MP in the Commons. The king promptly made him Lord Lieutenant of Worcestershire for his loyalty and his son, the sixth Earl, would serve as Lord of the Bedchamber, therefore an intimate friend to George II and George III. That, however, is another story and another chapter, for now the interest must lie in the detailed accounts which we have of the fourth Earl Gilbert and his intense seven years of formal gardening. Because his daughter, Ann, married a Carew of Antony House in Cornwall, most of the garden records are in the Antony Archives. Earl Gilbert married twice, but never fathered a male heir; hence the genealogical leap to the fifth Earl. But both those two wives brought in a considerable fortune, which could explain the garden.

The layout (*18*) was recorded by Henry Beighton in its youthful prime in 1714.[23] There are four ogee-roofed garden pavilions around the house, two flanking the south garden and two the entrance forecourt. The south parterre is not simply quartered, it is a starburst of six paths striking out, not from the house as at Westwood, but from John Van Nost's lead statue of Hercules. Earl Gilbert bought this for 50 guineas in May 1715, and in his usual lavish style the Earl had it gilded,[24] a reference to the gilded lead statuary he would have seen the year before in the open air theatre in the gardens of Herrenhausen, shades therefore, not only of Westwood, but of a brash North German Baroque. While the Beighton map records certain similarities between Croome's south garden and Westwood's starburst with four towers, the impression which it gives of an insistent and conventional axial line north and south of the house is a deliberate Beighton distortion. He shows the north forecourt opening up, beyond its two flanking pavilions, with a gate aligned to the south garden's gate. That was how Beighton thought the grounds should be laid out, but it was not how they were in reality. The north forecourt remained blocked by a substantial three-bay gatehouse with Westwood-style shaped gables until as late as 1750 when a bird's-eye view of the house (*19*) shows the starburst of paths in the south garden, but not a single one of the four ogee-domed pavilions.[25] As a further puzzle, the south gardens' gates and gate piers are missing on the 1750 view. Yet there is a description of these in the Antony Archives: iron gates 15ft high with a coat of arms, exactly as Beighton illustrates them, with eagles on the gate piers:

These eagles I presume ought to be in proportion with ye pillars 2 foot and 10 inches high, the Pedistoll they are to stand upon being 2 foot 5 inches square, so [that] they may be sent without any Pedistoll if carefully packed up.[26]

These divergencies could be solved if the dating for that bird's-eye view of the house mentioned earlier could be revised back to 1712.

The planting of the starburst garden was conventional and was meant to be viewed in the old-fashioned manner, like that in the Westwood quadrants, from the terrace walks on either side of it, leading from the house to the twin south pavilions. Earl Gilbert's nurseryman was George Adams of Stoke's Croft, Bristol, a confident gentleman who assured the Earl: 'I am positive I can furnish my Lord with all sorts of plants boath Domestick and Exotick upon better termes and better success than any other man in England'.[27] He had supplied carnations and those standard punctuation marks for every Baroque formal bed: pyramidal yews, almost 6ft high, and globe hollies with full heads and 3ft stems. Those at least do feature on the Beighton view. Adams wanted to know if the Earl had 'resolved on a design'. He had: a starburst, but Adams was still eager to be in on the action, 'having had great and Long Experience, and have saved some hundreds of pounds in carrying on large designes'.[28]

It would be interesting to know what happened to all the nurserymen in England when this standard Baroque planting of parterres became unfashionable as it would do at Croome

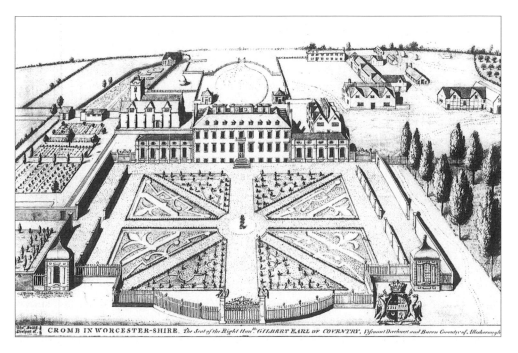

18 *Henry Beighton caught the formal south garden at Croome Court in 1714 in its brief maturity with that typical Worcestershire layout of six paths in a starburst.* By kind permission of the Croome Estate Trustees

19 *This 1750 bird's-eye view of Croome Court illustrating a sizeable north gatehouse calls into question the accuracy of Beighton's earlier, 1714, view with its open north axis.* By kind permission of the Croome Estate Trustees

in the next but one generation with the Arcadian reshaping of the grounds by the sixth Earl. For the meantime George Adams' income was secure. In that frenzy of spending before the fourth Earl died from 'gout of the stomach', one of those common but mysterious eighteenth-century maladies, he had bought a vine tree 'of an extraordinary kind' as well as orange and myrtle trees for a greenhouse, which one later plan shows perched up on the Kitchen Garden wall to the east of the house.[29] In addition a 1719 inventory refers to a Bowling Green House[30] and that, together with the new dog kennel and stables, would account for that clutter of service buildings to the east side of the house.[31]

In the perspective of garden design and changing fashions Earl Gilbert died at the right time. His formal garden, laid out with an eye to planting at Westwood that dated back to 1660, was out of date before George Adams got to work. His successor, William, the fifth Earl, would not be a gardener, being more interested in his broader responsibilities towards the county and compacting his estates by exchanges and purchasing. Croome Court's glory days in English garden history would come when he realised his inadequacy and handed over the estates in 1748 to George William, the future dynamic sixth Earl, three years before his own death in 1751. That gap between 1748 and 1751 will explain, in the next chapter, much that appears obscure and contradictory in a nationally important landscaping episode.

3

The earl, the landscaper and a morass

In garden history evaluations, Croome has the most important park in the county, which is not to say that it is the most beautiful, though it is interesting and it is very rewarding. Over two periods of time, one in the middle of the eighteenth century, and the other at the very end of the twentieth, Croome's grounds went through two unpredictable impositions of topographical rearrangement. The first followed 1748 when George William, the 26-year-old Lord Deerhurst, soon to become the sixth Earl, was given control of the estate by his father, William, the fifth Earl. The second shake-up followed 1996 when the National Trust bought what it describes as 'the core of the designed landscape'.[1]

In whatever way it is described, the 'core' is a challenge. Croome Park was very nearly a centre of inland drainage like the Great Salt Lake or the Dead Sea. Small streams do escape from it but not easily and not with any strong flow. It comes as no surprise to find a saline spring in Salt Baths Covert at its south-eastern corner. But only a mile away to the north, across several country lanes, and joined to Croome in the eighteenth century by a landscaped drive, is Pirton Court with its Old Park. Both properties were owned by the Coventry earls, and Pirton, with a large, attractive lake and a sharply defined ridge of wooded hillside, was a natural terrain for landscaping with a moated house as an ideal family seat with historic associations.[2] Yet it would be Croome, not Pirton, that had a fortune spent upon its grounds and two nationally celebrated architect-designers, Lancelot Brown and Robert Adam, doing their best, though in Brown's case at an early stage in his career, to make a silk purse out of a sow's ear by fashioning a handsome, trendsetting garden and park out of Croome's limp topography. If a sow's ear comes as too harsh a comparison, then we must remember the sixth Earl's description of the grounds in the Memorial he set up to Brown: 'Who by the powers of/His Indomitable/and creative Genius/formed this garden/Out of a morass', and the words of William Dean, who had served as Head Gardener at Croome for many years and claimed in 1824, quoting a correspondent to the *Gentleman's Magazine* of 1792, that the sixth Earl had contrived

> A vast extent of ground, formerly a mere bog, [which] is now adorned with islands, and tufts of trees of every species; and watered round, in the most pleasing, and natural manner, possible.[3]

What gives Croome an added melancholy distinction is that history has had to repeat itself. It needed to be rescued again, not from a morass this time, but from government planning. Before the National Trust intervened with such quixotic courage in 1996, the park had not just become dilapidated and vandalised. A wartime aerodrome had covered the land immediately east of the house, later lapsing into a science fiction horror movie backdrop of giant listening devices. More permanently damaging and intrusive, the M5 motorway was driven through the west side of the park, filling the air with that insidious undertone of traffic, cutting through Menagerie Wood and dividing the house from some of its most important visual landscape markers. For the Trust to attempt a rescue when Croome Court itself, with its pleasure ground and Rotunda, were still in private hands, was at least as gallant as the sixth Earl's first campaign. Whether either operation was well advised in the first place will make a valuable debating point in this narrative.

There can be no question over the will power of the sixth Earl. He was one of those rare people who, having an idea or an ambition, got things done. The more interesting questions are whether he was very intelligent, whether he had an informed taste and judgement, whether he got the right house built at Croome and the right landscape laid out for that difficult topography; and not all the answers to those questions are reassuring.

He had film star good looks, excellent dress sense and the confidence that goes with a handsome face; the 1765 Allan Ramsay portrait proves all three.[4] He was educated at Winchester and University College, Oxford, in virtual tandem with his adored elder brother, Thomas Henry, whose sudden, unexplained death in 1744, when George William was 22 years old, left the younger boy shattered and with a sense of having to make up for the loss to the family. In 1741 Thomas Henry had lost the parliamentary election for the county seat. In 1747 George William won it. To understand the strange shape of Croome Park's subsequent planning it is important to appreciate that the old fifth Earl gave George William, now his heir and Lord Deerhurst, complete control of the estate in 1748, three years before the old man died in 1751. Park events suggest that George William had really been in control a year earlier because it was in 1747 that John Phipps was taken on to sweep away Earl Gilbert's old-fashioned formal garden and create a long, serpentine canal, sleekly curved and by no means natural looking, in the park near the house. The serpentine would be in place by 1748. It is shown on Doharty's map of about 1751 (*colour plate 5*) as the 'New River' coming up close to the house where a little pavilion, the 'Evidence House', was sited on its bank, suggesting a combination of work over accounts and a pretty view of a 'Rococo' waterway, a miniature of that in Hyde Park. So this 'New River' was not a Capability Brown creation. It was in place when Brown was consulted first in 1751, which explains why it was so unlike the usual wide Brownian lake. All Brown did was to rough up its banks a little to make it look more of a river and less of a serpentine. Brown faced an exactly similar task with a serpentine at Longleat, but was not allowed to carry it through.[5]

That first firm action in the park proves that, well before he became sixth Earl, George William had seen the park's problem being one of drainage. It was noted in a previous chapter that Worcestershire had an underlying problem with many of its houses over an impervious layer of clay. This could be solved by a moat and it is obvious where George William hit upon the drainage solution. Pirton Court, the family property a mile away, where he is known to have lived while he was rebuilding Croome, had a quite complex system of moats around the Court with two little canal-like arms jutting into its small formal garden. An actual moat around Croome, dug in 1747, would have been an anachronism; the solution was the serpentine, a fashionable substitute for a moat, one which Brown would then have to bring further up-to-date by making it look natural. There remains one other question over this feature, a question staring in the face of anyone who looks at Croome estate maps, like John Snape's of 1796.[6] Was the Phipps serpentine (20) literally intended to look like a serpent?[7] That, with its long winding body and head and eyes in the wider section near the Grotto, is what it resembles; but there can be no conclusive answer.

Another important question does need an answer: once George William had become sixth Earl in 1751 and in absolute control of everything, who might have influenced his grand design for the park? That serpentine already indicates a feeling, quite fashionable in 1748, for Rococo or Arcadian features; and he would go on to create, at some distance from the house, an Arcadian area of classical temples and seats around that serpent's head by the Grotto. To reject a domed classical design when he was rebuilding the church on the marl ridge to the north-east of the house and to choose instead a Gothick scheme was eclectic and, again, fashionable. Brown would have difficulties

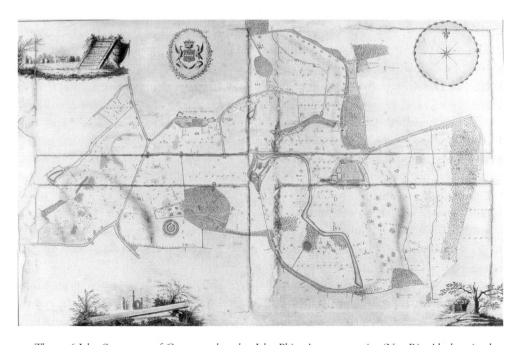

20 *The 1796 John Snape map of Croome park makes John Phipps' 1747 serpentine 'New River' look curiously like a monster with its head at the Grotto with its island.* By kind permission of the Croome Estate Trustees

with the design and Robert Adam would have to complete it, but there had to be other influential advisers behind these moves.

Unexpectedly for such a sexually conventional man, the sixth Earl was quite closely involved with the Strawberry Hill set. Horace Walpole, who was a confirmed bachelor, entertained George William and his dreadful first wife, Maria, at Strawberry on 2 June 1759.[8] 'Dickie' Bateman, who built that exquisitely ambivalent Gothick church at his Herefordshire seat, Shobdon, in 1746, almost certainly with the help of William Kent, was a member of the Strawberry group, and he visited Croome to praise the New River on 17 April 1750: 'I dare say Croomb is in great beauty....You have made a River where no water ever *ran* before'.[9] The chief influence on the sixth Earl must, however, have been Sanderson Miller with whom he was so friendly that he insisted upon Brown designing a new house around the old foundations and chimney stacks of Croome using as its basic form an uninspired, but safely Palladian, design roughed out for him by Miller. No one has ever quite explained the way Sanderson Miller, a minor Warwickshire squire of Radway, with no talent at all for careful practical architectural designs, but a man always ready to sketch something out, should have had such an influence – Gothick and classical – on gentry and aristocrats. He must have been charming and persuasive company. But it was he who urged George William to visit Hagley Hall to see what Lord Lyttelton was doing in his park. Lyttelton, for his part, was strongly influenced by the very minor squire, but much admired poet, William Shenstone, who had a landscape park at The Leasowes, Halesowen. There was, therefore, a Miller-inspired chain of connection between three Worcestershire parks: The Leasowes, Hagley and Croome.

That would have given the sixth Earl an eclectic awareness, hence the Gothick Church completed by Adam in 1763, with a Rococo elegance that makes Shobdon look jejune, and the Chinese Bridge over the serpentine near the house to a design by William Halfpenny of 1751 or earlier, certainly before Brown got to work.[10] It was Miller again who introduced the sixth Earl to Brown. He had been visiting Miller at Radway in August 1750 after Brown had shown Miller around the eclectic garden buildings at Stowe in November 1749, when Brown was still employed as Head Gardener at Stowe. The timing was perfect for the sixth Earl. He had already shown his awareness of drainage as Croome's big problem, and drainage was a speciality of Brown and his teams of workers. Bluff, northern Brown was the kind of man George William could cope with and vice versa; so for two intense, and expensive, periods: 1751-6 and 1762-6, Brown's trained teams were transforming that 'morass' or 'mere bog' into 'rich fertility'. Croome would never be the standard Brownian park with a gracefully swelling lake and a carriage drive around the entire perimeter. That was because Brown came in after Phipps and because the sixth Earl had an obvious fondness for Pirton, which already had a swelling lake. In a later consideration of the grounds of Croome as they work now, the strengths and weaknesses of the Brown-George William compromise scheme will be considered. For now it is enough to notice that the typical Brown carriage drive, admirably cambered and graded, with clumps of trees planted along its lengths, was not laid out around Croome Park, but to link Croome with Pirton.[11] It was implicit in George William's ambitious personality, his determination as Lord Lieutenant and Custos Rotulorum of Worcestershire, to cut a dominant figure in the county, that he wanted to site marker garden towers at the very limits of his estate, and even out 15 miles away on Fish Hill behind Broadway.

Most of our evidence as to George William's personal character comes from the very doubtful source of Horace Walpole, who was obviously attracted by his good looks and frustrated by his manifestly heterosexual inclinations. Even so, in his early manhood, the years when he was taking decisions to shape Croome's grounds, the sixth Earl does seem to have been as film star in his lifestyle as in his looks. Two Irish girls, the Gunning sisters, Elizabeth the elder and Maria, had hit English society with all the impact that Marilyn Monroe would have on America in the twentieth century; and even more. Seven hundred people are said to have sat up all night around an inn where one of the sisters was staying, only for the privilege of seeing her get into a coach after breakfast the next morning. The Duke of Hamilton snapped up the older girl as his bride with such haste that he had to use the traditional curtain ring on her finger. George William had to have Maria, the younger sister, which is a useful pointer to his character, but not to her influence on Croome Park. That was entirely negative as she disliked the country and loved London.

Although she was an exceptionally silly girl (she told the ageing King George II that what she was really looking forward to was the next coronation), George William seems to have truly loved her to the end and re-dedicated Croome Church from St James to St Mary in her honour. She embarrassed him at every turn and played ruthlessly upon his natural jealousy, but the physical attraction was so strong that she got away with it. Offered alternative sleeping accommodation to escape the bed bugs of a dirty French inn, Maria declared she would 'rather be bit to death, than lie one night from my dear Cov.'[12] Luckily for 'dear Cov' the marriage did not last long. Maria died lingeringly of tuberculosis in 1760 after a union of eight years. The sixth Earl's second marriage in 1764, a decent interval, was much happier. His bride, Barbara St John, Lord St John of Bletsoe's daughter, was a most cheerful lady, devoted to the country and to country fetes. Under her influence Croome Park prospered as her husband lavished garden gifts upon her. There were the usual park pleasures associated with ladies, a model diary with a model farm, but the second Countess's real interest was in her Menagerie which seems, by the time of the Royal Visit in July 1788, to have out-pointed every other feature in the park as the crowning element in a tour even though it was out on a limb to the west at Cubsmoor. It was begun in 1768 soon after the marriage and had become such an ambitious collection with red-headed parakeets, a 'Snow' bird, Cape geese, white turkeys, silver pheasants, Turkish ducks, a flying squirrel and two American deer, that when the Mayor and Corporation of Worcester visited it they were charged for the privilege.[13] At one point in 1780 a truly palatial design by Robert Adam was under consideration, but in the end the Countess settled for Adam's Keeper's House with a fine reception room for visitors.[14]

If all the important garden buildings at and around Croome are set out in their chronological order it becomes apparent why, for all the money spent on it, Croome has usually been considered an important rather than a strikingly beautiful park. Three well-known architect-designers – Lancelot Brown, Robert Adam and James Wyatt – all contributed to it, which suggests occasional bursts of interest rather than one united vision. The list of their works covers a long chronological span from 1754, when Brown designed the Rotunda[15] in the pleasure grounds at the back of the house, before the new house was constructed in 1757-62, to 1794 when the Broadway Tower was set up on Fish Hill to a bizarre 'Saxon' scheme by James Wyatt.[16] Both the time span and the area covered by those 16 or more park buildings or features were too great for coherent beauty to result.

In the 1760s there was a real campaign of park building around the serpent's head of the river. In 1760 Adam's elegant Temple Greenhouse went up (*21*), and in 1765 Brown's Dry Arch, to make the most visual drive to the house even more dramatic, and the Grotto was begun. But that was all, and none of those features group strikingly, while Adam's Island Temple would not be added until 1776. It is noticeable that when Richard Wilson painted the new house in 1758,[17] he could include Phipps' serpentine, Halfpenny's Chinese Bridge seen from a great distance, Brown's Gothick Croome Church (*22*) on the marl ridge to the north of the house and the Rotunda on the ridge to the south (*colour plate 7*), but there was no connecting vision, only a superb cloudscape and the boxy, Miller-Brown new house caught at a flattering side angle with a fine light effect.

At least Countess Barbara encouraged her husband's plant collections, said, improbably, to rival Kew's, and she arranged some wonderful firework displays over the water. She made him happy and, through the 1780s, relatively inactive over park buildings. When she died in 1804 he had just been indulging in a few long-range marker buildings: Wyatt's Pirton Tower on Rabbit Bank among a line of cedars in 1797 and the Broadway Tower in 1794. Her death disheartened him and he died two years later, honoured and respected by the whole county, which he is said to have enriched to the tune of millions by his investments in canals and turnpike roads.

We are privileged today to see Croome in something of that incomplete state of positive activity, which the park must have exhibited somewhere around 1755, when Brown was laying out the planting for strategic concealments and his culverts and pipes were draining the 'morass' into the New River. The National Trust has taken on here at Croome an even more challenging restoration than it has at Hanbury. A final aesthetic judgement must be witheld until the work has matured, but it may help to understand the problems the Trust faced if a visitor, having parked the car, looks over the fence at an ugly and dilapidated cluster of khaki-coloured sheds on the edge of ruin. These are the remains of the 1939-45 wartime aerodrome, but it is being seriously proposed that they too should be preserved as an historic relic.

Visitors will find themselves in a second aesthetic problem, one of orientation and incomplete planting, as soon as they leave the ticket office. A winding shrubbery walk has been replanted in 1999, lined with flowering shrubs, honeysuckle, wild roses, brooms and hawthorn of correct eighteenth-century provenance. It leads to the Church and is a valuable reminder that flowering bushes were finding a place, sweet-scented and intimate in scale, alongside the grand effects of lawn, lake, hillside and grove.[18] It will soon be possible, when the more recent Shrubbery Walk with its path leading across to the Grotto

21 *Robert Adam's Temple Greenhouse of 1760 housed an orangery and created an incident on Croome's inner circuit walk on the way to the Menagerie*

22 *Lancelot Brown's Gothick Church on the eastern marl ridge at Croome acted as an eyecatcher from the house and framed views of the valley with the Temple Greenhouse to the west*

and the Lake has matured, to enjoy that westward extension of this 'Church Walk'. What can only be appreciated by study of John Snape's carefully detailed survey (*23*) is that this Church Walk continued under the public road to a walled Flower Garden set out beside the lane to Pirton Court. Snape indicates a nursery and gardener's cottage across the lane from it, while the Flower Garden has a small round pool, two formally-placed pavilions among irregularly-shaped flower-beds and three further service buildings.

By its distant siting the Flower Garden could either have been intended as a feature to be enjoyed by both houses – Croome and Pirton – or else one of the ladies of Croome was a keen walker as well as a flower fancier and had created a floral route to a private retreat as far from the house as possible. Did the Church have some social role to play at the centre of this route? Was a walk before or after Morning Prayer part of Croome's social ritual when the sixth Earl's country-loving second wife reigned? It is from the churchyard that Croome's grounds begin to make sense with wide views across a flat valley to the Malverns in the distance and Croome Court below to the left. Brown had created several scenic drives to the house. The most direct ran almost straight to the Court from the public road. Adam enhanced this with his London Arch of 1779 where a panel of Day welcomed visitors and another of Night symbolically

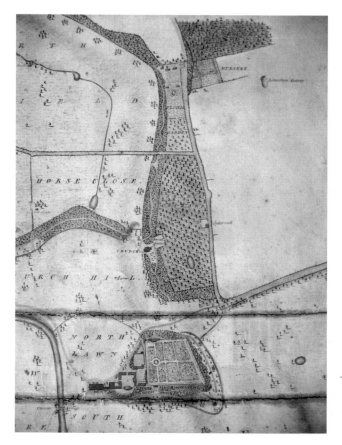

23 *This enlarged detail from the Snape map of Croome shows how formal in its pavilions but informal in its bedding was the Flower Garden far out north of the Church.* By kind permission of the Croome Estate Trustees

regretted their departure.[19] But the most visual drive was the one from High Green, which ran under the Dry Arch of 1765, again handsomely enhanced with Coade stone keystones, this time by Wyatt, in 1797. It would have afforded attractive glimpses of the most Arcadian part of the park at the top of the New River and then the house itself seen at an angle where the dull elevations would have looked their best.

The viewpoint by the Church is as fair a place as any to attempt an assessment of the National Trust's brave project. In its introductory pamphlet the Trust claims correctly that here Brown achieved a revolutionary combination of beauty and economic efficiency. What is less accurate is the next claim that: 'At Croome, Brown established the English Landscape Style which was admired and copied throughout the western world'. The 'English Garden', so widely copied on the Continent from France to Russia, was not so much Brown's open parkscapes with artfully clumped trees and ingeniously 'natural' lakes. It was the 'Rococo' Gardens, the Arcadias of eclectic garden pavilions dotted around such 'arti-natural' landscapes, that caught the imagination of French, Swedish, German and Russian aristocracies. Brown's speciality was not pavilion designing or even church designing. The evidence for that is here at Croome, where Robert Adam, William Halfpenny and James Wyatt were all called in for pavilion and lodge design. Even the New River is uncharacteristic of Brown's lake styling. Brown's forte was in draining, drive laying, tree clumping and the building of often vast earth dams, planted with trees to look completely natural. Croome needed no such dam.

Brown was not his own master at Croome. He was obliged, by his strong-willed patron, the sixth Earl, to engineer an Arcadia on an unsuitable site. The old house, which the Earl refused to abandon, lay too low for fine views of the Malverns, Bredon or the Forest of Dean; it did not even command the River Severn. Brown had to make the best of some very slight lines of rising land such as the marl ridge on which the Church was built. To compensate for an initial error, the Earl seems to have felt called, especially in old age, to build vista markers much too far from the house to work well. From the Rotunda on the rise behind the house it is just possible to see, with a spy glass, five markers: Pirton Tower, the Panorama Tower on Knights Hill at Cubsmoor, where the Court should ideally have been re-sited, the Park Seat (Owl's Nest), Broadway Tower and Baughton Tower – in no way do any of these pull together; they are mere assertions of ownership like those long avenues of trees so popular around country houses in the late seventeenth century.

A more recent misfortune is apparent from this vantage point by the Church. The Trust owns neither the Court nor its back garden with that scenically strategic Rotunda, and the boundary between Court lawn and Trust field is painfully obvious. Though there is no dividing fence or wall the Trust's grass is rough and tawny, the private land is immaculately green and shaven, an arbitrary and quite unhistorical division. What is more helpfully provocative is the wide swathe of bushes and young trees which the Trust has planted to link this headland by the Church with the distant cluster of park buildings around the Grotto at the top of the New River. Brown planted on exactly the same site but all his trees and bushes were cleared to give a wide open view north from the house. Has the Trust repeated Brown's error or his masterstroke? Was the new road with the new village a blemish which Brown was correct to hide? In a later chapter on modern gardens of the county this same problem is being faced in the grounds of Kemerton Court: to confine or not to confine? The sixth Earl made things happen in his park, but not always the right things. He seems to have imposed on the grounds his vision of two distinct visual circuits. One that we are looking at was a walking tour for the ladies. It ran from the house to the Church, with its oddly sited Shrubbery and orchard; then across to the Temple Greenhouse and the temple pleasures around the Grotto and the New River's widening: the Dry Arch, the Grotto, the Rope Ferry to the Island Temple, the two Boathouses (now lost).

It is easy to underrate the central role of the Grotto in this area (*colour plate 6*), because it now runs dry (*24*), stripped of the delicate shells and Derbyshire 'Petrifactions' which the Countess ordered for it,[20] the hollow cave has lost its magic. The Trust will, it is to be hoped, work hard on it in the future. It needs those shells, and that cold bath, which excavation has revealed, should be restored. Above all it needs the backing of evergreen trees, abundant ferns, the trickle of water, moist surfaces and that Coade stone statue of Sabrina, Goddess of the Severn, pouring her stream. These things have been restored in Stourhead's more hidden Grotto, Croome has the same need of them. It should be possible for visitors to sit here in a dark shade and look out at a templed island and riverbanks with mature trees. The restoration has taken us back to roughly 1765, and that is too early.

24 *In its present restored condition the Grotto at Croome awaits a sympathetic treatment with greenery and the return of its nymph Sabrina*

At this point in the walk, if the ladies were tired, the Chinese Bridge could take them back to the house, satisfied by an eclectic Arcadia of some charm (Wyatt's stone statue of the Druid has not yet been replaced).[21] If the ladies were vigorous their circuit could be extended to the Menagerie where there would be refreshment, and on to the Park Seat[22] and so back to the Rotunda and the house.

The riding circuit was much longer and much less connected. Horseback would have been likelier than carriage seat. It passed the Church, took the drive to Pirton Court then led by public lanes to the Panorama Tower (25) on Knight's Hill. This ingenious two-storey structure was planned in 1766 but not built to Wyatt's design until 1807. It had an upstairs room where a meal could be taken and a superb view of the Malverns and a real river, the Severn, could be enjoyed. Further public lanes would bring the riders to Adam's dramatic shell of Dunstall Castle (26).[23] There would be no more refreshment until the riders came up, by more public lanes, to the Keeper's House in the Baughton Tower and back at last by the impressive London Gate. Obviously this was anything but a park circuit. Brown, so fixated upon drives that circumnavigated a park's entire boundary with careful tree planting to reveal selected views, must have despaired of the sixth Earl's second circuit; not one of its markers was designed by Brown.

In perhaps 20 years we will be able to enjoy that inner circuit as the sixth Earl could have enjoyed it by 1780, when he would have been 58 years old. Perhaps it is wrong to

25 James Wyatt's 1807 Panorama Tower on Knight's Hill with its raised viewing room offered a view of the Malvern Hills and the Severn on the sixth Earl's outer circuit for horse riders or carriage drivers. It was actually planned in 1766

26 Robert Adam's 1766-7 Romanesque and Gothick composite at Dunstall Castle provided the next stopping place after Wyatt's Panorama Tower on Croome's ambitious outer circuit

express it in walking terms. There was a mile-long river, two islands, two Boathouses, a Rope Ferry and a fair scatter of temples, with the nymph Sabrina pouring the river out from her inverted vase. Fireworks by night, island picnics by day, music concerts in the flattering acoustics of Adam's Temple Greenhouse, with oranges to be plucked directly from the bushes: how little of an eighteenth-century Arcadia can we recreate? How enjoyable might that outer circuit have been if taken at an exhilarating gallop with iced wine waiting in the upper room of the Panorama Tower and buttered crumpets toasted by the keeper's wife in the Baughton Tower? The past is another country and we need to be wary in our assessments of it.

To appreciate the contrasts and the variety of these regions of parkland inspired by that vague Arcadian ideal, half-Horatian, half-Virgilian, it is helpful to move in the imagination directly from the high room in the Broadway Tower to The Leasowes estate of the poet William Shenstone, that leafy dell miraculously preserved in the urban heart of Halesowen. Croome was a triumph of the will, The Leasowes was a triumph of sentiment. Frankly it seems unlikely that the sixth Earl had an eye for the composition of Arcadias, but he had money and he could hire men to do his erratic bidding. We should remember him up there in the tower of his old age, looking down upon the county he had helped to enrich: an arrogant, admirable old aristocrat; then turn to a different version of Arcadia created by a sensitive soul with very little money, but a desperate need to be admired and visited for some visual achievement.

4

William Shenstone –
bad poet, great gardener

After reading second-hand assessments of William Shenstone's character and vague accounts of his 35-acre garden at The Leasowes, Halesowen,[1] it is difficult to say which then came as the greater surprise: his real character, as revealed in his headlong correspondence, or his real garden, as experienced when walking its circuit one August morning. To enliven their pages some garden histories project Shenstone as a whimsical poseur, putting him across as a versifier whose absurd garden was laid out on the cheap with multiple 'seats', coy inscriptions and gimcrack wooden temples. What is consequently hard to explain is how that parody of a garden caught the interest and attracted the visits of virtually all his contemporaries in the garden world, including, incidentally, the sixth Earl of Coventry, who planned a visit to The Leasowes in the summer of 1754, probably to see what all the fuss was about.[2]

A passage of Shenstone's poetry is often quoted to prove how fey he was:

Here, in cool grott, & mossy Cell,
We Fauns & playfull Fairies dwell,
Tho' rarely seen by mortal Eye,
When ye pale Moon, ascended high,
Darts thro' yon Limes her quiv'ring beam,
We frisk it near this crystal stream.[3]

The truth is that the lines were in no way ridiculous, but part of a witty mock curse by 'Oberon, King of the Fairies', pinned up at the public entrance to The Leasowes as a warning against picking flowers or breaking off branches. It ends:

Then fear to spoil these sacred Bow'rs;
Nor wound ye shrubs, nor crop ye Flowers,[4]

which was, no doubt, all very necessary, knowing how acquisitive visiting garden enthusiasts can be.

The real William Shenstone was, it is true, yet another of those confirmed bachelors of the high Anglican sensibility. There is no need to apologise for such an accumulation of gay gardeners, but the grouping does require an explanation and the key is literary. With no family or children to distract them, these bachelors were inclined to network for mutual support. A good case can be made for the Arcadian garden being the result of letter writing. In the middle years of the eighteenth century Horace Walpole, Thomas Gray, The Revd. Joseph Spence, Richard Bateman, to name just a few, devoted themselves to experiment with their gardens as instruments to shape and to respond to the mood of their visitors. Shenstone in particular, being short of funds for the raising of the usual stone temples, had to project The Leasowes as the eighteenth-century equivalent of a psychiatrist's couch. Its circuit was to be walked as an exploration of emotion – Sensibility – and as a training in the Picturesque lore for appreciating the minute subtleties of landscape composition. To come on a visit without a Claude Glass, which reduced a view to its essentials, was to betray an amateur status. Shenstone himself even used one, fitted up on a screen, to look at landscapes;[5] while one of his friends, Mr Dolman, was actually experimenting with a portable *camera obscura* that could, so he hoped, be used as he travelled along in a darkened, window-less carriage.[6] It was a very precious moment in garden history and the bachelors revelled in its nuances and the superiority its jargon gave them.

It cannot be stressed too much that this group of Arcadian gardeners was literary. Shenstone would have acquired no fame if he had not had a wide range of like-minded friends to whom he could write letters concentrating, first upon literary criticism, secondly upon his garden activities. Yet he had failed to gain a degree from Pembroke College, Oxford. Like John Betjeman, two centuries later, he exercised a witty, bumbling charm to create an image of the poet himself as the poetry, and to project the little notices and inscriptions which he set up on roots and tree trunks, as more essential to the garden than the trees or the views. In our present century, Ian Hamilton Finlay has pulled off a similar trick around his home at Little Sparta in the Pentland Hills of Southern Scotland.[7] Shenstone cleverly anticipated Hamilton Finlay's discovery that a short 'concrete' poem gains enormously by being set in a rich physical context of stone, wood and water. His was a true avant garde and that was why, between 1746 and his death in 1763, more than a hundred gardeners of wealth and influence, peers, merchants and militia men, with their wives and families, came to experience, not simply a garden phenomenon, but themselves into the bargain. It was a true advance in self-knowledge.

After the eye had been vista-trained over The Leasowes' modest Midlands prospects: the Clent Hills, Halesowen church spire, Hagley, Enville, the Wrekin and, further away, the Welsh Hills, these aficionados of the Picturesque could move on, Claude Glass at the ready, to the Lake District, the Wye Valley, the Derbyshire Peak and, for determined men like Dr Johnson, the Highlands of Scotland. Shenstone's The Leasowes represented a real move forward in sensitive human awareness of the environment. He was one of Worcestershire's greatest sons, and it is to the enormous credit of Halesowen that the town has preserved his subtle, underplayed circuit almost intact: a green, south-tilted bowl of land entirely surrounded by urban development. Whoever thought of replacing Shenstone's 'Farm', not that it ever was a serious farm, more a villa on the model of the Veneto, with a golf course, was a genius of practical compromise.

The quickest way to absorb Shenstone's sharp literary and critical qualities is to analyse a typical letter, one written to the Revd. Thomas Percy on 11 August 1760. Some indication of Shenstone's own literary ranking may be judged from the fact that, five years later, Bishop Percy published his *Reliques of Ancient English Poetry* which would prove a seminal influence upon the poetry of both Wordsworth and Coleridge. Yet here Shenstone is delivering firm, authoritative instructions to his friend. The two men had been discussing bizarre garden ornaments such as whitewashed trees:

> My good Friend Mr Spence intends a whole *Pamphlett of this kind*; which he calls ye *History* of false Taste: but I do not expect any great matter, from a subject of *Humouring* my Friend's Hands. *Dodsley* gave me this Intimation; who resides here for near two months, to correct ye edition of Fables begun by Baskerville. He has given me a Portrait of his head by Reynolds, ye Price of which I am asham'd to mention. He seems to entertain no doubt, yt your Chinese novel will excite Curiosity – You will perhaps be desirous to know what I have of late been doing about my Farm. One Piece of water below my Priory has *confin'd* me, *employ'd* my servants, and *enslav'd* my Horses all this year – I hope to finish it, the next week; but have often been *deluded* by such expectations. I have had a large conflux of visitants; and expect *more*, when Ld. Lyttelton brings all ye world to his new Palace.[8]

The 'new Palace' referred to was Hagley Hall, which had been completed to Sanderson Miller's characteristically uninspired Palladian design in that year. A half friendly, half maliciously competitive relationship existed as a constant between Shenstone and his neighbour, Lord Lyttelton, a courtier disappointed in his political ambitions by the unexpected death, in 1751, of the heir to the throne, Frederick Lewis, Prince of Wales. Sanderson Miller was a friend to both Shenstone and Lyttelton, relaying denigratory remarks about their gardens from one party to the other.

A critical sharpness, even an impatience, can be sensed throughout this excerpt from the letter. The implication is that Joseph Spence, a rival gardener and authority on Alexander Pope's poetry, has no sense of humour; Sir Joshua Reynolds overcharges for his sketches; Percy is unwise to press on with his Chinese novel (Shenstone was right, it was not well received); while garden operations usually run over in time and money. The relationship between Shenstone and his publisher, Robert Dodsley, was clearly more intimate than the usual one between author and publisher, with expensive presents and long residential working sessions. In the next 20 lines of the letter Shenstone went on to list and assess, usually witheringly, seven other recent publications in tones of the same confident authority: books on painting and poetry together with the discovery of a 'lost' Shakespeare play, *Edward III*, which he dismissed, correctly, as a forgery. Another

Dodsley publication was lauded and he promised to deal with a translation from Ovid. This was obviously not the writing of a scribbling amateur. Yet in his garden, this one-man literary magazine, cool to the point of arrogance, could indulge in seats and buildings of quavering sentimentality and in rapturous appreciation of relative visual trivia. It was of the essence of this period that things of nature and perceptions of the emotions were linked and sympathetic. The garden at The Leasowes was the poet's exploration of the soul, not for him only but for all visitors.

From the guide to The Leasowes which Dodsley wrote after his friend's death, it appears that he was behind Shenstone's project and that it was all something of a media creation. Dodsley stayed in the house for long periods, sharing it with Shenstone and Dodsley's frail brother Joseph. They were in the business of The Tully's Head, R. and J. Dodsley of Pall Mall, publishers, together. So it was in Robert's financial interest that his friend William should become a national celebrity, that some rather mediocre verse should go through several editions. If he were alive now Shenstone would be described as shamelessly camp, a Boy George of the gardening world. For his three volume *Works in Verse and Prose*, which went quickly through four editions such was his reputation, an extraordinary frontispiece was engraved (*27*). In it Shenstone, looking understandably

27 Robert Dodsley, William Shenstone's close friend and publisher, must have commissioned this startling frontispiece for his Works in Verse and Prose, *deliberately to excite a personality cult.* Bristol University Special Collections

complacent, stands close to the almost naked god, Apollo, who has the physique of a weightlifter. Shenstone appears to be reaching out to stroke the god's stomach as Apollo crowns him with a wreath. But the gesture is an illusion, the poet is only stretching out to play on a portable pipe organ which just happens to be placed in the garden.

All of this could be dismissed as camp showmanship on Shenstone's part, but in fact he was dead before the frontispiece was produced. The production gimmick was Robert Dodsley's. There is a tendency to accept the eighteenth century as a time of Reason, restrained, tasteful, and gentlemanly. But in real life it was an age of high camp, legs were exposed to the best advantage in hose with silk breeches and young men were expected to ape 70 year-olds with white powdered wigs; it was a time for unreserved emotional exploration. Moral sensitivity probably resulted much later, from the collision between Victorian religiosity and Oscar Wilde. Shenstone and his garden fitted their age like a glove, otherwise the family parties would not have come trouping in. 'I have been attending on a Sir J. Mostyn with a Party of Ladies & Militia-Gentlemen, yt have been long quartered at Bridgnorth', Shenstone told Percy in another letter. 'They seemed very good sort of People, without any great Depth of *Taste*':[9] perfect middle class fodder for his sensibility circuit.

What the confident, forceful sixth Earl of Coventry would have made of this extrovert poet and his pretty grounds is worth a question. Shenstone was, predictably, devoted to flowers, though guilty about his indulgence in them. 'I have been embroidering my Grove with Flowers', he wrote to his favourite confidante, the adulterous Lady Luxborough who lived nearby in her oddly styled house, Barrels, 'till I almost begin to fear it looks too like a *garden*'.[10] He had been reading Batty Langley's *New Principles of Gardening* (1728), and Langley's detailed plans had blurred the distinction between a park of 'groves' and a garden of flowery features. Shenstone must have caught himself looking at Langley's plans of winding paths and occasional features that resembled his own Leasowes circuit where: 'I have two or three Peonies in my grove, yt I have planted amongst Fern and brambles in a gloomy Place by ye Water's side. You will not easily conceive how good an Effect they produce, & how great a stress I lay upon them'.[11] Peonies will not last long amid brambles, so much of this campaign to naturalise garden flowers was doomed to failure. It would take William Mason and Humphry Repton to come to the logical conclusion of putting flowers like peonies in small formal beds, the epitome of the nineteenth-century Gardenesque style which would destroy the relaxed Arcadian air of a garden-park.

One of Shenstone's solutions was wild flower planting. 'I have been busy in paving a small serpentine stream & planting Flowers by ye side', he wrote, but added plaintively, 'I am afraid I shall find it impossible to preserve them. I would gladly enough compound ye matter wth ye Mob if they wou'd leave me about *Half*'.[12] He was writing about primrose roots. Visitors had only to see that one had been planted rather than growing naturally and they would pocket it.

He was a natural complainer, forever moaning about his inadequate income: the price of a 'Hermit's Seat will amount, on a moderate computation, to ye sum of fifteen Shillings & Six pence three Farthings'.[13] But he lived in a handsome Palladian villa (*28*)

28 *Much of Shenstone's Palladian villa at The Leasowes survives in the present clubhouse of a golf course; his Gothick stables have been demolished*

with large Gothick stables, a staff of servants and attractive grounds. Inheriting from his father in 1742 he had made his property, which he mockingly described as a *ferme ornée*, into a nationally appreciated artwork by 1744. Yet he still nursed a sizeable inferiority complex. He wrote sadly to the Revd. Richard Graves on 21 August 1748:

> instead of pursuing the way to the fine lawns, and venerable oaks, which distinguish the region of it, I am got into the pitiful parterre-garden of amusement, and view the nobler scenes at a *distance*. I think I can see the *road* too that *leads* the better way, and can shew it to others; but I have many miles to measure before I can get into it myself…My chief amusements at present are the same they have long been, and lie scattered about my farm.[14]

His problem was Hagley. Lord Lyttelton lived so near and had so much more money to spend on improvements. Shenstone wrote enviously:

> They are going to build a castle in the park round the lodge, which, if well executed, must have a good effect; and they are going likewise to build a rotund to terminate the visto. The fault is, that they anticipate every thing which I propose to do when I become *rich*; but as that is never likely to be, perhaps it is not of any importance.[15]

So much for Shenstone the man, his limitations and his uncertainties. Against all the odds his frail creation has survived in the care of an enlightened civic authority and can be enjoyed at any time of the day, with no entrance fee, unless the visitor wishes to play golf. There has been some thoughtful restoration work, but to experience that idyllic circuit with all its associations, a true time trip back into a garden of Sensibility, a visitor should obtain a copy of Dodsley's map (*29*) with 25 seats and ten garden buildings on its route. Dodsley prepared this and included, from his own experience of walking the route many times with his friend, a full and enthusiastic description of its pleasures.[16]

It is appropriate, therefore, to join the circuit at numbers 13 and 14 as they were dedicated by Shenstone expressly to his friend Dodsley. It is not easy to reach the circuit as it is hidden away in a bowl of land which Dodsley described as 'a punch-bowl, ornamented within with all the romantic scenery the Chinese ever yet devised',[17] a reference to those heavy pottery bowls of the period painted with garden scenes where young men in turbans poured rivers from vases and fed peacocks and pheasants under flowering trees. If the road signs are followed from Halesowen's busy main street to the

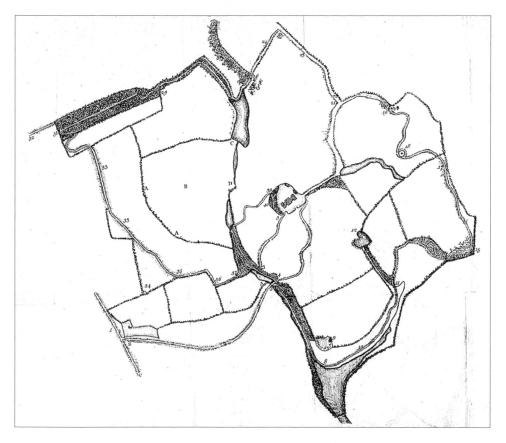

29 It is still possible, using a copy of Dodsley's map of The Leasowes, *to trace most of the sites illustrated here on its Picturesque circuit.* Bristol University Special Collections

local further education college the road heads steeply downhill into an unexpected rural tranquillity and a grove of dark yew trees outside the college's nursery gardens. This is Dodsley's 'forest ground...a landskip fit for the pencil of Salvator Rosa'.[18] Tiny channels can still be traced in the grass, rocky feeders to what was once a small serpentine below the house. Here, at number 14, was a statue of a faun, also visible from the house windows, and a tribute to Dodsley in the form of a small poem on a board:

> Come then my friend, thy sylvan taste display
> Come, hear thy Faunus tune his rustic lay.
> Ah, rather come and in these dells disown
> The care of other strains, and tune thine own.[19]

It was from a point just up the hill at number 15 that circuit walkers were supposed to get their first view of the Priory, low down in the bowl by the little lake. The circuit will lead right past the Priory's site but, in the perverse disciplines of connoisseurs of the Picturesque, visitors were urged not to look at that Gothick cottage or to bother the old couple living in it for a small rent. It was only to be enjoyed from proper distances as if from a Claude Glass. Ours is not to argue, only to absorb. From the yew grove outside the present Nursery the circuit path leads steeply down the valley of the North Stream, the lesser of the two streams that water the 35 acres and the little lakes. At first the path is a walk among holly bushes, yews and sycamore trees, typical planting of the period. Then quite suddenly the valley deepens (*colour plate 8*) and this surprising scale of the garden will continue for about a mile, until well beyond Virgil's Grove. The tiny stream is occasionally channelled and conducted; beeches and oaks of maturity close in. Here at number 11 was another cast of a Piping Faun and an Urn dedicated to William Somerville, author of a poem, *The Chace*, who died in 1742.[20] He was a friend of Shenstone's youth. 'I loved Mr Somerville', he wrote 'because he knew so perfectly what belonged to the flocci-nauci-nihili-pilification of money'.[21] He was obviously Shenstone's financial adviser.

This was the site of a lost feature of the garden, probably its most dramatic. At number 11 with the Faun and the Urn was 'a thicket of many sorts of willow' shaped around a large Root House inscribed to the honour of the Earl of Stamford. Shenstone advised the Earl regularly on the gardening of his Arcadian park, just over the border in Shropshire, and seems never to have felt as threatened by the developments at Enville as he was by those at Hagley, where he was not consulted, merely invited over to admire the superior Arcadian garden buildings. The charm of the Root House was that anyone sitting in it could look uphill and enjoy a little cataract tumbling down between wooded banks from a heart-shaped source at number 12. Dodsley reported: 'a more wild and romantic appearance of water, and at the same time strictly natural, is what I never saw in any place whatever',[22] but it should be appreciated that this romantic, wild water was unlikely to have been much more than 2ft wide and 2in deep. The Leasowes was, and still is, Arcadia in miniature.

1 *Birtsmorton Court, a house of medieval origins, not so much moated as islanded in an artificial lake below the Westminster Pool. One of many metal sculptures collected by the owner is in the foreground*

2 *Westwood's park is now one large arable field. The Gatehouse, composed of two linked lodges, was only one of five detached pavilions set around this former seventeenth-century hunting lodge of the Pakingtons*

3 *Sir Nicholas Lechmere's 1661 garden house at Severn End is set on the corner of a walled enclosure and had a study on its upper floor overlooking a formal garden*

4 *The National Trust has recreated most of the formal gardens at Hanbury Hall and the Sunken Garden of parterres before the west front, restored in 1995, composes cleverly between modern planting in a traditional pattern of box edging*

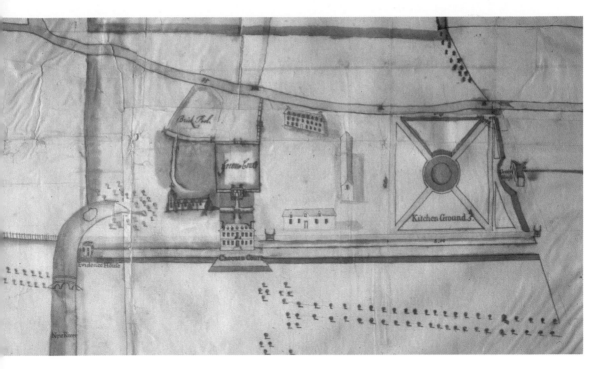

5 *The 1751 Doharty map of Croome Court illustrates the 'New River' overlooked by the 'Evidence House' and the short-lived formal garden before Lancelot Brown transformed the layout.* By kind permission of the Croome Estate Trustees

6 *The mid-1760s Grotto at Croome Court with the statue of Sabrina, goddess of the Severn, in romantic overgrowth of vegetation before the recent harsh restoration programme*

7 *Lancelot Brown's classical Rotunda of 1754 set on the marl ridge among cedars in the Home Shrubbery behind Croome Court*

8 *William Shenstone's paths around Virgil's Grove at The Leasowes miraculously retain much of their mid-eighteenth-century rustic charm*

9 *Sanderson Miller designed the Sham Castle at Hagley between 1747 and 1748. Seen here un-restored and without its modern car-park, it still exudes Horace Walpole's 'true rust of the Barons' wars'*

10 *Above the half-natural Cascade in Naboth's Vineyard at Arley Castle the circuit path crosses the stream dramatically on a cyclopean bridge of Regency date*

11 *The mid-eighteenth-century canted bays were added to the existing complex of Kyre Park deliberately to afford wide-ranging views of John Davenport's subtle landscape treatment of five lakes*

12 *A frisson of French naughtiness was added to Auguste Tronquois' 1869-75 Chateau Impney in Droitwich by the risqué statuary in its flower-filled garden*

13 *Madresfield Court's 1860s Gothic Revival ranges by P.C. Hardwick enclose the family's private Rose Garden. They are viewed here from Thomas Mawson's early twentieth-century Yew Garden*

14 *This view of the 1878-9 Pulhamite Rock Garden at Madresfield gives some idea of the scale of its Druidic monoliths and the modestly natural planting around its brilliantly disguised artificial rocks*

15 *Alfred Parsons built his reputation as a garden designer upon his exuberantly lush flower studies like this 1911 canvas of 'Orange Lilies, Broadway', which shows part of the garden at Russell House.* Royal Academy of Arts, London

16 *The Perseus and Andromeda Fountain, designed by W.A. Nesfield and sculpted by James Forsyth at Witley Court, illustrates the scale of the works undertaken by Samuel Daukes for the first Earl of Dudley in the 1860s*

17 *Alfred Parsons designed the layout of the garden at Court Farm, Broadway, in the late 1890s for his friend, the American actress Mary Anderson*

18 *The very Edwardian looking front garden at Rous Lench Court explains why it is so difficult to accept these grounds as a genuine survival of seventeenth-century planting*

19 *The multiple buttressed hedge in the lower forecourt to Rous Lench has been dated to 1480, but is more likely to be a replanting by the Revd. Dr Chafy-Chafy who bought the house in 1875. The Mercury is an early twentieth-century addition*

20 *Prince Charles might be flattered to see this replica of his Stumpery Temple at Highgrove now standing among tree ferns at Tim and Lesley Smith's Astley Towne House*

21 *The daffodils on the lawn at Bannut Tree House, Castlemorton, belong to a species that has not been commercially available for a century and must, therefore, date to the original 1890s planting for C.F.A. Voysey's only essay in timber framing.* Courtesy of Peter Reynolds

22 *What makes Veronica Adams' modern garden within the seventeenth-century walls at Birtsmorton is the contrast between her light-hearted planting and Mike Roberts' inventive ironwork, seen here in the Angel Gate.* Courtesy of Dianne Barre

23 *Rescued from the 1960s demolition of Strensham Court by Hubert Henry Edmondson and rebuilt between the double moats at Huddington Court, this Doric Orangery was of early nineteenth-century date*

24 *In the eight inventively designed, Carolean-style folly towers at Stone House Cottage Garden and Nursery, James Arbuthnott has created a grandstand for the appreciation of his wife Louisa's romantically casual planting*

30 *The Priory, seen here in a contemporary engraving of the ornamental farm, was the most substantial of the many incidents on Shenstone's otherwise flimsy and sentimental focal points on the standard circuit at The Leasowes. An old couple rented it as their home.* Bristol University Special Collections

Now the wooded valley opens out at number ten, with a seat and 'a fine ampitheatre' around Priory Lake (*30*).[23] The Priory, Shenstone's most ambitious park building has gone, which is just as well, as visitors were not supposed to admire it when they were within feet of its walls. Across the Lake, where in Shenstone's day there was a chain of monastic fish ponds, relics of Halesowen Abbey, there is now the high embankment of the Dudley Canal, pleasantly wooded, but blocking the vista of Halesowen church spire, which visitors were supposed to take in. Now the path begins to climb up the Beech Stream of the South valley, the noisy, babbling waters would have been a prelude to The Leasowes' most often drawn and painted attraction, the waterfall in Virgil's Grove. Shenstone's men had channelled the rivulet to run through an artificial cave and pour down several noisy feet into a pool, shaded with oaks. This feature could easily be restored as the water and the trees only wait for a subtle manipulation.

Dodsley gave Virgil's Grove his best descriptive effects:

the whole scene is opake and gloomy, consisting, of a small deep valley or dingle… through which a copious stream makes it's way through mossy banks, enamelled with primroses, and variety of wild wood flowers.[24]

Here was an Obelisk to Virgil's memory and a seat to the memory of James Thomson, poet of *The Seasons*. Lord Lyttelton had introduced him to Shenstone and the two poets had viewed Virgil's Grove together; Thomson died soon after. He had, Shenstone reported, 'praised my place extravagantly', but, 'proposed alterations'.[25] It is doubtful whether the visit was a complete success as 'Thomson was very facetious', Shenstone noted, 'and very complaisant; invited me to his house at Richmond. There were many things said worth *telling*, but not *writing*'.[26]

Dodsley was too tactful to propose alterations. He recorded respectfully that as the visitor entered the wood

> His eye rambles to the left, where one of the most beautiful cascades imaginable is seen, by way of incident, through a kind of vista or glade, falling down a precipice over-arched with trees, and strikes us with surprize…though surprize alone is not excellence, it may serve to quicken the effect of what is beautiful….. were one to chuse any one particular spot of this perfectly Arcadian farm, it should, perhaps, be this.[27]

The passage is worth examining closely for its revelation of how exactly, as in choreography, the Picturesque fancier was supposed to look and react. Up on the left of Virgil's Grove was a 'handsome Gothic Screen' in a clump of firs, dark Gothic trees.[28] From here the visitor could see 'a cascade in the valley, issuing from beneath a dark shade of poplars'.[29] The chalybeate spring which Shenstone favoured with a notice carved on a stone – 'Fons Ferrugineus Divae Quae Secessu Isto Frui Concedit' – still runs, dying its banks a rusty orange.[30] An iron bowl on a chain allowed visitors to sample its healthy waters, but that has rusted away. It was along the lost drive below this point that visitors entered the grounds, giving them a chance to be immediately impressed by Virgil's Grove. Today the most attractive reaches of the circuit still lie ahead up the quiet, tree-shaded pools of the Beech Stream. Visitors could either take the short route up to number 28, an Urn to the memory of 'Miss Dolman, a beautiful and amiable relation of Mr Shenstone's, who died of the small-pox, about twenty-one years of age',[31] or the longer route up to the viewing heights above the house. This last led to a pointedly unremarkable seat dedicated to Lord Lyttelton the unloved neighbour, and ended in Lover's Walk, a long rectangular grove of trees. This offered an Assignation Seat at number 27, close to Miss Dolman's Urn; the amatory and lachrymose were the two most stressed emotions of the Picturesque sensibility. There was also a Gothic Seat and a Rustic Building, but from this point onwards the emphasis was upon the views out towards rival parks. The second largest water in The Leasowes once lay immediately below Miss Dolman's Urn, but it no longer survives. A hollow of land once full of springs has had its water levels lowered by the Canal's construction and urban development.

Number 22 was a seat to view the house, Clee Hill and Enville. It is only today, up on The Leasowes' highest points, that Halesowen makes a visual impact. Until now the whole Arcadian hollow has been remarkably rural and inward looking. There was another Gothic Alcove at number 20; Shenstone clearly favoured the melancholy associations of a Gothic ruin (executed in lath and plaster) to a serene classical temple.

Number 18 was more cheerful: an octagonal clump of conifers in which visitors were invited to join in the traditional Shropshire toast: 'To all Friends round the Wrekin!' In Shenstone's day The Leasowes, though surrounded by Worcestershire territory, was an island pocket of Shropshire. At number 17, a seat again 'in the Gothick form',[32] there was an inscription on the back with poetic advice:

> Learn to relish calm delight,
> Verdant vales and fountains bright;
> Trees that nod on sloping hills,
> Caves that echo tinkling rills.
>
> Let not lucre, let not pride,
> Draw thee from such charms aside;
> Have not these their proper sphere?
> Gentler passions triumph here.[33]

Then, at last, at seat number 17, Dodsley's description acknowledges the hard fact that the garden is at the heart of the Black Country, a rich, industrial area: 'a glass-house appears between two large clumps of trees at about the distance of four miles', not looking industrial, but instead 'resembling a distant pyramid'.[34]

It was on this steep walk down to where this modern circuit walk began that visitors were allowed to take in the Priory ruin lying several hundred yards down below them; and therefore at the proper Claude Glass distance, where it could be enjoyed at the right perspective and in the best composition, with the little lake and the trees. The real value of a Leasowes walk is that it can bring one back into an entirely different, more fastidious, more analytical and yet less demanding way of looking at landscapes and assessing quite modest views. Whether it would be improved if the seats, the urns and the inscriptions were restored is questionable. The circuit today is pleasantly under-used and inscriptions invite vandalism. In an interesting experiment the latter-day Shenstone – Ian Hamilton Finlay – has set up a new stone Assignation Seat on Lover's Walk with a long quotation from Dodsley's account carved into it to remind us of the lost streams:

> Here the path begins gradually to ascend beneath a depth of shade, by the side of which is a small bubbling rill, either forming little peninsulas, rolling over pebbles, or falling down small cascades all under cover, and taught to murmur very agreeably.[35]

This is a substantial echo in stone of a frail echo in ink of the real thing. But then, are words more real to our intensely educated brains than the reality words describe? That is the question to which both Shenstone and Hamilton Finlay thought they had the answer. In another essay in the same issue of the *New Arcadian Journal*, Patrick Eyres defends obscene graffiti on a municipal 'seat' at the Leasowes. A conventional vandal has written 'FUCK OFF', but someone intent on restoring 'the Shenstonian ambience of a fairy realm' has altered it to 'PUCK OFF'.[36] Either inscription is resonant mentally, more possibly than a carving of Puck's head or a lewd scribble.

Some visitors, encouraged by this account, may walk the Shenstone circuit and become disenchanted by the absence of garden buildings. But as Whatley wrote: 'It is literally a grazing farm lying round the house; and a walk as unaffected and unadorned as a common field path is conducted through the several enclosures'.[37] As a garden it was intended to exercise and stimulate awareness of a real natural scene, not to gratify the age with substantial stone toys. Its first message is that Arcadia already lies around us; then comes the second message, an anticipation of Wordsworth's 'still sad music of humanity': dead poets and dead 21-year-old girls and helpful neighbours all recalled by a sensibility opened up by Nature. This is one of Worcestershire's five most important gardens and lies in its enchanted hollow to the eternal credit of Halesowen's civic integrity.

5

Lyttelton's Hagley and the
'true rust of the Barons' Wars'

Worcestershire is unusually fortunate in garden terms because it has two rival Arcadias, set up within sight of each other, both more or less surviving, and both described at length in their mid-eighteenth-century prime: The Leasowes by Dodsley, Hagley by Bishop Richard Pococke, the great traveller, who visited Hagley twice, leaving two accounts of it in contorted prose. As an additional bonus, if it can be described as such, Sanderson Miller, that local amateur architect of both Gothick revival and pedestrian classicism, offered his opinions on the comparative merits of the gardens of his two friends. In August 1749 poor Shenstone was surprised by an unexpected visit to The Leasowes by three of his most feared critics: Miller, the young George Lyttelton and John Pitt. They seem to have given his circuit a savaging, and he wrote woefully to Lady Luxborough telling her how he was thinking of pulling down his little Study by the stream, as it was so paltry. That was in a letter of 30 August 1749.[1] But then, in another Luxborough letter of 5 December in the same year, he was over the moon: 'Don't my Lady, speak of it; but Mr M[iller] tells it about yt my Grove exceeds any thing at Hagley of ye kind; but *yt ye Buildings at Hagley are better*. Is not this drole?'[2] Miller is likely to have praised the work of whomever he was speaking to, but it will lend an interest to any tour of the park at Hagley to bear this comparison with The Leasowes in mind. Hagley Hall is open to the public, but the park, with its large herd of beautiful deer, is not. I am most grateful to Lord Cobham for permission to walk those fascinating grounds with that celebrated Sham Castle immortalised by Horace Walpole: 'There is a ruined castle, built by Miller, that would get him his freedom, even of Strawberry: it has the true rust of the Barons' Wars'.[3]

It will be quite impossible to follow Bishop Pococke's two accounts of the park.[4] He seems to have been bewildered by its relatively simple geography.[5] The house lies well protected from the east and north-east by high ground, which is well wooded and irregular in its topography. A valley of small lakes leads east into these Clent Hills, curling slightly south to link with what the bishop calls a 'hanging ground' or plateau.

The oddity of the distribution of Hagley's park buildings is that they lie where the valley and the hanging ground meet, quite out of sight of the house. Cruelly divided from the main park by the dual carriageway of the A456 to Halesowen is Wychbury Ring, the hill where the first Lord Lyttelton raised the Obelisk that Shenstone could see from his Lover's Walk terrace and the Doric Temple, modelled on the Theseion at Athens by Athenian Stuart. So there is a bold dramatic backdrop to the house, but the only garden building closely connected visually with the house is Prince Frederick's Pillar up a shallow valley beside the cricket pitch and the bright red sandstone Victorian church.

The Doric Temple (*31*), constructed between 1758 and 1761, was, until recently, thought to be the first scholarly building of the Greek Revival in this country.[6] But it would seem that Stuart had already constructed a Greek temple at The Grove, Hertfordshire, for Thomas Villiers, 1st Lord Hyde.[7] Even if it has been eclipsed chronologically, Stuart's Temple of Theseus looks well from the main road. As Miller rightly said, Hagley's park buildings completely out-pointed Shenstone's extempore wooden seats and alcoves. But the Temple is disappointing when viewed close up. The light stucco rendering that originally made it look like a Greek marble structure has now all gone, revealing a sandstone scruffiness. The stone-coloured plasterwork cornice with its pea-green triglyph friezes is falling down, and the building lacks a full interior to support that strictly correct templar portico.

31 *This, one the first scholarly and accurate recreations of the front of a Greek Doric temple, was designed in 1758 by 'Athenian' Stuart who had drawn the Temple of Theseus at Athens*

Coming down the hill and turning off left to Hagley Hall and the main park results in a quite sudden confrontation with Miller's four boxy towers, correctly Palladian and executed in a lovely, anaemic, salmon pink sandstone. Its colour rather than its Burlingtonian façades tends to remain in the memory, as it exhibits no shred of an architect's invention or charm. It broods rather than presides over a park where buildings lie hidden away, up out of sight, and there is no clearly defined circuit. The best of the memorial urns, those to Shenstone and Alexander Pope, which once decorated that valley to the east, have been brought down to stand obscurely, but safely, beside the cricket pitch; they are best examined now. The cricket ground relates more closely to the house than anything else in the park, as if it had a vast Palladian cricket pavilion.

To simplify the site and force a circuit upon it, the best route is to climb up steeply above the deer park (*32*). This green carriageway leads up by Milton's Seat, a viewpoint, to the top of a broad hanging ground between two woods, one on the left of pine,[8] the other on the right, mixed deciduous, with much copper beech. In distant perspective, far away at the lower end of this open ground, is the Sham Castle which made Shenstone so jealous. Unexpectedly what first catches the eye is not the famous ruin, but a solitary sweet chestnut, planted, possibly to assert the distance of the ruin, though in reality it dwarfs it.

Miller's Sham Castle (*colour plate 9*) was a rare masterstroke of design, possibly the best thing he ever contrived and certainly the building which earned him the title of the

32 *Lord Lyttelton's Hagley had the flattering advantage of a small range of steep little hills – Pococke's 'hanging ground' – close to the house with a deer park at its front entrance.* Bodleian Library, Oxford, Gough Maps, fol. 56v

'Great Master of Gothick'.[9] Its contemporary impact is conveyed in a letter of January 1748 written to him by T. Lennard Barrett:

> If you have suffered in regard to this [the fall of Miller's Wroxton church steeple] you have, to make amends, got everlasting fame by the Castle at Hagley, so that I hear talk of nothing else. And now I mention Hagley all the three Lytteltons dined with me the day before yesterday and I can assure you we had a great deal to talk about you and by no means to your disadvantage and your health was drunk with more sincerity than most healths are.[10]

The Castle is vigorously asymmetrical with one tower, the one Shenstone claimed was too short, completely commanding the other three, which are impressively wrecked and ruined.[11] The stones for the construction of the Castle were taken from the ruins of Halesowen Abbey and in some places the courses have been cleverly varied in size to suggest partial rebuilding after slighting. When Coplestone Warre Bampfylde painted a view of it in 1762 the Castle looked even more authentic than it does today because the lawns around it had been cleverly littered with huge chunks of masonry as if time had brought them down.[12] Bishop Pococke thought that 'the Gothick windows rising above the ruins have a beautiful effect'.[13] They still do, but the remarkable collection of old bangers and functioning cars scattered behind the main curtain wall with its tall tower makes a stronger impression. Another unexpected feature is a sizeable cottage tucked away at the side of the mock Castle in a contrasting nineteenth-century vernacular style. One expects the Castle to be isolated and it is not.

The other curious planning feature of this high wooded plateau is the Ionic 'Rotund' (*33*), as Shenstone insisted on spelling it.[14] This was designed in 1748-9 by John Pitt of Encombe in Dorset, the man who frightened Shenstone on a visit to The Leasowes. While it is not far from the Castle and the adjacent cottage it does not relate to them, but lies at the very top of that valley of little lakes and, in Pococke's time, was one among multiple eclectic features. Before the trees grew up it may have created a bold visual goal for a 'Rococo' walk from the Hall; now roofless and battered it makes a feeble Arcadian note.

George Lyttelton's letter books, preserved at Hagley, prove that he had a very hands-on role when his park was being laid out. His relations with Sanderson Miller were close and flattering. He was forever requesting rough designs from Miller, but presumed cheerfully: 'yet I will make no apologies, as I know that these works are an Amusement to you, and that a Heart made like yours finds its own Happiness in doing acts of Friendship and kindness'.[15] One suspects that the two men found the touchy William Shenstone something of a bourgeois joke. Miller was to design 'Gothick form' chairs for the Sham Castle and he had sent 'Painted Glass' for its interior.[16] They were worried about the Rotunda as early as 1749. 'As you say', Lord Lyttelton wrote, 'the Rotunda now looks very white without Painting, do you still think it should be Painted? Hitchcock [Miller's mason] seemd to think that it should, both because of the

33 *The Ionic Rotunda at Hagley was designed in 1748-9 by John Pitt to stand commandingly at the head of a valley in the park close to the Sham Castle: Gothick and classical working visually together*

different colours of the stone, and to preserve it'.[17] The comment is hard to understand as the Rotunda's natural stone colour today is tawny; perhaps they were intending to cover it with a limewash shelter coat. There was talk too of a 'Tent' for the park, probably a Turkish Tent, though Lyttelton was anxious that it should 'not be left in the wood for fear of it being stolen, and there would be a good deal of trouble in carrying it thither and back again as often as we go there'.[18]

Lyttelton seems to have entrusted the planting of the park to his cousin Molly West who lived at Hagley, but he sometimes gave very precise suggestions as to the clumping of the trees. He wrote:

> I would have one Cedar of Lebanon, the finest we have, and two Silesia Larix's planted in a Triangular Clump between the Castle and the Lodge Pool but so as not to intercept the viewing the Pond from the Castle. Miss West will chuse the spott by her eye. It should be under the Brow of the Hill, so that the highest Tree may be still below the Terras. Let the Cedar be the lowest of the three. There should be a distance of 15 foot between each tree. Let two of the finest New England Pines be planted within ten foot of the Water, one on each side of the Lodge Pool, but not directly over against one another. Let three more of the same be planted at the Tail of the Pond twelve foot from the Water in a Triangular Clump either on the right hand or the left, or about the middle, as Miss West shall determine.[19]

It may seem to be a sweeping generalisation, but a Rococo-Arcadian design works best in an enclosed valley or hollow, like that at The Leasowes, Stourhead or Painswick, not in an exposed upland of the Clent Hills where the eye is always straying away to wide, distant views. The valley down from the Rotunda to Hagley Hall is an ideal Arcadian space the deeper it gets; and when Pococke walked it there were eclectic features of much charm every few yards. It is still an exciting area to study, but also a disappointing one as so many urns have been removed and rocky alcoves of mineral and slag have been lost. We need Pococke's enthusiastic words now to appreciate what once enlivened the chain of little ponds overshadowed by mature trees.[20]

There is now no path to guide the visitor, but below the Rotunda, which Pococke described as having 'a view of two lawns and two pieces of water' and a 'rustick building', there is a pleasant pool with yellow water lilies and, to the side of it, by a vast Wellingtonia and an oddly spreading beech, there is a dry, rocky cascade bed. The bishop saw a 'little dip adorned with a variety of flowers in a constant succession'. Did he mean by that a regular planting in flowerbeds or was Lord Lyttelton imitating Shenstone's attempt to naturalise peonies among brambles? Further down the valley were 'an alcove seat covered with pebbles curiously figured, in which are represented a cross, beads, and ornaments of pots of flowers', a 'hermit's fountain, cover'd with an old trunk of a tree, and so leads to the Hermitage at the south-east corner made with roots of trees, with a seat round it cover'd with matting, a rail and gate before it made of rude stakes'. Lord Lyttelton was, like Shenstone, a published poet whose verses were dismissed by Dr Johnson in his *Lives of the Poets*: 'they have nothing to be despised, and little to be admired'; but the lines inscribed, Shenstone-wise, on the Hermitage, were from Milton:

> May at last my weary age,
> Find out the peaceful hermitage,
> The hairy gown and mossy cell,
> Where I may sit and rightly spell
> Of every star that Heav'n doth shew,
> And every herb that sips the dew;
> Till old experience do attain
> To something like prophetick strain;
> These pleasures, melancholy, give,
> And I with thee will choose to live

which was modest and retiring on Lyttelton's part.

The Palladian Bridge stood, according to the Historic Gardens' Register, at 'the west end of the westernmost pond'. That pond ends in a high earth dam, now attractively wooded and, by hanging over the bank at a point where a trickle of water flows out it was possible to make out the frosted keystone of an overgrown arch. The 'rock-work of rough materials of the glass-houses and quarries', which Pococke describes, may have been here. He speaks of 'a hollow in the middle and rising up about 20ft, the water comes out of the rock-work in several streams in a fall of about 15ft. Below this to the right is a grotto where the water runs, and there is a statue of a Venus of Medici as coming out of a fountain'. Horace Walpole, who disliked Lyttelton, wrote more lyrically:

> Then there is a scene of a small lake with cascades falling down such a Parnasus! with a circular temple on the distant eminence; and there is such a fairy dale, with more cascades gushing out of rocks! and there is a hermitage, so exactly like those in Sadeler's prints, on the brow of a shady mountain, stealing peeps into the glorious world below.[21]

I had to make do with that frosted keystone and a pilgrimage up to the nearby Prince's Pillar (*34*) where Prince Frederick stands on a Corinthian column dressed in Roman military uniform. Lord Lyttelton had been secretary to Prince Frederick, and briefly Chancellor of the Exchequer.

Of the two circuits: The Leasowes and Hagley, Shenstone's works most satisfyingly so Sanderson Miller's remark was not just mere flattery. Both circuits have lost virtually all their eclectic adornments, but Shenstone's retains that firm sense of direction which a sylvan Arcadia needs.

34 If Prince Frederick had lived to succeed George II, Lord Lyttelton would have been his chief minister. This pillar with the prince in Roman costume records frustrated hopes

6

Hermit-hollowed, Gothick-castled, Brownian grand

Each English county seems to have reacted to the Picturesque aesthetic according to its own topographical strengths or weakness. If the lie of the land was unadventurous then Lancelot Brown, or more likely one of his less expensive imitators – Richard Woods, William Emes, Adam Mickle or Nathaniel Richmond – was called in to dam up a likely small stream into a lake and make a gentle rise in the contours look memorable by planting a strategic line of trees. In that case the resulting parkscape would be conventionally fine – the English ideal – and not a few hundred, but literally more than a thousand such 'improvements' were laid out over the eighteenth century. In his travels, Bishop Pococke lists them with conventional approval at every turn.[1] The more individual parkscapes resulted when a picturesque composition, the essentially frame-worthy view of rocks, lakes, steep hills and narrow valleys, was there already, waiting only for landscape adjustment: the contriving of a surprise revelation on turning a corner of woodland, or the building of a bridge to carry the drive at exactly the right point for viewing a cascade or a gloomy widening of dark water. Certain areas, like the Wye Valley below Ross-on-Wye, cried out for viewing, and were readily given it. There were boat trips down its mild 'rapids', and there were landscape parks poised along its limestone cliffs. Then there was the picturesque lure of soft sandstone, riddled naturally with caves and ledges to link hermits' cells with 'giants' castles' and 'holy' wells. Hawkstone Park includes a line of sandstone hills that never rise more than a few hundred feet above the levels of north Shropshire, yet it had that sculptural quality and could be coaxed into delivering shock and awe in acceptable miniature measures.[2] Its Picturesque trails offered honeymoon couples, who stayed at a local hotel, a White Tower, a Red Castle, a Swiss Bridge, the Foxes Knob, Reynard's Walk and a thrilling squeeze up a rock passage, the Cleft, into a largely artificial grotto-cave with viewing holes; also, inevitably, it had a hermitage.

Worcestershire had its own version of all three Picturesque possibilities. At Hewell Grange the great Lancelot Brown and his team worked full time on massive earth engineering and lake creation. The county never contrived to turn the too-commercial Severn into a second Wye Valley experience, but it went one better: instead of creating a panoramic walk, it built a panoramic linear town, not one Malvern but five: Little Malvern, Malvern Wells, West Malvern, Great Malvern and Malvern Link, a unique belvedere community of five consciously genteel units for middle class living, laid out with a spa of exceptionally pure, sterile, flavourless water as its excuse. Almost every house in that airily refined urban complex commands a stunning natural vista to the east of half Worcestershire. Its fortunate residents had then only to turn their backs and look up westward to find lively granite hills, pretending to be mountains, rising up out of their main shopping street. Richard Lockett's *Survey of Historic Parks and Gardens* lists 12 interesting gardens in the five Malverns.[3]

There was also the county's hermit potential. Shenstone's Leasowes and Lyttelton's Hagley both claimed a hermitage, but they had to build them from scratch. Elsewhere in north Worcestershire, in the soft sandstone hills around Kidderminster, there was no need to scoop out a cave to imitate Hawkstone. The county had not one genuine medieval hermitage but three, all watertight and habitable. In 1732, when George II's gardening Queen Caroline persuaded William Kent to build a fantastic classical hermitage in Richmond Park as her retreat, hermitages became instantly fashionable. Three years later, when Spenser's *Faerie Queene* was enjoying a literary revival, the queen followed up her Hermitage with Merlin's Cave.[4] This was not a cave at all, Richmond had no soft sandstone cliffs; the 'Cave' was a thatched, triple-domed Gothick pavilion containing waxwork representations of historical figures who could, by a generous stretch of interpretation, be seen as ancestors of the House of Hanover. Inspired by royal example, Worcestershire took stock of its own native anchorites' dens.

The best known was the Blackstone Rock Hermitage on the east bank of the Severn opposite Ribbesford. Then there was Redstone Rock Hermitage on the west bank of the river on the outskirts of Stourport, the Astley Hermitage, near Areley Kings and, hidden above the Teme valley, the Southstone Rock Hermitage, with the remains of a chapel of St John, tucked away in rough woodland which also enclosed a 'Devil's Den' and a 'Hell Hole' for Gothic authenticity. There was also a medieval hermitage at Wadborough, first mentioned in the thirteenth century,[5] but only Hermitage Farm survives north of Pirton to record its thirteenth-century evidence.[6] That was not all. The pretty wooded hills around Wolverley are literally riddled with caves and cave cottages at Blakes Hall, Vales Rock, Kingsford, and the Cave Cottages at Drakelow. Worcestershire, in its north-western areas, is a cave county. They are not deep, watery limestone caves, but shallow, dry, easily extended caves with the advantage of an even, unchanging temperature. In Worcestershire it was not necessary to pay some old retired gamekeeper to grow a long beard and pretend to be a real hermit. It was a county where labourers would pay rent to live in a cave with all mod cons, garden included. One ill-drawn view (35) by the antiquary, William Stukeley, of 'Blackston cave, River Severn, by Lord Herbert's house, near Bewdley', dated 23 September 1721, illustrates a prospect garden at the side of the Hermitage Cliff.[7] It is fenced, planted with shrubs and has one gentleman in a tricorn hat sitting to make a sketch while another strolls. Even before Queen Caroline and William Kent's indulgence in a fake hermitage the

35 *Stukeley's naïve illustration of the Blackstone Rock Hermitage indicates the strange fascination that the idea of an old, holy man in a cave had for the 1720s.* Bodleian Library, Oxford, Gough Maps 33, fol.70r

Blackstone Rock had been given a scholarly examination and illustrated professionally in the same year, 1721, as the Stukeley sketch was made.[8] The engraving was published showing a trow sailing past its wooded cliffs together with a 'Ground Plot and Section' of its chapel, altar and five adjoining apartments. These included a 'common Room', a 'Study' with 'Shelves for Books' and a 'Belfry', to let neighbours know the hours of prayer. So Worcestershire hermits lived in some style.

One of the most impressive of these cells is that at Radston's Ferry, Astley, where Thomas Habington reported in the 1580s that the Hermitage consisted 'of a Chappell and other roames, the altars and all formed out of the Rocke....Over the Altar is paynted an Archbishop sayinge Masse before all the Instruments of our Savyour's passyon'.[9] On the rock face outside were the 'Armes of England betweene Beauchamp, Earle of Warwicke...and Mortimer...and howe lounge Bauchamps and Mortimers have vanished awaye let Antiquartyes iudge, but thease monuments of Honor are here so woren as they are instantly perishinge, whearefore with others fadethe thys worlde's glory'.[10] The Redstone Rock Hermitage at Stourport (*36*) is readily accessible through a caravan park and suggests the scale of the cells and apartments at Astley where Bishop Latimer reported in 1538 that the system could 'lodge 500 men, as ready for thieves and traitors as true men'.[11] This must have been an exaggeration, but it suggests that such caves already had a romantic, even infamous, reputation locally.

In his *History of Worcestershire*, Treadway Nash was alert to a hermit's need for a picturesque view. Writing on the Blackstone Rock at Ribbesford he noted that the hermit

36 *The multiple caves and galleries of the Redstone Rock Hermitage, down river from the Blackstone, at Stourport*

'had a fine view of the Severn, and of the woods which overhung its banks: a situation very fit for one disposed to lead a life sequestered from the ways and busy haunts of men. It is now profanely turned into a cyder-mill and cellar'.[12] Protestant England was able to show an interest in the Catholic trappings of religion because a hermit sounded more like an enthusiast for picturesque views than a priest. Edmund Spenser had popularised hermitages soon after the break with Rome, by describing them poetically in his *Faerie Queene*, though there again, as in Bishop Latimer's words, there was a hidden, Gothic, threat as Spenser's holy hermit turned out to be the wicked magician, Archimago, in disguise.

To appreciate the influence which one of the county's genuine hermitages could have on Picturesque garden design, it is only necessary to look across up river from the Blackstone Rock to one of Worcestershire's most interesting, though least accessible, garden-parks. The grounds surrounding Winterdyne House (*37*), just south of Bewdley, lie up above a steep, wooded cliff, one field west of the Severn. T.B. Freeman's 'View of the Winterdyne Rocks'[13] was engraved shortly after Sir Edward Winnington had laid out the Picturesque walks to surround his gaunt new classical box of a house and to command views of the Blackstone Rock on the other side of the river.

Working down its cliff walks from north to south, Winterdyne still presents the perfect Savage Picturesque park, only damaged at its extreme southern edge by the concrete bridge of the Bewdley bypass. Freeman's view shows the cliff newly planted with mixed conifers and deciduous trees. Today both Winnington's house and the rock faces are hidden in a mature woodland that allows tantalising framed views of the Severn. A drive leads directly from the West Lodge to the house, but from the Lodge a delightful viewing path also winds, first north, along the edge of the escarpment, but then bends

A View of the WINTERDYNE ROCKS *with S.ʳ Edw.ᵈ Winnington's Seat near Bewdley,*

To whom this first N.º of Views upon the River Severn is most respectfully dedicated (by permission) by his obliged hum.ᵇˡᵉ Serv.ᵗ   *T.F.Freeman.*

37 *T.B. Freeman's view of Winterdyne Rocks shows Sir Edward Winnington's eighteenth-century villa commanding his Savage Pictuesque cliff top walk with its Gothick Fort high above the Severn.* Bodleian Library, Oxford, Gough Maps 33, fol.70v

sharply south, dividing to enjoy the thrill of views from the cliff edge across the river. The paths below the cliff edge are now completely inaccessible, but they originally passed below the house to a little Tea House pavilion of eighteenth-century date, and wound on, double and sometimes treble, to the Fort, a sandstone tower, just visible on Freeman's view. This has collapsed and a pile of rubble stones surrounded by Scots pines marks its site. Sale particulars of 1903, which include a map of the site (*38*), report that this fifteenth-century structure was then used as a billiard room, but it is supposed originally to have been a feudal toll house exacting payments from cargo trows passing up and down the river.[14] Next in the walks came a Summerhouse, obviously sited for its views, now spoilt, of the Blackstone Rock. The tour would have ended in Winterdyne's Kitchen Garden next to a Model Farm, which would have offered the usual pleasures of dairy produce and refreshment. So there were three architectural viewing points on contour walks, with variable alternatives, overlooking the river and the Hermitage cliffs on the opposite shore.

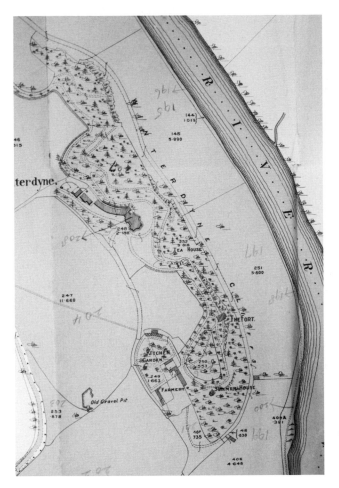

38 *Overgrown and dangerous today, Winterdyne's grounds are mapped here with a serpentine of paths to a Tea Pavilion, the Fort, a Summerhouse and the Kitchen Garden and Farmery set in a hollow.* Worcestershire Record Office

With its narrow, sometimes quite frightening, ledge paths cut back into the sandstone, Winterdyne presented the Savage Picturesque. Areley Kings Rectory, a few miles down the river, offers a mild, priestly Arcadian picturesque. The heart of the Rectory is Caroline, but later it was Georgianised and the living of St Bartholomew, Areley Kings was being passed down from one younger son of the Vernon family to another. In 1728, the Revd. Richard Vernon, whose wife had produced only daughters, became so overwhelmed with female chatter that he built what he called the 'Outstout', a three-storey brick garden house (39) overlooking a fine view of the river valley.[15] It has the arms of the Vernons carved over its garden door and served him as a retreat from his womenfolk; it was later used as a parish office. He was, apparently, so devoted to rural views that he had a second Picturesque viewing alcove dug out from the hillside below his Outstout. It is a shell-shaped recess, a Grotto or an Echo where alfresco meals could be taken. On the Rectory's entrance side is a little building with two more Westwood-style gables and a vine draped over it; possibly it was a dairy, but it is interesting that

39 *The Revd. Richard Vernon of Areley Kings built this three-storey garden house, the Outstout, in 1728 to escape his womenfolk and enjoy views out across the Severn valley*

Westwood's distinctive forms seem to have been considered right for playful structures. Incidentally the next Rector, Thomas Vernon, was more happily married. He put up a monument in the church to his wife Hannah, who passed her days 'in the uniform exertion of an excellent understanding and a benevolent heart'.

The grounds of Winterdyne and Areley Kings Rectory both respond to picturesque settings. Clent Grove, a lost house near Hagley, and Castle Bourne, at Belbroughton, have no cliffs or valleys to enliven their grounds, but created instead a home-grown, towered Picturesque. What unite them are their bold Gothick castle garden buildings, heraldic in their design, like houses for the King of Clubs in a pack of cards. Their unrecorded architect was too sophisticated to imitate Westwood's dated Jacobean-Carolean. He had absorbed the William Kent vocabulary of ogee arches and quatrefoil windows, and then added his own distinctive Maltese Cross fenestration. They are not merely very large and visually dominant as garden buildings go, but aggressively sited, not out in the grounds to focus a view, but slammed down close to their parent houses to boost their profiles, as if in protest at the humble simplicity of Palladian classicism. The garden Castle at Castle Bourne is actually attached to its house by three arches; the other garden Castle at Clent Grove is planted down just above the entrance drive where it must have confronted and dramatised the now demolished house a few yards down the hillside.

In an effort to modify this immediate impact the Castle at Castle Bourne has been painted a dull green;[16] but the Castle at Clent Grove (*40*) has been left in its shameless light pink brick, though there are traces of white render on its walls, which would have made the building even more unavoidable. One other oddity about this intensely characterful building is that, now its parent house has been demolished with its platform marked only by a stone urn, the Castle works perfectly as an eyecatcher for Field House, Clent, an eccentrically sub-Palladian house a quarter of a mile away to the west. Was it designed to please one house and to overawe the other, or would Clent Grove originally have hidden the Castle from its neighbour? This whole area around Clent and Belbroughton was Birmingham's equivalent of London's Chiswick: a desirable housing area for the wealthy as they fled from smoke and fumes.

A pencil plan of Clent Grove gives the only clue to the Castle's dating.[17] It shows the 'Castle' and the 'House', one on either side of the drive, with 'Garden' in between them; and someone has noted 'must be after Thomas Hill bought the property as it shows Castle'. So Thomas Hill built the structure; but while the *Victoria County History* gives precise details of when a church was endowed in the middle Saxon period, it records nothing of Thomas Hill's purchase or of his picturesque building. For the dating of Clent House generally it hedges its bets, by attributing the house to both the early eighteenth century and the late eighteenth century; allowing the reader to choose.

At Broome House, another in the tight cluster around the Clent Hills, an owner, most likely Samuel Hellier, who owned the estate in 1762,[18] decided to change the

40 *The elegant brick 'Castle' at Clent Grove serves equally well as a folly to the Field House, Clent, and has a similar twin with Maltese Cross openings at Castle Bourne, Belbroughton*

character of his existing house, not by setting up a giant garden castle next to it, but by applying wild Gothick detail to the house itself. As a result Broome House is an inventive delight of entirely illiterate Gothick detail with Westwood-style Jacobean gables as an extra stylistic impropriety on one side and alternative Palladian classicism on the main front. Such wanton confusion of second-hand styles may have shocked Nikolaus Pevsner, but in his *Worcestershire* he dates the façades, plausibly enough on their styling, to between 1760 and 1770.[19] Is Broome House before or after the castles at Clent and Castle Bourne? The church of St Peter across the lane is also eighteenth-century and equally amateurish, but far more restrained. At a guess, Broome House preceded the two Castles, which though clumsy in their siting, are of delightful Kentian Gothick in their styling.

The garden at Broome may complicate the picture with its omnipresent geese, but if any small layout in the county can be held up as an example of Worcestershire's Picturesque garden-park then this is it. Broome supports a whole flock of Toulouse geese and is now a pleasant, welcoming home for retirees. The grounds are heavily shaded with trees, dark evergreens for the most part: middle-aged yews, pines and firs, while a teardrop-shaped lake fills up most of the open space. A circuit of this lake, which has been turned a deep, dark green by goose droppings, must serve the old people for an admirable morning constitutional. Out across the lawn, from the unexpectedly Adamesque porch on the classical front of the house, the perimeter path threads a shady route through the yews to a wooden bridge spanning the lake at a point where the teardrop narrows down. The rust red gables, triple ogees and battlements of the Gothick façade and the pediment and Diocletian window of the classical front of the House are still clearly visible through the yew trees, so it works like an intriguingly playful garden building. One specimen Wellingtonia towers up above the lesser growth to mark the circuit's western limit.

On the walk back along the north shore there is a second smaller bridge over a narrow stony leat and there, fronting Broome's only dull façade is a lively little garden consisting of a lawn with a reedy stream proceeding through it in a succession of small pools below a grass terrace. It has urns and cherubs and the pools are rushy. Even here the garden never quite escapes tree shadow. Beyond is a walled Kitchen Garden with a ruined stable range. The church tower peers over them like a stable clock tower. It is, the word is hard to avoid, bijoux, yet still undeniably picturesque, even with the geese.

Before turning to the two real heavyweights of Worcestershire's Picturesque parks, at Hewell Grange and Kyre Park, there remains one charming lightweight park to Bevere House, a mile or two north of Worcester. Bevere's grounds do not belong with the distinctively Worcestershire, Gothick and Westwood-influenced parks. Though slight and absorbed within minutes, Bevere is, like Hewell and Kyre, in the great English mainstream of the professional Brownian Picturesque, following the formula of handsome, pared down compositions of woodland adjusted to the contours of the land and enriched with artificial waters.

A drive dips downhill towards a belt of mature woodland with Anthony Keck's spankingly smart Bevere House still hidden. Then, as the trees close in, an elegant little bridge of ornate, white-painted ironwork takes the drive over a clear stream by a tall clump of bamboo. It is a moment to pause to enjoy a carefully created picture of a wooded dell. Out in the sunshine, on the other side of the tree belt, Keck's villa bursts in upon the view: high walls of pale stone at the top of a gentle rise, with tree clumps strategically set behind it. The view creates a second picture and that is all; but the approach has been controlled to the best visual advantage, which is the essence of the Picturesque.

In its present form the House dates to around 1756.[20] The John Doharty junior map of 1751, drawn before Keck revised the house, the bridge and the grounds, shows Bevere in its forecourt and a long straight avenue of trees leading to it from the east. But in a Picturesque composition there should be surprise views and the house should lie comfortably in an apparently natural landscape. Keck used the bridge and the tree belt just as a director would use the curtain in a theatre. So Bevere corrects the atypical impression of Picturesque garden design which the earlier parks of this chapter may have given. A professionally laid out Picturesque garden does not drop a theatrical castle tower into the back garden; it improves existing landscapes by careful planting, curves the drive to take advantage of the best views and creates memorable pictures, as does Keck's bridge over that wooded dell.

After these minor, though enjoyably individual Picturesque grounds, a major Picturesque landscape park, one which was not only dammed up, contoured and ordered by Brown, but then trimmed, re-planted and made more picture-worthy by Brown's self-appointed successor, the pedantic, intensely competitive Humphry Repton, may come across as overwhelmingly ambitious. Hewell Grange is the inappropriately domestic sounding name for an enormous, quite un-Grange-like house; also one most easily experienced if you are a criminal. Since 1946 its Brown and Repton grounds have been developed to house not only a borstal, but also two large adult prisons. Permission is occasionally given for small groups to tour the grounds.[21] This is still a rewarding experience as the trees are in superb maturity and the park has been kept in reasonable trim, and includes several notable garden features delivered with the added frisson of high fences and barbed wire.

Opinions differ sharply on the Victorian Jacobethan, but the red sandstone house, actually more purple than red, broods monstrously over a forecourt of busy lizzies planted around an 1825 Coade stone statue of the Dying Gladiator painted in convincing flesh tones. It is a bizarre introduction. Lord Windsor,[22] who brought in Bodley and Garner to build this demonstration of Jacobethan pomp between 1884 and 1891,[23] had become understandably bored with his plain classical house lower down the hill, but then, incomprehensibly, he kept its gutted, hardly ruinous shell as a kind of garden memento rather than as a garden ornament. In his 1812 Red Book, when the classical house was still in use, Repton thought the building deplorable. He wrote:

> had the whole building been raised on a Terrace....the site would have been less objectionable, at present the house appears to stand low, but the greatest objection is its Northern Aspect. In this climate we do not require that state so persistently extolled by the poets and painters of Southern Latitudes.[24]

In his usual clever before and after paintings Repton suggested improving the old house by adding or revealing an impressive stable block with a turret behind it. As an approach he recommended a drive running picturesquely through the quarry to emerge through a big rough arch, which would supply a surprise view of the lake, and a classical urn to lend a Roman dignity. The little island in the Brownian lake was created at Repton's urging, but his plan to make the lake irregular with two inlets was not carried out.[25] All his watercolours suggest that bushes should enliven the banks of the lake. He hated, or claimed to hate, Brown's 'one great naked lawn, miscall'd a Park'.[26] By 1812, with Brown long dead, Repton was in tune with Uvedale Price's call for rough, natural landscape. He urged that:

> a lake like that at Hewell derives its greatest interest from rough margins enlivened by cattle wading near its shores, for which shallows should be made by putting stones or gravel in spots where cattle come to drink.[27]

Repton was a weathervane always eager to be fashionable, and he was frightened of Price and Richard Payne Knight, the two apostles of the Savage Picturesque. In fact today there are very few open lawns along the lakeside and, though there are no wading cows, it does seem that Repton's advice to conceal the bare edges of Brown's lake was eventually taken. Repton copies, almost word for word, Price's appeal that the rough root systems of fine old oaks should not be covered up and cosmeticised with soil.[28] By 1812 he has decided that Brown had '5 leading defects viz. 1. The Ha Ha, 2nd the circuitous approach, third the Belt, fourth the Clump, fifth the bald and naked lawn': which list includes virtually everything that Brown had stood for.[29]

Immediately to the east of the Grange the ground collapses sharply into the Quarry Garden where the sandstone, from which the hidden foundations of the house were hewn, positively smoulders in the shadows of overhanging yews and beech trees.[30] A cyclopean pivoted gate (*41*), which no longer pivots, if it ever did, gives entrance to this atmospheric pit, and the narrow side elevations of the Grange hang over it. Nothing else in these rich grounds is quite as mood creating, with scalloped-out rocks, a throne of stone and overgrown paths scrambling between boulders. An arch as crude and pitted as the cyclopean entrance adds a pre-Roman note. The Quarry Garden was in place before Repton arrived, but he gives an illustration of the entrance arch in his Red Book, so he must be presumed to have improved it.[31]

Beyond, and only a few feet above the level of the lake, is the shell of the house that the second Earl of Plymouth had built in Baroque style in 1712; Andor Gomme attributes it to Francis Smith of Warwick.[32] Its heavy Doric portico was added in 1816 for the sixth Earl by Thomas Cundy whose lodges survive, now equally desolate, at the north entrance before the long, 1890s, double avenue of trees which line the drive to the Grange. Why this earlier house was allowed to linger on, roofless but intact, so near the sinister new Jacobethan palace, it is hard to say. Enclosed in scaffolding, as if it were about to be repaired and re-used as some palatial prison for offenders who could afford

41 *The most dramatic section of the grounds of Hewell Grange is its Quarry Garden hacked out from dark red stone with a swinging monolith gate and the arch Humphry Repton wanted to use for an entrance drive to the house*

superior accommodation, the house is not lovely and never has been. A fire of 1889 conveniently gutted it; the new house was built in the garden of the old.

At this point the scale and the mature grandeur of Hewell's woodlands begins to bear down on any visitor following the prescribed route around Capability Brown's great lake. The woods are majestic and vintage in the variety of their planting. As usual the plane trees reach a commanding stature, but the play of delicate acacia against copper beech, and Douglas firs rising out of dark yew jungles are what remain in the memory. For a time the lake circuit is without structural incident, though steps leading up into the Planted Hill west of the lake indicate a lost network of viewing paths.

At the lake foot the waters run out under a battlemented sandstone bridge and over a domed brick sluice in a reed bed. It is then, as the path begins to follow the old carriage drive along the top of Brown's prodigious earth dam that one begins to appreciate what Brown and his skilled team of labourers were paid for. Repton bewilderingly and, probably dishonestly, claimed in his Red Book for Hewell not to know whether Brown had preceded him at the park. This was a convenient ignorance as it then allowed this most venomous of garden designers to attack virtually every feature of Hewell's park without seeming to attack Brown by name. He wrote disingenuously: 'Whether Hewell was originally form'd & planted by this ingenious self taught Landscape gardener, or by one of his school, it certainly bears strong marks of his System & Practice'.[33] Yet in 1812, many still living at the house must have been alive when the lake and dam were created 30 years earlier. Repton is a fascinating, but most unreliable, writer on gardens, often coming across like a character in Dickens: Uriah Heap for instance, 'ever so 'umble', but actually feline.

What an extraordinary eighteenth-century engineer Brown must have been. He was commissioned between 1759 and 1761, after the fourth Earl of Plymouth had attempted, with advice from William Shenstone, to create a lake below the house.[34] Shenstone first visited Hewell in 1753 to see the earl's new pool and wrote disparagingly:

> I only wish I had known his Lordship before he began that Piece of water. I told both him & Ldy P. my mind very emphatically & *ingenuously* ye very Day I came, & they both had the good-sense to hear me, and to thank me for it. That side ought apparently either to have been coverd with water, at any expence, for near 100 yards lower; or it ought to have been thrown into a broad serpentine River, the fens drein'd; & the ground slop'd down to it, from about the Present haha. The stream is sufficient for any sort of purpose. The *Cascades* might have been *display'd*, or the *stoppages* where they *were*, conceal'd wth aquatick Plants, as had been thought most agreeable; & I think, by proper *management*, the expence of these Schemes might have been less than the Present. The Reasons I go upon will appear yet more striking when the opposite ground becomes Part of their Park, wth garden Seats; from wch the House will make a very magnificent Figure.[35]

After Shenstone's visit to Hewell, Lord Plymouth went to The Leasowes to see the improvements there and to seek further help. Shenstone later wrote to his friend Richard Jago repeating his views of the 'Piece of water' and gave a warm character sketch of the young Earl: 'I think him such a sort of character as may *shine* in Company, upon growing older – he is & must be belovd already. He has been here once since, & talks of causing me to come & design for him in his Park'.[36] Interestingly, in this letter of January 1754, Shenstone mentions having met Mr and Mrs Winnington of Stanford Court on his last visit to Hewell and that the party went off to visit Thomas Vernon at Hanbury where they met 'Lord Coventry, & a deal of other Company',[37] proof of the close connection between these landscape enthusiasts.

It would appear that the improvements around the pool did not entirely satisfy Lord Plymouth, so Brown and his team were brought in to rescue the situation. Brown did not contrive the serpentine that Shenstone had suggested, but dug out the triangular lake with its naked banks that is so typical of his style. The earth dam, which created the lake, is completely wooded and appears like an entirely natural feature; it is some half a mile long and often 130ft high from its base. The planting along the carriage drive along the lakeside is subtly varied. Brown was at Hewell again in 1768, no doubt to supervise the planting up of the sides of the lake and the pleasure grounds around the house.[38]

Repton may have been responsible for the finer touches.[39] At least three species of oak – Common, Sessile and Lucombe – are flourishing, with suggestions that their planting was originally grouped to back a statue, an urn, or a seat, as Shenstone had suggested, to focus on a view across the water. Because the trees are so mature it is possible to pass along the whole east side of the lake without being aware of the scale of Brown's achievement or its subtle recession into the natural landscape. At the head of the lake a fine iron bridge (*42*) from the Horseley Foundry is modelled in its circular supporting beams on the original Shropshire Iron Bridge. It crosses a river of reedy grey water. The carriage way is blocked now, but the clustered iron spears, like those of a Fascist Rome, gathered into its ornamental side piers, indicate that this was the formal entrance to that gutted, earlier Grange. The high wire fences and prefabricated units of one of Hewell's several prisons rise up unexpectedly in this remote corner of the park.

The formal gardens on the south side of the Grange belong largely to the Edwardian chapter. What does belong to the Picturesque sector of the grounds is the Royal Tennis Court, now the prison gymnasium. This handsomely austere building by Cundy is fronted by four giant caryatids copied from the Erechtheon at Athens (*43*). It makes a resounding classical note above and to the side of an actively un-classical house. From the bridge that leads to it, a green drive winds away up into the woods which are such

42 This cast iron bridge with its roundels and spear railings set in romantic decay marks the original carriage drive to the old eighteenth-century house at Hewell. Today its neighbour is a fenced-off secure unit

43 *Cundy's early nineteenth-century Royal Tennis Court, set above the old house at Hewell, acts a garden pavilion with its Erechtheon loggia overlooking the pleasure grounds*

a feature of Hewell. Nothing in these grounds is quite like the usual surroundings of a great country house, as there are so many unpredictable changes of mood.

After walking and admiring Brown's work at Hewell it would be satisfying to be able to attribute Kyre Park, Worcestershire's other great lake-park, to him and his team. But we have only a later, wishful family legend that Brown was involved there, and the terrain is so complex and ingenious that the lakes, all five of them, cannot be given to Brown on stylistic grounds. Their layout is so playful, even perverse, that they make as much a Rococo as a Picturesque impression. Though one of Brown's most important commissions, Hewell Grange is rarely noticed in books of garden history simply because it contains three prisons. Kyre is equally un-remarked, but for a different reason. It lies on the road to nowhere in the county's panhandle, a lost, bucolic finger of territory reaching out towards Wales, above Bromyard, which must be Herefordshire's most isolated market town. Kyre Park house is as unpredictable as its park, a muddled oddity of stone elements, half-overlaid in later brick, but never grand. The Hiorne brothers, William and David, built most of it in 1753-6 around a half-digested medieval and seventeenth-century core.[40] Their additions offer the best evidence for the dating of the park of lakes immediately around and below the house. The two boldly canted bays which the Hiornes applied to the structure were clearly designed to command and enjoy existing ponds, so there can be a fair assumption that Sir Edmund Pytts, who commissioned the Hiornes, also supervised the subsequent reshaping of those ponds into the strange, stepped lakes of the park after he had completed the additions to his house.

Another complication hindering research into this important, but relatively un-noticed park, is that it is only one of two. The park of the five lakes, which we are considering, lies to the west of the B4214, Bromyard to Tenbury road; to the east of this road is a much larger Kyre deer park with three more pools, one of them big.[41] A drive cutting across the road links the two, but all the architectural and design interest is concentrated within the west park.

The actual contractor who laid out the park of lakes for Sir Edmund was a Shropshire nurseryman and designer, John Davenport. A letter from him of 1784 reads: 'I am now employed at Mr Pytts at Kyre and have been for many years and we never had any disputes in settling acts. Or in any other business'.[42] Davenport lived at Burlton Grove, near Wem and enjoyed a successful career as a landscape designer and architect in many parts of the country. In 1790 he claimed to have been in business for 22 years and is recorded to have worked at Pitchford Hall and Mawley Hall, both in Shropshire.[43] That would date his commission at Kyre to the late 1760s where he must have given shape to Pytts' ideas over a long campaign of delving and conducting. The presence of the Hermitage and a reference to a Chinese Bridge, now lost, are further evidence of the Rococo or eclectic nature of the scheme, as are two Grottoes, one on the Top Pool, the other, restored and imaginatively repaired, by the Lily Pond.

Walking on a clockwise circuit from the church, which is attached to the house by a pentice, the first, largest and longest of the lakes is The River. This lies almost on the same contour as the house. There is also a Top Pool with a Grotto which feeds The River and is set above it in deep woodland; the other three lakes – Hanning's Pool, The Lily Pond and the Fish Pond – all lie well below Kyre House down across the gentle slope of the Central Meadow (*colour plate 11*), composing together one of the most subtle of all eighteenth-century waterscapes, and one most imaginatively enriched over the last ten years. After winding along the south bank of The River the circuit walk comes to a thatched Summerhouse, restored in 1998, and the wreck of a Hermitage, which once had a Gothick façade. Here a path leads up to the Top Pool with its Grotto and the first of Kyre's many cataracts.

At the end of The River the grounds falls steeply away to Hanning's Pool. Here the waters of The River tumble into the lower pool down a long, narrow rock cascade. On the far shore of Hanning's a recently cut break in the tree-line damages the composition, which proves how important tree planting was to the creation of the Picturesque. Now the path leads, with fine visual effects, along an isthmus of land between the upper Hanning's and the lower Lily Pond. Here a twisting cataract runs alongside, the stones set into its bed to produce modest white-water effects. Dominating the Lily Pool, yet concealed from the house by a gloriously dark cedar of Lebanon, is Rapunzel's Tower. As a recent rebuilding, part of the campaign to restore Kyre to its rightful place in the tourist trail, this will be described in the chapter on modern gardens in the county.

However, it was here that Edmund Pytts and John Davenport contrived the ingenious Rococo climax to a park tour, with a tunnel under the hill which would have brought the excited visitor out of the darkness of a half-lit Grotto onto the waters of the Lily Pond with its island and, before that cedar grew so tall, a glimpse of the house at the top of the Central Meadow.

On the other side of the tunnel the path leads to a trim bridge of Stourport ironwork. Well shaded, it crosses the smallest of the five lakes, the Fish Pond, which appears more like a river than a lake. Above it a long straight vista leads down from the house and one of the Hiornes' two canted viewing bays, proof again of the carefully Picturesque interconnection of house and park which was achieved in the 1760s. At the foot of the slope was an eighteenth-century Bath House, demolished in 1900, which was, most unusually, supplied down a pipe from the house, apparently with heated, soft rain water. It would be interesting to see the evidence for this self-indulgent luxury. On the left of the slope behind a brick wall are the Kitchen Gardens of 1753 and the gardener's cottage. The big tree on the right is a Cut Leaf Beech with the largest girth in Britain. Even that has not exhausted the focus points of these remarkable grounds. To the east of the house is the Archery Lawn. This is a terrace below the great brick Tithe Barn of about 1618 with the dovecote moved here, apparently to create a picturesque grouping, which it certainly does. According to Pytts' family tradition the dovecote was originally sited on an island in one of the lakes, but which of all the possible sheets of water in this double park system is not known.

If Kyre Park stood to the side of a main A-road like Berrington Hall or Great Witley Court, it could become a show place. As it lies on an obscure, though attractive, B-road the success of the brave and imaginative restoration work carried out since 1993 must hang in the balance. It certainly deserves to succeed as a private venture to stand alongside those of the National Trust at Croome and Hanbury. Fortunate visitors will not forget quickly that amazing vista from the church pentice, of lake, below lake, below lake, with the lovely green nothingness of the Welsh Border stretching away to the west and the intriguing new shape of the Rapunzel Tower stabbing up at the far right, backed by woodland. This could eventually be a Picturesque-Rococo garden, half-Savage, half-Arcadian, to offer a subtext to the very different Rococo Garden at Painswick in Gloucestershire. All that is required is the restoration of that Chinese Bridge and the Gothick Hermitage.

7

Bonaparte, Mountnorris and gardens on the cusp

The most rewarding gardens to explore, though more for their interest than for their achieved beauty, are those caught on the cusp of change from one flagging style to another one which is moving in, revolutionary and experimental, to replace it. Probably the most interesting cusp, because it is the least predictable, is that between the Regency Picturesque and the High Victorian or, as the encyclopaedist, John Claudius Loudon, named it, the Gardenesque, that garden style when virtually every innovation could be tried out, and often was.

Worcestershire has two garden-parks poised on that last cusp: Thorngrove in Grimley parish a few miles due north of Worcester, and Arley Castle, much further up the Severn, almost in Shropshire. What makes them particularly fascinating is that the same designer, Richard Varden, a local Worcester architect, certainly remodelled the house and grounds at Thorngrove and perhaps did the same for Arley when he was building a dramatic Gothic Revival castle for the second Earl of Mountnorris alongside the existing Jacobean house.[1] Though born in 1770, before the Regency, Lord Mountnorris developed, by his obsessive scientific interests, into a typical experimental, rather than aesthetic, gardener. He exemplifies, therefore, the Gardenesque, though he also created several backward-looking Picturesque features of great beauty and interest at Arley in one of the county's most important, but only half-known layouts.

At Thorngrove another owner was employing Varden in 1835 to reshape yet again that satisfying formula for the Picturesque, which Capability Brown had established 80 years earlier. There are, however, some variations upon that Brownian pattern and a startling possibility exists as to exactly which owner of the property was responsible for the landscape. For a few years, between 1811 and 1814, Thorngrove was the family home of Lucien Bonaparte (44), soon to be Prince of Canino and the third of the five Bonaparte brothers who shook the thrones of old Europe. Joseph was the eldest, Napoleon was the second, Louis and Jerome were the two youngest boys; but only Lucien ever lived at Thorngrove. What a name the house would have if

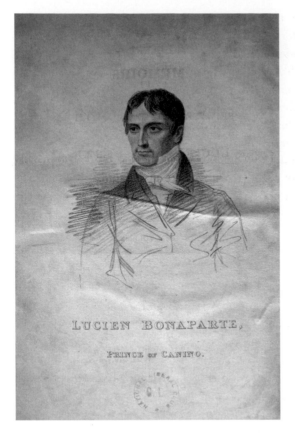

LUCIEN BONAPARTE,

PRINCE OF CANINO.

44 *This frontispiece portrait of Lucien Bonaparte, Napoleon's brother, is taken from his memoirs which describe life at Thorngrove during the Napoleonic Wars.* Bristol University Special Collections

Napoleon had been confined upon one of its several lake islands instead of on Elba or St Helena.

The whole saga of Prince Lucien Bonaparte's exile in Worcestershire reads like something from the early operations of MI6, with the Foreign Office playing a most dubious role. Lucien had always been the wild card in the Bonaparte family.[2] He was treacherous, also the most devout of the five brothers. It was Napoleon's policy to create an imperial house of the Bonapartes, setting up his brothers on the thrones of the kingdoms he had conquered. For Lucien he intended the artificial Kingdom of Etruria in the middle of the Italian peninsula. But to give his brother some royal dignity he proposed first marrying him off to a Spanish infanta. Lucien, handsome and wilful, had other ideas. He had been conducting an adulterous affair with a Madame Jouberteau, whose husband he had sent off to the West Indies to die of yellow fever. She had become pregnant, not by Lucien, who thought he was the father, but by a valet. So, believing that he was about to become a father, Lucien promised to marry her. Napoleon, who was kept well informed by his police system, was furious, dismissing Jouberteau, not inaccurately, as 'a mere trull'.[3] In an angry dispute Napoleon ranted at his brother: 'I wish to place all my brothers on thrones; and you, whom I love, who ought to second my views, your only delight consists in running after women: and now to finish all, you are going to dishonour yourself'.[4] With surprising firmness Lucien refused the crown of Etruria and refused to abandon Madame Jouberteau. Frustrated in his plan to be married by the Mayor of the 10th Arrondisement, Lucien drove his beloved off to Plessis Chamont in the suburbs where a *curé*, who later got into terrible trouble for his involvement,[5] put the bridal couple through both civil and religious ceremonies.

Lucien obstinately refused to put his bride away and the new Madame Bonaparte proceeded to appropriate all the fine pearl necklaces which Napoleon had lavished on his two nieces, Lucien's children by his first wife. In an effort to settle in neutral territory, Lucien retired to the Papal States only to see French armies sweeping into, first Rome, then Naples. Napoleon arranged a meeting of reconciliation, offering Lucien another crown, probably that of Tuscany, if he would abandon his wife. Again Lucien refused and began plotting to obtain a passage to the United States of America, anything to escape his brother. Now the British secret service joined the conspiracy. No sooner had Lucien and his family boarded an American ship, *The Hercules*, than an English frigate pounced, took the Bonapartes on board and sailed them off to captivity in Malta. The Marquis Wellesley, future Duke of Wellington, arranged for another frigate, *The President*, commanded by Captain Warren, to bring them all, as prisoners of war, in a stormy, one-month voyage, to Plymouth, where they were put up at the Kings Arms Hotel. As mementoes of a good relationship, Lucien gave Captain Warren a gold watch and the Captain gave Lucien a beautiful double-barrelled fowling piece, which he would use frequently at Thorngrove.

The Bonapartes soon attracted too much interest in Plymouth, so they were moved up to Ludlow, where they occupied Lord Powis' town house. Once more Lucien's charm worked social wonders. He was lionised so much locally that the British government persuaded him to buy the Thorngrove property for £9,000 and settle there in secure isolation. Mercurial as ever, Lucien was now determined to achieve lasting fame as a great French poet. He had already written 14 of the proposed 29 cantos of an epic to be called *Charlemagne: or the Triumph of Christianity*.[6] At Thorngrove he became very regular in his habits. Every morning he got up at eight, breakfasted with his family at nine and then retired to the gardener's cottage on the estate to write his poem. The family – there were two girls by each of his two wives from their previous marriages – were allowed visits to the cottage, and in the afternoons he went out shooting with Captain Warren's gun.

He was still wealthy and in the sale,[7] which followed his return to France and Rome in 1814, there is a mention of a Herschel telescope in a building set up as an observatory, also of a 'large and commodious pleasure boat'. So it appears that the Lucien years may have left some mark on Thorngrove. The evidence for this lies in those sale particulars and in the assurance of his *Memoirs* that:

> his mode of living in England was conducted on a totally different principle [to his scrupulous economy on leaving Italy], being both magnificent and expensive: the senator appeared to be desirous of shewing that he was the brother of a great sovereign.[8]

It seems likely, therefore, that he added some features to Thorngrove to satisfy that 'large and commodious pleasure boat' and to house the Herschel telescope. But before considering Thorngrove as it exists today, it would be a story half told to abandon Lucien and his entourage on their return to the Continent after Napoleon's exile to Elba and the Peace of Paris in 1814.

Predictably, he improved his circumstances. Forbidden entry to Bourbon France, he travelled through Germany and Switzerland to Rome where he was received with joy by the Pope and created Prince of Canino, the name of an estate which he had bought while on his previous residence in Rome. Then, by letter, he effected a reconciliation with his brother Napoleon on Elba, and plotted with him a return to France for those fateful Hundred Days that would end in the battle of Waterloo. Lucien had completed his *Charlemagne* poem while living at Thorngrove; so he immediately had it printed and sent a copy to the French Academy. The Academicians were, predictably, embarrassed and gave no acknowledgement until 1815 when, upon Napoleon's unexpected return to Paris, they hastily sent a deputation to Lucien 'to express how much flattered the Academy would feel, by his *excellency's* consecrating a few moments of his valuable time to its proceedings'.[9] Lucien had, therefore, a brief hour of literary fame.

After Waterloo Lucien tried desperately to persuade Napoleon not to abdicate, but to take refuge in America. When Napoleon, crushed by his defeat, insisted upon resignation, Lucien proposed to the two governing French chambers – deputies and peers – that they should swear allegiance to Napoleon II, Napoleon's young son. Lucien was hoping to insinuate himself into the position of Regent, but the debates went against him. Once more he fled, this time under the incognito title of Comte de Châtillon. Failing to find a packet boat to take him to America he took on a second incognito title as Conte di Casali and eventually found his way to Rome and the forgiving arms of Pope Pius VII. The allied powers – England, Austria, Russia and Prussia – had generously decided upon a policy of mildness to the Bonaparte family and in Rome, the Prince of Canino was allowed to stay.

Little is known of Richard Varden, but he came originally from Godalming in Surrey, was a contributor to J.C. Loudon's *Encyclopaedia* and was recommended as an architect and landscape designer by Loudon in the *Architectural Magazine* of 1836, just after he had set up practice in Worcester.[10] A detailed view of the house and plan of the estate at Thorngrove (45), as it existed just after 1835, was prepared by Varden,[11] and almost everything survives as the architect recorded it. The usual route to the house today branches off from a little side lane off the A443, Great Witley to Worcester road, passes a range of vaguely Gothick brick stables and swings abruptly out onto the front of Thorngrove House. This is unlikely to have been Lucien's ceremonial entrance. That leaves the A443 directly between austere classical twin lodges and proceeds, in its picturesque curving sweep, to reveal virtually everything of charm and interest that the estate can offer.

Initially there is a fine view, one illustrated above Varden's plan of the layout, looking down across an islanded line of lakes, then up the whole expanse of the main meadow to the façade of the House which, while hesitant and unsure in its elevations upon

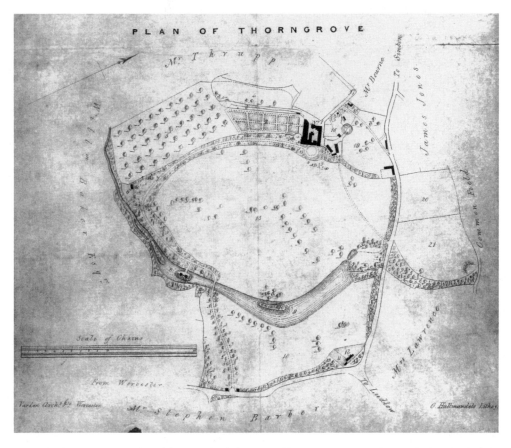

45 *Richard Varden's 1830s plan of the grounds of Thorngrove illustrate a Picturesque layout of lake, islands and island pavilions threaded by a typical Brownian-style main drive*

close inspection, puts on a brave show from this distance. But there is much more visual entertainment before the drive reaches the House. It is not, technically, a Brownian encircling of the entire park, but a more subtle, Reptonian-style preparation piece. The drive hurries down between trees, saving the best views for later, then leaps out dramatically across a narrowing of the serpentine lake on a grandiose stone and ironwork arched bridge (46) with wheeled standards supporting lamps at each side of the balustrade. To the left, the waters widen into a lake with a wooded island, and there is a glimpse up to the House, but then the trees close in again as the drive swings left, along a river-like reach with three more wooded islands, each linked by footbridges to the drive and inviting exploration or picnicking.

The first of these islets is the most intriguing. A frail iron bridge, stamped 'Stourport 1805', with a lion's head on its handrails, must, by its date, be pre-Lucien, But Varden's plan marks the island with linked twin pavilions. These have left no trace; but was this the Observatory for Lucien's telescope, or were they twin classical pavilions for that pleasure

46 *As Thorngrove's drive in from the Worcester road crossed the lake on this surprisingly grand bridge it opened up briefly a wide view up to the house and down to the lake*

boat to visit with a family of laughing Bonapartes aboard? Each of the next two islands has its unremarkable little brick bridge; so how were they used? As the drive bends right to turn uphill, Varden marks another pavilion tucked away in the woods against the fence of the very large orchard. The belts now on either side are planted with mature specimen trees, a Kitchen Garden rises up to the left. Its walls were once heated by flues and it possessed a central fountain, now removed; the yew hedges and herbaceous border are recent.

At last the House is reached, appearing suddenly at the top of a rising curve on a terraced shelf from which it looks out, like Holt Castle, to the sunken, shifting course of the Severn. It is a likeable, indeterminate building of late Georgian classicism reshaped by Williamane additions. In its interior simple architectural elegancies pop up curiously under figurative plasterwork, where the fruit and leaves have been carefully painted in natural colours, although not by Lucien Bonaparte. There is a close stylistic connection between house and garden, both here at Thorngrove and at Arley Castle. At Thorngrove the façades of the house are largely classical, but lurch occasionally into unexpected Gothic ogival arches; and the park, while generally Brownian, has those islands linked obsessively to the drive by illogical bridges. In both house and grounds the eighteenth-century predict-abilities hesitate at times. Arley Castle was, before its demolition, commitedly Gothic Revival, but it retained a Jacobean wing; and its grounds, though very Gardenesque with a great Arboretum, still have one complete area of Picturesque charm, where Gardenesque features like the Fernery manage to infiltrate the eighteenth-century Picturesque of cliffs and waterfalls, and yet contrive, by a brave show of rocks and boulders, to suggest the savage side of the Picturesque. That is what being on the cusp involves.

The Earl of Mountnorris, who began building the new Castle at Arley impulsively in 1843, a year before his death, was an Irish peer, the second holder of a brash new political title. His mother Lucy was a Lyttelton, so his maternal grandfather was that Lord Lyttelton who had built the celebrated Sham Castle at Hagley; his Irish father had rescued his mother from drowning in the Severn at Arley when their pleasure boat was rammed by a barge and sank. Castles and adventurous projects were in the blood, but for his very ambitious castle project at Arley, Mountnorris consulted Varden rather than his Lyttelton relations. Until that time Mountnorris' interests had been exclusively and intensely botanical and scientific, which makes him a typical early Victorian even though he was born before the Regency. As Viscount Valentia, he had inherited Arley Hall from one of his Lyttelton uncles in 1779 while he was still a child. But before his twenty-seventh year he had been made a fellow of the Linnean Society and the Royal Society, and was travelling as far afield as South Africa, Ethiopia and India in quest of new plants and trees.[12] By 1801 he had 'lately much ornamented' the grounds at Arley Hall 'with a variety of considerable plantations, etc, as well as added much to the comfort and convenience of this respectable mansion, beautifully situated on the richly wooded banks of the Severn'.[13] He suffered from that general Victorian condition of being too well informed to follow traditional patterns in the arts and gardening. If that sounds a paradox it is only necessary to consider the complete collapse in the Victorian century of architectural taste into a welter of eclectic and unrelated styles. Scholarship and educated awareness results in eclecticism. From their travels, their research and the innumerable illustrated publications, the Victorians could build authentically in Venetian, French and English Gothic, in Flemish Renaissance or Louis Quatorze. All styles were available for a moneyed patron, therefore the guidance of tradition was lost.

It was the same with garden design. Adventurous plant hunters, among them Viscount Valentia who, in 1802, was writing letters back from his travels to Sir Joseph Banks,[14] were bringing in a treasury of flowering shrubs, trees and bulbs from China, Indonesia and the Americas. Horticultural societies competed to display them. Where the colour of flowers had been limited to the low carpet design of a parterre in earlier gardens, now bushes of flaming colour, rhododendron, camellia and azalea took over, while greenhouses rose up to protect orchids, palms and delicious soft fruits; gardeners became technicians and engineers. Industry could now supply cheaply, mosaics, statuary, fountains and ironwork. When everything was available for display there was a real danger behind the Gardenesque of vulgar profusion.

At Mountnorris' Arley estate the cultural divide in gardens was unusually well defined. The grounds of Thorngrove had more or less preserved the Brownian decencies. Lucien's Observatory had been tucked away, probably on that island with the 1805 bridge. The landscape at Arley was, in contrast, two very distinct horticultural worlds. Below the Castle in the valley of the Kettle Brook, Lord Mountnorris, who had succeeded to the earldom in 1816, had behaved like an arrogant eighteenth-century improver, straight out of Goldsmith's *Deserted Village* of 1769. A flour mill and several cottages were cleared away, but one old lady held out until her death around 1816; hence the name Naboth's Vineyard, given to the valley in memory of Naboth in the Old Testament who refused wicked King Ahab's demand: 'Give me thy vineyard, that I may have it for a garden of herbs, because it is near unto my house'. Not that anyone suggests that Mountnorris had the old lady starved to death, as Ahab did to Naboth. Indeed her cottage became a showpiece in the new Picturesque valley between the two waterfalls. Thatched and tricked out with bought-in Jacobean panelling, it became a viewing pavilion for alfresco meals, its bow window perfect for enjoying the upper waterfall, with a little round lily pool in the garden as a Gardenesque concession to a Picturesque area.

Entrance to Naboth's Vineyard is by a long stone-lined Fernery which strikes again a double note: a Fernery is Gardenesque, but if it is lined with rough boulders it becomes Savage Picturesque.[15] But where the Arboretum on the other side of the Castle is outward looking, Naboth's Vineyard is an inward world, loud with falling water and directing visitors to its own intimate vistas. On one occasion its path brings the startled visitor to a vertiginous halt on the edge of a small cliff above a dark pool and a cascade (*47*). In a playful spirit it is sometimes truly Savage Picturesque, as when the circuit path

47 *The circuit walk around Naboth's Vineyard, the Picturesque sector of Arley Castle's grounds, comes to two 'Savage' viewpoints over the Kettle Brook. This is the lower Cascade with the first frightening drop*

crosses a cyclopean bridge built deliberately on the actual brink of the theatrical upper waterfall (*colour plate 10*) where the Kettle Brook tumbles down a 20ft cliff, part-natural, part-enhanced.

After that giddy experience the path winds away up among Lord Mountnorris' real love, specimen trees – Corsican and Crimean pines, Maples, Redwoods, Mountain Magnolia (*Magnolia acumulata*) and Bitter Nut (*Carya amara*) [16] – with two small quarries, cut for the building of the Castle in 1843-4, a yew circle and an ice house for diversity before descending down into the valley again. It is on this reach of the path that the loss of the two lakelets, silted up years ago, is so evident. They would have dramatised the whole valley with bamboo and flowering shrubs on their banks. It is to be hoped that the Trust, which now administers the grounds at Arley, will turn from its first love, the Arboretum, which is admirably tended, and restore the lake. There would be few other Picturesque gardens to equal Naboth's Vineyard for compact contrivance of multiple vistas.

North of the Castle's platform, now occupied by a discreetly elegant modern house, a lime avenue leads into the Arboretum, which is neither a wood nor a garden, but a tree laboratory or museum where trees are measured to record their growth and are preserved primarily for their rarity rather than their beauty, though beauty follows as an inevitable end product. [17] A noble profusion of prime specimens takes over. There is an extraordinary layered beech whose trunk has resigned, but whose branches have rooted themselves to take over its original role. A great Cedar of Lebanon, a Wellingtonia, planted in 1860, and Mountnorris' favourite Crimean Pine crowd each other so that it is hard to do individuals justice. There is distraction too from the idyllic views out over the Severn valley but one tree, not a very large one, remains in the memory: this is the famous *Sorbus domestica* or True Service Tree. It stands quite near to the house, but visitors have a ceremonial approach. This northern, tree-sodden area of Arley Castle's grounds is almost completely surrounded by a high battlemented wall as for some medieval town. Before the Vardens' Castle was demolished in the 1960s the two features must have worked atmospherically together. Even today the ghost of that short-lived Castle, Worcestershire's counter to Cheshire's Peckforton Towers, haunts the site and its vistas. The Gothic Gatehouse (*48*) leading in through garden walls has survived, framing a fine view of a melancholy range of trees. The Trust, which was set up by Roger Turner to save Arley after his death in 1999, has created a visitor centre with a formal Italian Garden between disciplined rows of White Lime, *Tilia tomentosa*. It is after this that the *Sorbus domestica* must be approached with reverence. It is descended from a specimen discovered in the Wyre Forest in 1678 and was thought for many years to be the only tree of its kind. Resembling a sturdy Mountain Ash, it has green-to-brown small fruit, from which a native beer can be brewed. Another name for it is the Chequer Tree and any public house called The Chequers is likely once to have stood near a grove of such beer producers. Rather sadly another specimen of *Sorbus domestica* has been found in the Wyre Forest and one romantic theory has it that these trees were introduced by a French hermit who possibly brewed his own beer.

48 *A Gothick Gatehouse out into the park, sited at the end of a massive bastion, is a reminder of what was lost when Arley Castle was demolished in the 1960s. Only the fortified inner garden survives*

Roger Turner, it should be explained, was a Birmingham philanthropist who bought the Arley estate from the Woodward family who, in their turn, had bought it from Mountnorris' heir, Major Arthur Lyttelton McLeod. Mountnorris did not finish his new Castle and, ironically, the splendid garden interlocking sections of that building which remain today – the great Bastion Terrace and the Barbican Gatehouse – were McLeod's creations before he sold up his uncle's vast collection of Egyptian antiquities, shells and botanical specimens. Lord Mountnorris' best memorials are his trees. The tower of the parish church, St Peter's, has to stand in today for Mountnorris' 120ft keep. A solid, brilliantly green wall of yew separates the graveyard from the lawns and rose beds of that modern house, which now cowers, self-effacingly, as if apologising for a well intentioned regime that valued trees above castles.

8

Great trees and artificial stones –
the county's Gardenesque

Ombersley Court, like Arley Castle, was completely reshaped in the first 40 years of the nineteenth century and stands, like Arley, in an arboretum of the same period. Both parks are arranged around minor tributaries of the Severn at a point just above the union of the rivers. Yet it would be difficult to find anywhere in the county two houses or two parks so unalike.

It seems too clinical to refer to Ombersley's park as an arboretum. It is a garden of trees, where each mature giant can be appreciated at a distance and enjoyed for itself alone. Only one tree, a Swamp Cypress, undersized for its age because it does not have its feet in the water, lowers the tone of the great cedars, redwoods, Golden Larch and other choice specimens that rise above Ombersley's perfect lawns, each one demanding individual attention. For instance, the Wellingtonia in front of the house, planted in 1853, is 124ft tall with a girth of 21ft 3in. Consequently it commands the park as completely as would a soaring Gothic folly tower or a large domed classical temple. It even has an interior, being blessed, unusually for that species, with a low, sweeping skirt of branches. To stand within that skirt and look up into the tree is to experience the internal structure of a natural skyscraper; and the Golden Ash (*Fraxinus excelsior aurea*) that stands respectfully a good 50 yards away, planted in 1860, works like a contrasting flower in a garden for godlike titans.

The Court is another matter, a severe neo-classical box of extreme austerity. Yet the house, or at least its Regency reshaping, and the arboretum-park all around it, were both commissioned by the Dowager Marchioness of Downshire & Baroness Sandys from the same man, John Webb of Lichfield. Like Richard Varden, Webb was both architect and garden designer, consulted at Eton Hall, Cheshire, Ashridge Park, Hertfordshire, and at Lowther Castle in Wetsmorland.[1] He was a pupil of William Emes who was himself a pupil of Lancelot Brown. It has to be accepted that the desperate restraint of that seven-bay façade and the displaced reserve of the lovely park stem from the same neo-classical spirit. Webb was working here between 1811 and 1821;[2] Richard Varden was raising the theatrical complexities of Arley Castle for Lord Mountnorris less than 20 years later, after 1843, but what an aesthetic somersault has been effected between the styles of the two houses and their parks.

The Marchioness must have been deliberate in what she commissioned from Webb. There was no need for that icy new façade. Francis Smith of Warwick had built, between 1723 and 1727, a quietly attractive Baroque courtyard house, but Webb may have been influenced to employ self-denying Protestant aesthetics by her son, who was altering the exterior of Hillsborough Castle, County Down, at the same period, 1810.[3] Whatever influence it works for the garden even if it chills the exterior of the house. To go in under that coupled Ionic columned Webb portico into Smith's rumbustious Entrance Hall, which was allowed to survive Webb's glaciation, is like walking out of a refrigerator into warm sunshine.

An engraving (*49*) in Nash's *Worcestershire* of 1782 shows the entrance front of the house with simple, quartered grass lawns leading up to the public road, beyond which a tree-lined avenue stretches out into the park. Immediately prior to Webb's arboretum treatment of the park there was a formal round pool in front of the house and then a

49 A late eighteenth-century view of Ombersley Court, showing the formal garden to the east front, the public road and formal tree avenues. All this was to be swept away in John Webb's Regency remodelling of the grounds. Bodleian Library, Oxford, Gough Maps 33, fol.63r

fine chain of four long ponds, part of that dammed-up tributary; and the drive went east between the two upper ponds to meet the main road at a surviving lodge.[4] John Webb and the Marchioness were not interested in such flights of Picturesque indulgence, so Webb's utilitarian drive goes directly north to the church and the village.[5] All the Picturesque pools have gone except for a marshy survival – the Black Pool and Fish Pond – down by the Turn Mill dam which initially created them.

On the garden front of the house to the west grows one of those weirdly engaging 'apprentice trees', whereby a young eighteenth-century woodsman proved his skill in the craft of bringing off a successful, bizarre graft. This is one of a lime tree compounded with a hawthorn bush. Now fully grown, it bears in mixed bursts, the leaves and flowers and seeds of two species. An improbably abrupt copper beech seems to have been another apprentice piece. The European Larch (*Larix decidua*) was planted in 1738. It and its brother at Krief Mongie in Scotland both came from the Tyrol. To be taken around the great trees of the park by Lord Sandys was rather like being introduced to older members of the family. The only reservation he expressed over his demesne related to the ice house of the later eighteenth century. As we were making towards it he hesitated. 'If I might suggest', he paused with old world courtesy, 'there are...horse flies'. We did not visit the ice house; but then one ice house is very like another.

In another sharp change of garden mood the park at Hadzor Hall on the eastern outskirts of Droitwich, is of 1827, by Matthew Habershon who was building the house for John Howard Galton. In that 17-year interval between Ombersley and Hadzor the Gardenesque has gone blowsy, Victorian even before the young queen was on the throne. To be correct its gardens should be described as Williamane, as the 'Sailor King' reigned from 1830 to 1837 and houses of that brief period tend towards the Italianate, as does Hadzor and its gardens.[6]

I came to the Hall almost too late. The developers have closed in and all the rising ground of the park below the house and facing north has been parcelled out into mildly attractive courts, drives and cul-de-sacs of outdated Post-modernist housing. On its south side, however, the park and gardens are still intact, if a little decayed. The new brick houses give way and a curious, quiet spell settles upon the Italianate garden front of the house with its belvedere tower, its terrace with broken balustrading and multiple steps and, most unexpected and *Brideshead Revisited* of all, the spiky Regency Gothic, Roman Catholic chapel of St John the Baptist. This is in absolute stylistic contrast to the house, though not much younger.

Although Habershon was responsible for the remodelling of the Hall and the adjacent church in the late 1820s, the balustraded, terraced garden that was under construction in 1831-33, when Galton was in Rome, is not the garden that survives today and which was recorded in early *Country Life* photographs.[7] Kenneth Lowe, the agent at Hadzor, kept his employer informed of progress on the original terrace garden which was planted with dahlia beds, box edging, penstemons, 'polyanthus, tulips, crocus, snow drops, anemones, double hyacinths, [and] early sulphur narcissus'.[8] Habershon's initial design featuring massive vases and statues seems to have been altered by his employer, who had his own design ideas, and then Alexander Roos was brought in to give the grounds a more consciously Italianate atmosphere. Roos was associated with Thomas Hope at The Deepedene in Surrey, one of the earliest Italian-style houses and gardens in the country, and later worked with Charles Barry at the celebrated Shrubland Park in Suffolk, where he designed the suitably Italianate Barham Lodge in 1841.[9] An undated water-colour by Roos for Hadzor shows the existing garden[10] and he is known to have added Pompeian decoration to the main reception room. The balustrade with its curious stone seats and the Roman-style stone basin with its imperial lion's head spout (50) are similar in design to garden features published by Robert Wetten and P.F. Robinson in contemporary pattern books.[11]

Until recently there was also an ironwork garden pavilion on the terrace, which was originally a greenhouse, but used for a time as the chapel of St Richard's College. Now its Corinthian columns lie in a heap to the side, waiting, it is to be hoped, a reconstruction sometime soon. An air of latent Catholic religiosity hangs over the remainder of the pleasure grounds. These were reshaped before 1901 when Lady Hindlip was in residence.[12] There are very thick yew hedges to the entrance front of the Hall, wrecked garden urns, surprisingly well-kept lawns, one tall, absurdly isolated conifer and the predictable scatter of specimen trees lower down the slope. But instead

50 *An Italianate balustraded terrace by Alexander Roos surrounds Matthew Habershon's Italian-style Hadzor Hall. The lion's head spout and basin suggests its consciously Pompeian ancestry*

of a garden temple there is a Temple Memorial to the young men of the family killed in the 1914-18 War. It is a gaunt structure intruding impressively into the conventional steep lawns and yew hedges. Down to the right is Hadzor Wood, thick with nettles, but retaining a pool, which must once have been the romantic destination for woodland paths. Most disturbingly of all in this atmospheric garden of bereavement and change is a high-walled yew rectangle, an empty, shadowed garden room for a statue of Our Lady. When the Hall has been restored the gardens will flourish again. They are far from lost, merely in between periods and I caught them in a forlorn but memorable state.

A more relaxed and Anglican version of a religious garden was created by the Revd. Robert Landor, less ebullient but perhaps more scholarly brother of Walter Savage Landor, who came to The Rectory, Birlingham, in 1829. He immediately put in hand the construction of a small Chapel at the northern end of the garden with an elaborately decorated façade and space for three stained glass windows. Nearby he erected a sandstone column with barley-sugar spirals. Landor lived in his Rectory like a lesser prince bishop and enhanced the garden by a lime avenue, a nut walk, a gazebo and extensive plantings of cyclamen and aconites. His passion for gardening was maintained by his family until the death of his great niece in 1945.[13]

Abbey House, Evesham, was, on my visit, weathering its near-suburban situation more confidently than Hadzor and more dependent on big trees for its effect. Its scholarly Gardenesque qualities were not essentially botanical, like Arley Castle or Ombersley Court, but historical. Its park covers the site of that ugly Battle of Evesham in 1265 when the Lord Edward, Henry III's ruthlessly capable son, moved fast to separate Simon de Montfort's army from its likely supporters, and smashed the aspirant constitutional reformer's troops in a violent thunderstorm. The old king was rescued, frantically pleading his identity just in time to avoid a descending mace; Simon de Montfort was killed, but the Lord Edward, soon to be crowned Edward I, was left with the unavoidable precedent de Montfort had set: that of a Parliament with two knights from every shire and two representatives from every borough. It would be a precedent that had to be followed in future whenever a king felt the need to raise taxes, and from it a true parliamentary democracy would flower.

So it was an important defeat constitutionally and de Montfort, who may have been no more than an intelligent manipulator of the popular will, was seen in the nineteenth century to deserve a memorial park of great trees. Today a well-signposted pilgrimage can be followed to de Montfort's memorial Tower and then on to a memorial Obelisk in a Victorian shrubbery. It is not a usual landscape garden. As at Hadzor, the dead from an earlier war cluster around it; and, as at Hadzor, the developers have moved in, though not quite as overwhelmingly, only a few discreet middle class houses have been tastefully set back along the drive to the Abbey Manor House.

The park lies within a long triangle of roads lined with thick belts of mature trees. These give it an unexpected privacy so near to a sizeable market town; the sharp wedge end of the triangle points north-west towards Worcester and a public path, with helpful information boards, leads from The Squires side of the triangle across open parkland to the Leicester Tower (*51*). This rises in a curious Gothic octagon high above the chestnut trees. Overlooking the path, indeed dominating virtually every point of the park, is the Abbey House, one of Pevsner's rare errors in dating. He suggested loosely: 'The house seems to be of *c.* 1840',[14] when anyone with an eye for the pinnacled, spiny refinements of the true early Regency Gothic would have dated it to no later than 1820. But Pevsner was never as sympathetic to the revived Gothic as he was to the genuine article. Abbey House was built in 1817-8 and looks exactly that date: a beautifully spare, elegant building, still clinging nervously to classical symmetries despite its Gothic clothes. It has been the home of the Rudge family since the sixteenth century.

The Leicester Tower is, as its date of 1842 suggests, a little rougher in detail, but a splendid park marker. 'To the Memory of Simon de Montfort Earl of Leicester' its inscription reads, 'The Father and Founder of the British House of Commons', and, if that is not entirely accurate, it is what most chroniclers believe and that is what matters. There are more historic reminiscences ahead. A path leads alongside the chestnut bands until it comes opposite the Abbey House. Then it climbs steeply uphill to the wood around the gardens of Abbey House. There is a large oval fish pond in these trees, placed at the end of a formal garden layout, but that is hidden.[15] The path leads through the Victorian shrubbery instead to an Obelisk, set within a contrived woodland glade straight out of that well-known painting by Constable. On the faces of the Obelisk are carved representations of events in the battle (*52*) and this, apparently, is where either King Henry was rescued or de Montfort was slain. It is not easy to become emotional about either man. Henry reigned for such a long time, 1216 to 1272, doing very little except being weak and aesthetic, but he did give us the coronation theatre crossing of Westminster Abbey, even though he was himself crowned in Gloucester Cathedral. Here in this grove of trees, on 4 August 1265, he got the chance to reign for another seven years, and simply by being weak, he became, accidentally, a useful shaper of the English constitution and the excuse for a bold Gardenesque memorial park. In retrospect the Abbey House park is most unusual for a nineteenth-century Worcestershire designed landscape in its general avoidance of specimen trees from West Coast America. Perhaps native trees, if chestnuts can be called native, seemed more appropriate for such an historic English park.

No such reservations were felt when Pull Court's grounds were being planted out to provide a suitable frame for the grand Tudor to Jacobean country house that Edward Blore designed between 1834 and 1839 for Canon Dowdeswell on the site of an earlier house, at Bushley, just west of Tewkesbury.[16] Being ruthlessly honest, it was much too sumptuous a house for a mere Canon and far too large a park. Richard Lockett gives it the tribute of a double page spread in his *Survey* and there is even a tradition, with no documentary evidence, that Lancelot Brown had worked on the deer park, which is first mentioned on Isaac Taylor's county map of 1772. Ever since it was laid out the park around Pull Court has been shrinking. Looking out from the garden front of the house over Blore's battered, pierced stone balustrade there should be a great sweep of parkland to Hill House on the horizon; but the land has all been divided up into agricultural fields with one or two improbable cedars still hanging on here and there.

51 The Gardenesque in one of its historicist moods is captured in the octagonal Leicester Tower built in 1842 below Abbey House, Evesham, to recall the heroic death of Simon de Montfort fighting for the liberty of Parliament

52 On the Obelisk, set in the shrubbery walks of Abbey House, representations are carved in earnest detail showing the rescue of the cowardly King Henry III and the gallant death of de Montfort. Victorian historicism acknowledged no shading of truth

On the other, north, side of the house the huge park has been even less fortunate, as the M50 now cuts the Court off from its church, St Nicholas, at Queenhill. It was the planting of the inevitable dark, boldly profiled, specimen trees close around the house that gave the Court itself an oasis of dignity. Once a few Wellingtonias have moved in and there are rhododendrons to supply some ground cover, then a pompous Victorian Jacobean Revival construct like Pull Court can begin to feel correctly framed.

There is an extremely long drive in from the south, where a public road pretends for at least a mile to be a private drive by having a Jacobean-style Lodge built by its side. This crosses the bare farmland for a while, but then redwoods rise up, the drive sneaks in through the rhododendrons and Blore pulls off quite a visual coup with a forecourt screen of arches and pinnacles, attractively planted with climbing shrubs, while the Court puts on a brave show of gables. Pull Court has only one garden feature on offer after its forecourt. This is the Rose Garden which straggles away to the east and then unexpectedly ends with a pair of fine eighteenth-century wrought iron gates, good enough with their flowering urns and stylized fleur-de-lys to have been made by William Edney. They do not really belong here. Canon Dowdeswell's son William, who served briefly as a mid-nineteenth-century Chancellor of the Exchequer, presented them to Tewkesbury Abbey. Where he got them from is not recorded, but one suspects that they were a Bristol cast-off. When William heard that Tewkesbury had been given another set of gates he took his own gates back and set them up here at the end of a long terrace in the Rose Garden. Traces of original 'invisible' green paint and gilding survive on them. William ended up as a Governor of the Bahamas, like the Duke of Windsor; an extensive Empire can be a real social convenience for the disposal of unwanted notables.

To appreciate what the Gardenesque could really achieve at its best, it is essential to be at Witley Court on those occasions when the fountains are playing. Without a breath of chauvinistic exaggeration, Witley's fountains are superior in their rising profile, their theatrical figures and their multiple spouting jets to those at Versailles. They are probably Worcestershire's supreme garden treat. As at Pull Court and Hadzor, the actual grounds of the park have shrunk, arable fields have crept back in; woodlands have been felled; the house has been gutted; but the fountains play again, and that fabulous Baroque Chapel still holds Anglican Church services. Wrecked and ruined as it is, Witley remains one of the county's top five gardens; it is the great survivor.

There is no better justification for the Gardenesque's insistence upon uniting horticulture and technology than William Andrews Nesfield's fountain groups at Witley Court: the masculine Perseus rescuing Andromeda from a monster and the feminine Flora and the Tritons (53), carved by James Forsyth in 1860. Some Worcestershire gardens, like Croome Court and Arley Castle, celebrated applied science with firework displays. Arley had a full-time powder-monkey, Witley showed off with equally expensive water displays twice a week. Nikolaus Pevsner was most prescient in his account of Witley Court. He was there when the statuary of the fountains stood dry and apparently dead in rough meadow grass. I remember them too on an earlier visit in the 1970s, but never dreamed that they could ever work again. Pevsner was wiser; in a footnote he quoted a *Country Life* article

53 *Only the muscular, trumpeting tritons survive on James Forsyth's Flora and the Tritons Fountain which awaits restoration at Witley Court*

by Captain M.J. Gibson, who had delved down into the Piranesian guts of Witley Court's waterworks to find out how such ambitious fountains functioned. In 'a ramshackle building deep in a steep-sided dell', he had found, 'huge wheels, larger than one can take in at a view, ropes, chains, hooks, bars, spikes, crumbling walls and shafts of light amid darkness'.[17] Such antique technology was irresistible to an age devoted to the restoration of steam engines and threshing machines, dockside steam cranes and crashed Spitfires. Now Perseus is ready to slay again and his dragon to fume, while Flora and the Tritons are waiting to live once more in violent waters for a precious 20 minutes or so. The theatrical performance takes place at regular intervals in the day and the wait on the terraces between the great, gutted palace and the Perseus Fountain far below gives expectant visitors an opportunity to weigh up Witley Court's Gardenesque pluses and its minuses.

The bones of the Court are seventeenth-century though its walls, columns and parapets are largely nineteenth-century. Between 1843 and 1846 the house had been let to Queen Adelaide, so it was a truly superior Williamane residence with King William's actual widow as its principal ornament. After her departure, William Humble Ward, eleventh Baron Ward of Birmingham, moved in and he had the existing house and gardens remodelled in the 1850s and 1860s by Samuel Whitfield Daukes and Nesfield.[18] Lord Ward was created first Earl of Dudley in 1860. Even though ravaged by fire, his reshaped Court, on its multiple stepped terraces, has the movement of a

Vanbrugh house like Seaton Delaval in Northumberland. Coarse in its detail, it is refreshingly un-English in its movement, the swirl and embrace of those pavilioned arms. Such architectural animation needed a responding movement from its gardens. James Forsyth's fountains gave them just that: palatially scaled architectural events to match the sprawling Italianate palace (*colour plate 16*). But when it comes to Nesfield's work at Witley Court I have to express reservations.

Nesfield's parterre design is the one technological excess of the Gardenesque that I find hard to admire. Nesfield came into garden designing sideways.[19] He had been an army officer and had developed a precise finicky skill in map-making while fighting America in that odd, little-noticed war of 1812. In addition he was a skilled water-colourist. But most of his commissions to design gardens came from his brother-in-law, Anthony Salvin and, since Salvin was the architect of many ornate Jacobethan houses in that overwrought, hybrid style that the Victorians loved, Nesfield developed monstrously elaborate, expensive and overblown parterres, to accord with Salvin's houses. The paradox is that Nesfield's *parterres de broderie* were inspired by French seventeenth-century models, whereas Salvin's houses were either Tudor, Elizabethan, Jacobean or a mixture of the last two styles, but always historicist versions of English architecture. Victorian grandees like the Earl of Dudley loved Nesfield's Franco-Jacobethanry gone wild because he could spend their money for them and produce gasp-making tapestries of box and bedding plants. All those brash formal parterres with patterns of slate, spar, brick and coal dust delighted the Victorians and, with his map-making background, Nesfield wove the most complex Paisley-style patterns for them on a scale the Elizabethans and Jacobeans could not have imagined. At Witley Court he had a great employer. The Earl of Dudley was seriously rich. His coalmines and ironworks brought him, in modern monetry values, more than a million pounds a year. He owned 25,554 acres. His central heating at Witley Court consumed 7 tons of coal a day in winter. The 'Michelangelo' Conservatory which he added to his palace is as large as a small country house; but it was this excess of money which turned Witley's gardens into something resembling a municipal park.

The Gardenesque was basically about what gardeners liked doing if they worked for patrons who had the funds to indulge themselves. Nesfield pandered grossly to their obsessions with the south and east parterres at Witley Court.[20] Even he described his projects there as his 'Monster Work'.[21] Some of his bedding intricacies were outlined in stone; if they were in box then the plants had to be 4in wide and 4in high. Later in a tour of the grounds, on the far side of the Baroque Chapel, visitors will see the greenhouse complex required to sustain such plating.[22] There were flowers in the patterns: perlagoniums, vibernum, godetias and cotoneasters, but coloured gravels endure for all 12 months of the year, so stone in gravel, statuary urns, pools and ornate walling predominated. At its height Witley Court was a garden of stone and metal and engineering, the epitome of the Gardeneseque, what Nesfield called 'Architectural Gardening'.[23] It was typical of the period that Nesfield's two almost Baroque pavilions on the slope behind the Perseus and Andromeda Fountain had domes of amber-coloured glass to cheer their users, and that there are Hindu touches to their architectural detail.

At their eclectic worst, and Nesfield together with the Earl of Dudley represented their worst, the Victorians could not leave well alone.

As it stands today in theatrical ruin with just the Perseus and Andromeda Fountain in the South Parterre garden restored and functioning, Witley Court is in its real aesthetic prime. It would be a dreadful waste of money to attempt a complete restoration of the 'Monster Work'. Nesfield was not a great gardener; labour for labour's sake is not a good garden principle.

The Witley deer park was enormous with four pools, but it is a comment of the park's design that the fifth, or Front Pool, is the only one of any landscape significance. With its 1733 Chapel also serving as the village's parish church, the Court lacked privacy and to compensate for this a Wilderness was planted not, as is usual, behind the house, but between it and the main road. Two drives, each with a spatially lively Italianate lodge, plunge into this thick woodland and break out with pleasant drama near the house and overlooking the impressive, river-like Front Pool which had a cataract and that Piranesian Engine House at its head. Various estate buildings of Witley Court's golden age under the Earl of Dudley survive out in the park, but the elegant classical Keeper's Lodge that Henry Flitcroft designed for the second Lord Foley before 1762 was demolished around 1950.[24]

In a curious way Witley Court has been visually out-pointed by a neighbouring house, Abberley Hall, built for James Moilliet in 1845-6, Italianate in style again and also by Daukes. All was scenically well until 1867 when Joseph Jones of Severn Stoke, the archetypal brash industrialist, bought the estate. His cousin, John Joseph Jones, succeeded him in 1880 and employed J.P. St Aubyn, not just to extend the house, which already had the usual Italianate belvedere tower, but to build in 1883-4 a rival to Big Ben up on his hilltop: a thrusting Gothic tower with 20 bells and a repertory of 54 tunes, all in pious memory of his father. What could an Earl of Dudley do to counter that? It is a landmark from Tenbury in the north to Worcester in the south and Abberley's grounds, with their lime avenues, shrink at its feet.

Nevertheless the grounds immediately below the house are terraced and enlivened by mature, even at times overgrown, Pulhamite gardens of great interest. To the rear of the Hall is an Italianate South Terrace of three levels lined originally with balustrading, statuary and urns, now mostly ruinous. There are steps down at its eastern corner to the pleasure grounds where the terrace supporting the house is tunnelled with grey, stalactitic Pulhamite caverns that lure the curious into their low passages, only to expel them a few yards further along. The precise dating of the Pulhamite rockwork is not known, though sale particulars of 1867 mention 'a spring, fountain, rockery and alcoves',[25] so it must have been constructed during James Moilliet's residence at Abberley. The *Journal of Horticulture and Cottage Gardener* of 1887 described the passages as a 'series of small caves, delightfully cool in the hot weather of early August'.[26] More impressive in a planting of berried bushes and Japanese maples is the Pulhamite Quarry with what has once been a sizeable Water Garden (54) that has now run dry. As usual with the Pulhams' work the craftsmanship displayed in these artificial rocks is remarkably convincing, and the whole

54 Half-natural rocks and half-clever Pulhamite imitations of real stratification in the Water Garden at Abberley Hall are still impressive now that the waters have run dry and the site is overgrown

area on the lip of Abberley Hill deserves to be repaired and restored. With its cascades running it would make a delightful Gardenesque period piece.

The Lodges to Abberley's main drive are unfashionably High Victorian, of 1883 by St Aubyn. In time they will come to be valued as rich period pieces. That same cloud of the nearly, but not quite, fashionable still hangs to a degree over Droitwich's period piece, Chateau Impney. Just the improbable collision between those two words – one French, one earthy English – tends to raise a smile, and its brilliantly coloured, even crammed gardens give the impression that they would be happier in Vichy, supporting hot springs and hopeful invalids.

A small park threaded by the Salwarpe gives the hotel which bristles with symmetrical, and obviously alien, French pavilion roofs and turrets, a little of the dignity of a country house, but not much (55). There is far too much flower colour, yellow and blue bedding plants, nodding larkspur, peonies and roses, for it to look native; even the bulbous shrubs clash violently between bright golden privet and thunderous dark yew.[27] The statuary too is outrageously of the fun-to-be-shocked-by variety: naked cherubs, young men and a half-draped Venus (*colour plate 12*) pose on the cast iron fountain to give the guests some distraction from what they are eating. Very recently a modern Water Garden has been added below the set-piece floral terrace and, unlike so many water gardens, it

55 *The garden of Chateau Impney is a flowery alien in Droitwich, setting up the brazen airs of France as the Victorians liked to imagine them: semi-nude statues and lavish horticultural effects*

enjoys a generous bubbling flow down small cascades. Although modest in scale and impact, it seems too lively for the ordered colour just above it. The architect of this transposition from Normandy was Auguste Tronquois and it went up between 1869 and 1875. At that time it was very English to be French, but the Chateau's grounds can hardly be called Gardenesque. They are pure Napoleon III, and of Second Empire date. John Corbett, who made his money out of Droitwich salt, built the Chateau as a house, not a hotel, to please his wife who had been a French governess. There is nothing else like it in the county, but it seems appropriate to Droitwich which, like Malvern Wells, has a detached, other-worldly and un-Worcestershire feeling about it.

One distinguishing mark to the county, which only becomes apparent after viewing 80 or more of its gardens, is that it has a much richer profile of Gardenesque work than any of the other counties in this series. Could that be the industrial, technologically dense influence of Birmingham and the Black Country: new money pouring into Worcestershire from men who had made their wealth from machine management? That theory is not supported by Worcestershire's greatest Gardenesque park, which has to be that at Madresfield Court. Witley Court has Gardenesque fountains, Arley Castle has a Gardenesque arboretum, Abberley Hall has a Gardenesque rock and water garden, Abbey House, Evesham, has cultivated a Gardenesque historic scholarship, but Madresfield has the lot. Its indigestibly picturesque moated house (*colour plate 13*), constructed as if to offer King Ludwig of Bavaria a holiday home, and its cleverly wooded garden make up together a whole that should convert even the most hostile critic to Victorian garden ideals.

It is not easy to decide who was the horticultural hero behind Madresfield's nineteenth-century planning. Family histories modestly give most of the credit to the two head gardeners, William Cox and William Crump who presided, between them, at Madresfield for 76 years.[28] If they were the real shapers then Cox was the more influential as he was Head Gardener from about 1840 to 1883 when the principal avenues and most impressive features were laid out. But if the successive sixth and seventh Earl Beauchamps – Frederick and William – were, as seems likely from their active natures, responsible for the grounds, as they certainly were for the alterations to the house, then Frederick, the sixth Earl, rather than William, the more hubristic and poetic seventh Earl, was probably the garden genius. The seventh Earl of *Brideshead Revisited* and Evelyn Waugh associations was, together with his wife Lettice, an Arts and Crafts enthusiast, and his garden contributions were Edwardian, post-1892, when his father died. While there are minor Edwardian areas to Madresfield's grounds its bones are tougher and uninhibited by the Jacobethan constraints of the Edwardian ideal garden.

I have a personal debt to Madresfield. While Cornish gardens made me aware of the power of exotic flowering bushes, it was Madresfield which converted me to the parkscape of Victorian specimen trees: redwoods and the like.[29] What were once Californian intruders now seem an essential dramatic addition to parks of native trees like Abbey House, Evesham. Without their fierce outline and aggressive darkness a park seems bland and lifeless.

Madresfield delivers everything with little or no help from its site, a level plain with one small stream crossing it inconspicuously. The Malverns are virtually ignored; if anything the vistas are to the east. There are four insistent avenues of trees, three of them linked in a triangle with schloss Madresfield, the house itself, double moated, down at the bottom right-hand corner, not tucked away at the centre. The fourth avenue, the only one carrying a main drive, drops away down south from the main entrance to the house, but the usual way in follows a drive that winds its own undirected course from the North Lodge.

Everything to do with the sixth and seventh Earl is very superior, they were aristocrats of self-conscious taste and fashion, always demanding the best. In 1852, Pugin rebuilt their Norman parish church, but they pulled it down after a few years and had F. Preedy build them another one in 1866-7 on a site where their privacy would not be tainted by anything so common as worshippers, when they had, in any case, a jewel-like chapel within the house for family eucharists. Richard Norman Shaw was called in to design the North Lodge in 1872, Charles Annesley Voysey designed the South or Gatehouse Lodge in 1901. Both are minor masterworks, aesthetically greater than the parent house. Shaw's inventive Lodge of black-and-white timbering with warm red brick exudes sophistication while still declaring the lower class status of its keeper. Never visit Madresfield if snobbery is a problem; the place is the epitome of aristocracy and needs to be enjoyed as just that. Voysey's Gatehouse Lodge is fastidious and perverse, a complete domestic rethinking of the concept of a gatehouse. It leads to a Home Farm complex of pure Cheshire creative charm with a Dairy and Pigeon House. The seventh Earl's wife was a Grosvenor from Eaton Hall outside Chester, and she clearly had a fondness for John Douglas' estate buildings, half-vernacular timbering, half-brick Germanic, that make the approaches to Eaton Hall such a visual pleasure.[30]

Immediately upon entering the inner front garden by the North Lodge a visitor is overwhelmed by the billowing profile of specimen trees, more cedars, pines and redwoods than deciduous, all lending a dark funereal richness to the approach. One rare failure of the grounds lies a little of the left: the reedy thinness of young poplars planted when the elms of the Temple Avenue, one side of the triangle, fell to Dutch Elm disease. Poplars were not the right answer, the grounds at Madresfield demand weight. The entrance bridge to the Court looks south down that fourth avenue of Tulip Trees to the Gatehouse Lodge, passing a grove of specimen trees clustered about the ruin of Pugin's church and the graves of the sixth and the eighth and last Earl Beauchamp with their tall cross. Then comes that very Worcestershire second moat which half encloses the inner one.

The Cedar Avenue, planted between 1866 and 1868, draws the garden decisively away from the moat to the north and is the most grand and memorable feature of the grounds, un-English in its faint blue tints, each tree a mature sculptural form. Half way along its magisterial course there is on the left a half-circle of pleached limes, a briefly scented indulgence around a lawn. Across the way, an unusually acrobatic nude Mercury by C. Giddings stands poised for action on a woman's head. Slight notes of decadence run like a descant through these gardens and these Beauchamps. Was it predictable that the seventh Earl, on being appointed Governor of New South Wales at the age of 27, should have occupied himself by carving a naked golfing boy at the high point of his stroke, or that his sister's voyage accompanying him out to Australia should have inspired the wistful thirteenth of Edward Elgar's 'Enigma Variations'? This is Worcestershire's garden of aristocratic echoes.

At the north end of the Yew Avenue it meets the almost equally fine Oak Avenue which forms the third side of the avenue triangle, striking back to meet the feeble new Poplar or Temple Avenue at the Greek Doric Temple of 1870, put together from columns of a lost 1814 lodge. Just outside this angle of the two avenues is the Pulhamite Garden of 1878-9, the wildest, most imaginative and ambitious of its kind (*colour plate 14*). Half-concealed behind hedges, beset with ferns, hostas, hellebores and ice plants, it rears its entirely convincing artificial boulders into a Druid dance of shapes, as if the monoliths of Avebury were partying. It is in the Henry Moore category, delicious little winding ways and steps and small green pools make it a children's paradise and the stratification of the different 'sandstones' has been meticulously observed; no one would take them for fakes of rubble and artfully applied cement and pebbles unless they had been forewarned. This is just another of Madresfield's garden features, like its cedars and its hedges, that has to be described as the best of its kind.

On either side of the Oak Avenue (Turkey and Red Oaks) lies the Wild Garden of the 1880s which works best, as usual, in Spring with orchids, fritillaries, anemones and cowslips. In the midst of it a wooden bridge rather arbitrarily crosses a canal on the way to the Maze, a formidably bewildering feature with head-high yew hedges and a raised central platform essential for planning an escape. To the side of the Greek temple, where oaks and poplars meet, is a sinister Arthurian-looking island, densely wooded in its pond, its access bridges broken. At this point, with the triangulation of the inner wooded garden complete, it is necessary to remind the reader once again of the omnipresence at every stage, except the Yew Garden, of the superb specimen trees. Western Red Cedars, Sweet Gums, Ash leaved Maple and Dawn Redwoods in this Temple area, Incense Cedar, Wellingtonias, London Planes and Continental Redwoods rising everywhere.

With the Maze the chief features have been covered, but it would be a mistake not to go down that fourth avenue of new Tulip Trees to enjoy the Home Farm complex with its Dairy, its Shippon and its Loire French tower for the less favoured pigeons who have not secured a place to nest hanging over the moat on the east wall of Madresfield's chapel. Out to the east beyond this farm lies an enormous park, a mile wide and three quarters of a mile long. The Gloucester Drive, a mile of lime tees, runs across it, planted to replace the elm avenue. Its level featureless expanse is a reminder of how hard the Beauchamps have had to work to make the grounds about the Court so memorable. This was a park where man did everything and nature virtually nothing; but this was the essence of the Gardenesque. It was not a style of gardening that related to existing nature. In the nineteenth century a landowner had so many technical and historical resources that the temptation was, particularly among the very wealthy, simply to roll out trees, exotic bushes, statuary and buildings over the given topography. Was there, one wonders, a conscious rivalry between the two really old aristocratic families, the Beauchamps here at Madresfield and the Windsor-Clives at Hewell Grange? The Beauchamps had the inestimable advantage of a dramatic moated house, and skilfully played their gardens around it. Until 1884 the Windsor-Clive Earls of Plymouth, who with their Welsh industrial enterprises were far wealthier, in the multi-millionaire league by modern values, had only a lame classical house. To make comparisons even less favourable that vast lake which Brown had dammed up for them had made the house damp and even unstable.

What happened next was most unusual. The sixth Earl of Plymouth, who had consulted Repton, was more Gardenesque in his tastes than the man he had paid to advise him. He spent a small fortune on Coade stone urns and statuary and laid out a Dutch, an American and an ambitious French Garden. His was the royal tennis court with its Coade stone caryatids, the Medici and Borghese vases, the statues of the Four Seasons in the French Garden and the Dying Gaul, now sited at the entrance front.[31] These gardens in the several national styles were typical of Gardensque aspirations.

The *Gardeners' Chronicle* of 1843 described the Dutch Garden as a special preserve of the Countess with five brightly coloured walks radiating from a central circle. Box hedges and white pebbled paths separated the wedge-shaped flowerbeds creating a pattern of 'very great beauty'. The general effect thus obtained is enriched by a profusion of vases and Dutch porcelain boxes, holding small plants, disposed in lines along the main paved walks, and by a double row of umbrella Acacias, placed between the garden and the tennis court'.[32] Only a sad wreck of this actively artificial little garden survives now next to the once balustraded, now breeze-blocked, bridge over the drive. The American Garden was national by the trees planted in it; it lay north of the Maze. But it was the French Garden, laid out on the site of the old Kitchen Garden west of the house, which proved so magnetically attractive that the damp old house was abandoned completely and Bodley & Garner's overpowering pile was built expressly to command that new French Garden and enjoy its richness. Thus a Gardenesque garden called into being a house considered fit to stand above it.

The Hewell complexities do not end there. As it was first laid out the French Garden of the sixth Earl, planned in 1827 or earlier (the Four Seasons statues (56) at its core are dated Croggan, Lambeth 1825) were plausibly 'French', with four great lawns enriched, in the style popularised by Nesfield, with intricate parterres 'of all gay flowers, interspersed with crowds of Roses, pinnacles of Holyhocks, small groves of Dahlias, and

56 The 1825 Lambeth Coade stone statues of the Four Seasons in Hewell Grange's lavishly planted French Garden have been prudishly hidden in tents of trained branches and the elaborate parterres laid to plain lawn

ranks of standard Roses, placed as sentries all over'.[33] But then in 1833 the sixth Earl died and the estate passed through one of those accidental vacancies that sometimes occur when heirs fail to produce children. His uncles, the seventh and eighth Earls, both died, childless, in 1833 and 1837; and all that wealth and land passed to his sister, Harriet, who was made Baroness Windsor. She died in 1869 to be succeeded by her grandson, Robert Windsor-Clive who did not come of age until 1878. But he and his wife Lady Alberta, belonged to a new generation of aesthetes and garden fanciers, that exclusive social group known as 'The Souls', which tends to be seen as centred on Arthur Balfour and is popularly associated with exquisite life-styles and a permissive attitude to adulterous love affairs. The Souls needed gardens with high concealing hedges and many private nooks in which to pursue their flirtations and assignations. Consequently a Gardenesque 'French Garden' with low, trimmed parterres and no places of concealment needed to be rethought in the next age of garden styling, that usually described as 'Edwardian', though it was gathering pace in the 1890s or even earlier.

9

Alfred the Uncertain and the American invasion of Broadway

It is possibly harder for twenty-first-century readers to empathise with the spirit of late Victorian and Edwardian Britain than with any other period over the last 200 years. That is because of its imperial chauvinism. After a century of industrial wealth, with an empire expanding to cover almost a quarter of the globe and with a navy unchallenged on the oceans, patriotism had become virtually the national religion.[1] The Boer War would be a stumbling, but the relief of Mafeking and the subsequent wild rejoicing would be a reassurance, after which it would take the horrific casualty lists of the Flanders trenches in the 1914–1918 War to bring sobriety and some general disenchantment. Even now the writings of Kipling and, to a lesser extent, of Sir Arthur Quiller-Couch, create an unease, an incomprehension in the minds of readers brought up on Dr Johnson's quotable: 'Patriotism is the last refuge of a scoundrel'. Yet to understand the art and the mind-set of Alfred Parsons, this intense and unquestioning love of country has to be taken on board, not uncritically, but rather as an historical phenomenon, like Puritanism in the reign of Charles I or the Cult of the Virgin in the fourteenth century.[2]

Even in his appearance Parsons was patriotic, sporting loyally on his plump face the brisk naval moustache and pointed beard of the future King George V.[3] He was an Edwardian aesthete, but one more addicted to lemonade than to absinthe. Yet for all the overwhelmingly wholesome nature of his paintings, the photographic accuracy of his exquisitely embarrassing flower studies, that beard and his little steam launch on the Avon, there is just the slightest whiff of decadence about him: a 'confirmed' bachelor and a good friend of the unquestionably homosexual Henry James. It was that side of his nature and the friends it brought him which resulted in Parsons, far more of an artist than a garden designer, becoming the first man in Worcestershire since William Shenstone who can be said to have had a national, as opposed to merely a county, influence upon garden styling.

In one sense he was born into, if not decadence, then into defiant aestheticism. His father, a doctor of Frome in Somerset, was not only devoted to flowers, but a good friend of a wild Irishman, William Robinson, the controversial journalist and garden polemicist. Not surprisingly Parsons and Robinson would work together to their mutual advantage in the 1880s and 1890s, though it would be a union of convenience rather than a marriage of minds, a favour to a father's friend, not a labour of conviction.

Dr Parsons had intended his son Alfred for the civil service but, after a brief spell in the Post Office, Alfred escaped in 1867 to study at the South Kensington School of Art. By 1868 he was exhibiting his luscious gardenscapes in an exhibition of the Society of British Artists and, being such a reassuringly establishment and true Victorian artist, he exhibited at the Royal Academy in 1874 and would continue to do so in every year until he died in 1920.

All that may sound staid and plodding, but Parsons' watercolours have to be seen to be believed. They are utterly seductive, birthday-card art, so entirely pretty and photographically accurate that, in the climate of modern art criticism, one feels mildly sinful for even looking at them. If they are studies of cottage gardens then those were very superior middle class cottages. Parsons took over where Repton left off in his illustrations anticipating the Gardenesque style of J.C. Loudon, but done as early as 1803 for *Observations on the Theory and Practice of Landscape Gardening*. Both Parsons and Repton loved trellis-work alive with roses, backed by towering hollyhocks and beset with bird baths and sundials. Neither could resist a few white doves; but Parsons' paintings are much lighter and more technically skilled, there is a shimmering transparency to his paint and a general avoidance of dark colours. William Robinson may have found them irresistible justifications of his own garden theories.[4]

In 1879 Parsons encountered a soulmate and his career immediately took off. On 27 January at a party in the home of another artist he was introduced to Edwin Austin Abbey, one of those anglophile Americans who, like Henry James, relish the history, the architecture, the patterned countryside and the fixed class system of England so much that they determine to break into that system and become more English than the English; all the while preserving a little corner of their New England superiority. 'What a lucky fellow I am', Abbey wrote in his diary, 'to drop right into the society I most enjoy and from which I can learn so much'.[5] He was a good looking young man, beardless, but with a long, soft moustache, rimless spectacles and hair parted in the middle. In no time at all the two artists were working in a shared studio and had moved into a house together, a pleasant Regency villa, No.54 Bedford Gardens, Kensington.

Artists are very dependant upon social connections for their commissions, so No.54 was the making of Parsons. Another American artist, Francis D. Millet, joined them and they entertained a cheerful and cleverly chosen circle of friends like George du Maurier, Lawrence Alma-Tadema and the American actress, Mary Anderson, the woman who would later give Parsons one of his best garden designing commissions at her converted farmhouse in Broadway. Abbey and Millet were leading illustrators for the American magazine *Harper's*, which resulted in Parsons being given several commissions in that prestigious publication.

Did they have a gay relationship? It is unlikely. Millet joined them at No.54 with his whole family and Parsons struck up a combative flirtatious relationship with Millet's wife,

Lily. Marion Mako suggests that Parsons might have written a poem about her in which he imagined Lily as an angler with hook and line and himself as the fish. It ends:

It's little trouble she would have
In bringing me to book
Right gladly would I spring to bank,
Unheading her faint cries,
Content to see in my last gasp
The triumph of her eyes[6]

which hardly sounds gay. Cheerfully homosocial might be a better description of the relationships, and in 1891 'Ned' Abbey married Gertrude Mead.

It was Parsons who introduced the Americans to Broadway and Worcestershire; not the other way round. They adopted him because his representations of English gardens were the images they required. Henry James, who employed Parsons to design his garden down at Rye in Sussex, found Parsons a kindred spirit, and wrote an article on his paintings for *Harper's Magazine*.[7] He speculated on whether, during his visits to the USA with Abbey, Parsons had cleverly analysed what the Americans wanted England to look like and chose his compositions with that in mind. 'The England of his pencil', James wrote, 'is exactly the England that the American imagination, restricted to itself, constructs from the poets, the novelists, from all that delightful testimony it inherits'.[8] Before dismissing those paintings as 'chocolate box', what else do gardeners aim at? One mark of Parsons' confidence in the cottage or 'chocolate box' image was his comparative indifference to Japanese garden aesthetics even though they were fashionable at the turn of the century and he had spent a year in Japan, writing a book on his observations.[9]

Abbey and Millet were under the direction of Laurence Hutton, *Harper's*' literary editor who wanted to place his two favourite illustrators close to Stratford and the Shakespeare industry. William Morris was another draw and Hutton took Parsons along with him in the summer of 1885 to interview Morris and Edward Burne-Jones who were camping out for the fine weather in the airy rooms of the Broadway Tower up on Fish Hill. It had been designed by James Wyatt for the sixth Earl of Coventry in 1794 for just such civilised holiday use.[10] Parsons' impressions of Morris were not recorded, but in the great Blomfield-Robinson debate Morris occupied very much the same compromise position as Parsons.[11] He loved old-fashioned flowers, fruit trees and vegetables, but still wanted a garden to be quite distinct from natural fields and woodlands. In addition he loved vernacular English buildings and would have approved Parsons' half-rotunda pavilions. It was during his stay at the Tower in 1876 that Morris drafted his letter to *The Athenaeum* which led to the formation of the Society for the Protection of Ancient Buildings (SPAB), the anti-scrape society devoted to preserving the texture of old buildings.

Hutton and Parsons returned from their visit with a rapturous report on the mellow textured beauties of Broadway village and, at Hutton's urging, Abbey and Millet hurried out to see the village for themselves. It had the bonus of a main line railway station and easy Stratford connections, making it a dream site for weekending. The charms of that amazingly varied main street and the promise of half-hidden gardens seduced them and they promptly rented Farnham House, a late seventeenth-century yeoman vernacular building with two enormous dormer windows.

Soon Parsons was weekending with them at Farnham. Because he was often away from London at this time he had begun lending his London studio out to John Singer Sargent, and after Sargent had suffered an accident Millet brought him out to Broadway to recuperate. In the garden of Farnham House among Lily Millet's prized carnations, Sargent painted one of his best works: 'Carnation, Lily, Lily, Rose' where the two little Millet girls are holding paper lanterns among the lilies and carnations of the twilight garden.[12] If Parsons could have felt visually for half-lights and small children as strongly as he responded to China Roses in full sunshine he would have become a more celebrated artist, but we all live within our limitations. Sargent is unlikely to have had Parsons' linear talent or his accurate eye for flowers and foliage.

Aesthetic worth is hard to evaluate. Sargent's 'Carnation, Lily, Lily, Rose' remains one static canvas on the walls of the Tate Gallery, but the reverberations of the argument between Parsons' visual interpretations of Robinson's *The Wild Garden* and Francis Inigo Thomas' visual interpretations of Reginald Blomfield's *The Formal Garden in England* are still being felt. Armies of daffodils are planted along half of the village roadsides in Britain. Even the railway embankments on each side of Crewe station are golden with them. It is commonplace to plant an orchard with bulbs by initially throwing them out in casual handfuls: unwitting tributes to Robinson's theories and Parsons' illustrations. Similarly the metallic abstracts and stony severities of modernist gardeners like Geoffrey Jellicoe are tributes to Blomfield and Thomas. There are divergent possibilities within all garden design, equally valid, order or nature, both artfully controlled. The debate was important, it was a significant mark of national maturity, and Parsons played a key role in it.

The general outlines of that debate are well known, but not everyone is aware of Parsons' part in it: the long drawn-out timescale of its unfolding or the way Alfred Parsons helped William Robinson to understand exactly what Robinson himself was proposing. Simplifying the struggle to its essentials, both sides were right, no one was wrong. Both Robinson and Blomfield were expressing valid and valuable aesthetic concepts of how a garden could be designed and function. The difference between them was that, though Robinson, publishing in 1870, had a 22-year lead on Blomfield, publishing in 1892, Robinson was a confused, poetic blunderer; and while Blomfield had a clear vision of precisely what he wanted to do, Robinson was initially unsure of what he was suggesting and was, therefore, often wildly impractical and environmentally destructive. He was in desperate need of an artist, someone informed on both wild and garden flowers, to demonstrate the real potentials of 'natural' planting which was, of course, not natural at all; as tiger lilies towering in Parson's illustration of the grounds of Great Tew, Oxfordshire, dramatically conveyed.[13]

On the other hand many, indeed most, of Parsons' illustrations for the de luxe 1894 edition would seduce and educate readers into imitation of their enchanting practicalities. For the frontispiece he drew wild kingcups and primroses grouped with cultivated daffodils on the banks of a stream. How many thousand sowings of daffodil bulbs have resulted? With his graceful black-and-white compositions he made sense of Robinson's vague claim that his

object in the *Wild Garden* is now to show how we may have more of the varied beauty of hardy flowers than the most ardent admirer of the old style of garden ever dreams of, by naturalizing many beautiful plants of many regions of the earth in our fields, woods and copses, outer parts of pleasure grounds, and in neglected places in almost every kind of garden.[14]

That was the shock therapy which the Victorian Gardenesque needed: an end to prim, regimented beds and a clarion call for imaginative planting. Not hundreds, but many thousands of gardeners must have responded, setting roses, honeysuckles, wisteria and clematis 'scrambling' over old stumps and ugly outhouses. A freedom that we now take for granted was persuasively demonstrated for Robinson by Parsons' illustrations. Robinson was strongly opposed to the Gardenesque, not only to neat red, white and blue bedding out, which left the beds bare for half the year, but to rockeries like Madresfield's mini Avebury:

'rock-works', as generally made, are ugly, unnatural, and quite unfit for a plant to grow upon....'rocks' are piled up with no sufficient quantity of soil or any preparation made for the plants, so that all delicate rock-plants die upon them and the 'rocks' are taken possession of by rank weeds.[15]

Most disturbingly of all for the Victorian gardeners of Worcestershire, a county unusually devoted to specimen trees from California, one thinks not only of Madresfield, but of Ombersley, Kyre, Overbury and Hewell, Robinson despised them. He wrote angrily and imperceptively: 'money is thrown away like chaff for worthless exotic trees like the Wellingtonia, on which tree alone fortunes have been wasted'.[16]

It is easy to understand how the book roused such strong feelings and opposition. If the Beauchamp earls associated Parsons with Robinson it would explain why the seventh Earl turned eventually in 1902 to Thomas Mawson rather than to Parsons for his angular Yew Garden at Madresfield. Robinson's love was for native trees, the 'prim shape' of Irish Yew was 'too often seen'; he opted instead for holly 'which in no country attains the beauty it does in our own'.[17] Parsons did his illustrative best to support this view with full-page drawings, finely observed, of White Willow (57), a Robinson favourite, the Black Poplar and Crack Willow.[18]

Viewed in the light of later experience Robinson made some bad errors. He set Parsons to drawing a flattering illustration of the appalling Japanese Knotweed, which neither

57 This Alfred Parsons illustration for William Robinson's The Wild Garden *was drawn to support Robinson's belief that our native trees deserved to be admired and planted more than foreign exotics*

poisons nor pile drivers can control today. Robinson observed smugly: 'P. cuspidatum is most effective in flower in autumn. They are fine plants for deep soils and certainly can take care of themselves';[19] they can indeed come up through concrete, so Parsons must take some share of the blame for the invasion. Robinson was on his most uncertain territory when making a case, not for the wild planting of sturdy garden flowers, but when he urged gardeners to go out into the country to uproot wild flowers, some of them like Lady Slipper Orchids extremely rare, and replant them alongside garden species. To support his scheme Parsons drew the rare Cheddar Pink, Solomon's Seal and Herb Paris with 'Star of Bethlehem in Grass'.[20] But Robinson was prepared to give a garden home to some very rough weeds like the common willow herb, 'in a wood or out-of-the-way spot, where it cannot overrun rarer plants, it is very pretty';[21] and he set poor Parsons to drawing Giant Cow Parsnip 'for rough places only' and even 'Giant Horse-Tail', 'the numbers of slender branches depending from each whorl look most graceful'.[22] He can, however, be forgiven for his anticipation of the late twentieth-century's delight in wild meadow gardens:

> *Not* to mow is almost a necessity in the wild garden…quite as good an effect is afforded by unmown as the mown Grass – indeed, better when the long Grass is full of flowers. Three-fourths of the most lovely flowers of cold and temperate regions are companions of the Grass.[23]

Obediently Parsons drew delicate 'Crane's Bill. wild, in grass'.[24] The artist left no record of his relations with his extraordinary employer; Robinson was, incidentally, another bachelor, though he was briefly engaged to be married. In addition he was a vegetarian, graciously declined a knighthood, launched 8 horticultural journals, put his *English Flower Garden* through 15 editions, died, by some accounts, of syphilis in ripe old age and was buried in the grounds of the Golders Green crematorium which he had himself laid out.

It is easy to underestimate the influence of Robinson's ideas and Parsons' demonstration of them in *The Wild Garden*. This is because the 'hard' Edwardian gardens that Blomfield advocated tend to survive well and can be visited today in almost every county, with their yew hedges overgrown but intact, their terraces commanding and their Jacobethan garden houses as charming as when they were built. Blomfield appears to have won the debate. Yet for every modern gardener who shapes a terrace or plants a yew hedge for the next generation there are a thousand gardeners, working on grounds great, medium and small, who plant exotic flowers casually and scatter bulbs at random over orchards or grass in the manner Robinson urged and Parsons illustrated. If anyone won it was Parsons; he did, however, if three of his Broadway gardens are analysed, tend to hedge his bets and compromise between the disciplined garden and the relaxed. His artistic response to flowers in crashing conflicts of colour pulled him one way, his membership of the Art Workers' Guild tugged him the other.

The Guild was far more interested in stone and metal, in the revival of old English crafts and building techniques than in flowers. Blomfield's *Formal Garden* is often seen as the book behind hard landscaping, but John Dando Sedding's *Garden-Craft Old and New* came out in the preceding year, 1891; and Sedding had put his imaginative ideas on hard landscaping over to Guild members in a lecture of 1889 entitled 'The Architectural Treatment of Gardens'. The profuse illustrations in Sedding's book offered very hard garden designs with topiary work at Levens Hall, grand flights of steps with fountains at the Villa d'Este and practical plans for modern gardens with tennis lawns, parterres, sundials and lawns.[25] 'A garden should be well fenced', Sedding wrote, 'and there should always be facility for getting real seclusion'. He wanted 'cedar-walks' with 'the wisardry of green gloom', the bower, the maze, the alley and the wilderness: the historicist garden in fact, 'an old English pleasaunce, hidden happily and shielded safe', so he was perfectly in tune with the national mood of sentimental patriotism.[26] Sedding had already laid out an ambitious axial formal garden at The Downes in Hayle, Cornwall as early as 1867-8.[27] With all these influences working on him what else could Parsons do when he came to design gardens for his friends in Broadway but wobble between flowers and formality?

When his three Broadway gardens are considered, Russell House, post-1886, Court Farm, post-1896, and his own Luggers Hill after 1903, Parsons seems to have had a vocabulary of garden features which he applied when patrons and space allowed. There was a standard rose garden, circular for preference, a pergola, generally in wood, not stone, a nut walk, a battlemented yew hedge and other oddly shaped topiary, stone terraces to dramatise even slight falls in land, pleached limes, vernacular garden buildings of modest size, yew houses, tennis and croquet lawns, a rectangular pool, mulberry, walnut and robinia trees and a general openness to any landscape outside the garden. This last feature, together with a fondness for utility – espaliered fruit trees and vegetable plots – modified the formal elements.

Russell House is on the main street at the entrance to the village from the west with its prying Gothick Gazebo commanding a slight bend in the road. Parsons was not really in control there. Lily Millet loved flowers as much as Parsons and bred carnations successfully so the brick wall and the Flowery Way that linked Russell House to The Grange and the artists' studios was lined with an herbaceous border of Jekyll dimensions.[28] The border is visible in the 1911 *Country Life* article on the house and Parsons had his way, lining the buttressed wall with espaliers for utility. Whether or not he added the double slate covering to the wall is uncertain, but it lends an air of Elizabethan authenticity. Even though Russell House already had two characterful garden buildings, a Gothick Belvedere (*58*) and the gabled Gazebo, Parsons, no great architect, was allowed to add a semicircular vernacular Loggia with sub-classical columns and pyramidal roof. This, unfortunately, has been lost by subdivision and redevelopment and stands in the grounds of a former telephone exchange (*59*), but the espaliers are a reminder of William Morris' earnest dictum that 'nothing can be a work of art that is not useful'.

As usual the hard landscaping, the Loggia and a low terrace wall, have survived, but the difficulty in assessing Parsons' aim is that most of the floral effects probably disappeared

58 The Gothick Belvedere tower stood in the grounds of Russell House, Broadway before Alfred Parsons was asked to model the gardens on his own flower paintings

*59 The simple Arts and Crafts
vernacular Loggia, which Parsons added
as a focus to vistas at Russell House,
has been cut off by a lane from its
original setting*

over one autumn week of digging, weeding and clearing.[29] Nothing emphasises this
transience better than two of Parsons' paintings, works of 1890 and 1911: 'China Roses,
Broadway' and 'Orange Lilies, Broadway' *(colour plate 15)*.[30] They record two corners of
the garden at Russell House in its prime. Today the garden is soberly pleasant with the
pale green of lawns, wisteria and the darker green of trees. When Parsons captured them
they were radiant with pink roses, harsh orange lilies, geranium and campanula. Doves
littered the sky and the lawns. Two white cypress trees that have grown together in an
arch, were originally small and separate; the circular rose garden covering an ice house is
not of Parsons' designing but they would be a feature of his later commissions. Trees make
no great showing but a geriatric walnut survives in the small area of woodland to the rear.
What remains at Russell House is a tastefully subdued ghost of Parsons' original vision.

Another inevitable loss is that of the atmosphere of a Virginia Woolf house party, an
Edwardian gaiety of events. An 1886 letter from Austin Dobson describes Russell House
just after the Millets had moved in:

We have really had a gay summer, pretending to work and sometimes working (for
there are numberless places with easels in them to hide away in – if you really do want
to work) until four, and then tennis until dinner time, and after dinner dancing and
music and various cheering games in the studio – but mostly dancing.[31]

The Arts and Crafts period was very much one of open-air living: external balcony bedrooms, croquet and tennis, unheated swimming pools, tea in the garden pavilion. These were happy gardens, alive with games, gossip and horseplay. The serious sketching and illustrating was punctuated by picnics and adventures upon the Avon in Parsons' little steam launch. Nothing is so revealing of the real, pipe smoking Parsons as the book Sir Arthur Quiller-Couch wrote in 1892, *The Warwickshire Avon*, recording the voyage which he made in a Canadian canoe down the river with Parsons. It was P and Q together. Benighted in Brandon, a remote village, after missing the last train back to Coventry, Q wrote that: 'P, who under a rugged exterior hides much aptitude for human affairs, announces that he has a way with landladies, and tries it', in the event unsuccessfully.[32] It was all very *Two Men in a Boat* in feeling. Q wrote: 'As our tobacco smoke floats out on the moonlight we can dwell, we find, with a quite kingly serenity on the transience of man's generations; nay, as we sit down to dinner at our inn we touch the high contemplative, yet careless mood of the gods themselves'.[33] How cosily pompous the Edwardian gentry were! But this is the essence of that conservative mood behind the Arts and Crafts movement: a retreat back into an Olde England of roaring fires, mine host of the inn and the quaffing of ale. It accounts for the early Tudor details, the avoidance of classical direction, the double stone slate capping, the big topiary peacocks at Court Farm and the box-edged borders at Luggers Hill. One 1886 Parsons' painting, 'Russell House, Broadway', shows the courtyard with its dovecote wall steepled with hollyhocks,[34] but the bones of these gardens were hard and Blomfieldian or Seddingesque.

There is one strangely solemn moment in Q's book, one fortunately that can still be recaptured. The canoeists had paddled to Cleeve Prior where Q suddenly became positively reverent. When he saw the Manor House's front garden that patriotic religion set in:

> the garden walls coated with lichen and topped with yellow quinces or a flaming branch of barbary…the clipped yew trees that abounded in all fantastic shapes…but best of all was the manor farm itself and the arched yew hedge leading to its Jacobean porch, a marvel to behold. We hung long about the entrance and stared at it.[35]

Parsons did one of his many careful illustrations of the yew hedge, capturing its arched structure symbolizing the 12 Apostles and the 4 Evangelists. Very little has changed today (*60*) even though the 'manor farm' has been dignified to a 'Court' and adapted tactfully into a condominium. It is intriguing to find that, for Q's generation, there was something awesome about a yew hedge, a living link with a revered past, age, gloom and control. It gave that privacy that Sedding seemed to require, the house extended out into the open air. It is possible to walk up to the Court's Jacobean porch without getting even a glimpse of the two gardens, one on each side of the stone-flagged path.

Parsons, perhaps because he had nothing to hide, no flirtations or adulteries, only pipe smoking, seems not to have stressed privacy when he designed the gardens behind

60 *This is the yew hedge of the Twelve Apostles and the Four Evangelists that so awed Parsons and Q when they paused from their canoe trip to visit Cleeve Prior Manor*

Court Farm at Broadway for his American actress friend, Mary Anderson, now Mary Anderson de Navarro, married to a Basque husband. The house is at the other, east end of the village as the street rises to Fish Hill.[36] The complex was originally two vernacular houses, Court Farm and Bell Farm, which were linked after 1901 by a music room designed by Andrew Prentice, who was later to build Luggers Hill for Parsons. Much more of Parsons' planning survives here than at Russell House, and Mary Anderson's book, *A Few More Memories*, adds valuable detail of authentic Parsons planting, her writing brimming with the same cloying sweetness as Parsons' watercolours. Beyond the formal, stone-flagged courtyard with its box parterre and two guardian topiary peacocks (*colour plate 17*), was the regulation Rose Garden, planted in 1897, with its sundial and then 'a coppice with flowering cherries, aspens and Lombardy poplars – my favourite trees – hollies, lilacs of all colours from the large double whites to dark vinous purple; the ground carpeted with anemones: a cool, perfumed place'.[37]

Alma-Tadema mentioned Parsons' planting there of wide drifts of larkspur 'as though a patch of the blue sky had come to rest in the garden', so Parsons was decidedly Robinsonian in his escape from trim bedding plants, preferring flowering bushes and generous clumping.[38] In a sense he appears to have worked like a William Kent with flowering bushes, easing the garden out into a wider landscape to frame a view of the

Broadway Tower high up on Fish Hill and not, therefore, entirely of a mind with Morris or Sedding, who both wanted their gardens to be distinct enclosures, demarcated from fields and woodlands.

Scattered behind Court Farm are a slender wooded rose Pergola (Lutyens would have made one of solid stone columns and heavy beams) with an Arbour Seat at one end, a square Swimming Pool, a pleached Lime Avenue, a Nut Walk (replanted), a bay tree taken from a cutting on Morris's grave at Kelmscott, and a Croquet Lawn and a bastioned, raised terrace above a Tennis Lawn. There is a daffodil slope, but no sky blue drift of larkspurs any longer. That chocolate box lushness of Parsons' painting has toned down into English greens upon greens with some bursts of colour in the newly replanted borders. Finally there is a linear garden extension to the east range of the former Bell Farm where a secret yew-hedged enclosure is accessed from Mary Anderson's own private sitting room. This rises in shallow grass terraces with stone steps and low walls punctuated by small yew pyramids of recent planting. This must be of Mary's devising for it has none of Parsons' openness to nature, but everything of Sedding's sense of privacy, 'hidden happily and shielded safe'.

At Court Farm Parsons was pleasing Mary Anderson, at Russell House he was controlled by Lily Millet, at Luggers Hill he could please himself in both the house, which Prentice designed for him, and in the gardens lapped around it. Luggers Hill, together with Great Chalfield in Wiltshire and Wightwick Manor outside Wolverhampton, have the gardens on which to judge him.

Luggers Hill is at the west end of the village, opposite Russell House, but set back from the main street behind a high hedge and an orchard. There is a gate in the fence across the road from Russell House through which Parsons would pass on his way to dinner and card games with the Millets. The house was designed by Andrew Prentice on an irregular H-shaped plan in a subdued Cotswold Arts and Crafts style and built between 1903 and 1911. Entrance from Springfield Lane is between high stone walls with Prentice's courtyard front in view. Parsons' studio was in the left-hand wing with a tall tripartite window giving his room an artistic north light. It is an interesting comment on modern sensibilities that, when a turn is made out of the courtyard through the trees into what should be one of the two homely vegetable gardens, the area has been transformed into a cutting garden with an Italian fountain. Then, built onto the entrance wall, comes another semicircular Loggia (*61*), barely classical like its neighbour across the road at Russell House, tucked away in a corner and aligned on the east terrace of the house. To its side and parallel with the modern cutting garden is one of Parsons' standard features, a Rose Garden, which has been created by the present owner, Kay Haslem.[39] This is enclosed near the Loggia by a billowing cloud-like yew hedge, contrived by Diana Baskerville Clegg very much in the manner of Parsons' hedges at Court Farm. From here the Broadway Tower can just be glimpsed through trees that have grown too high. One of Parsons' post-1912 watercolours, 'The Artist's Garden at Luggers Hill, Broadway' records the view as originally open to the fields below the Tower with a serpentine gravel path threading through the yew

61 *Never a professional architect, Alfred Parsons copied his Russell House Loggia for the garden of his own house, Luggers Hill, where it works better aligned with the east terrace*

hedges flanked by drifts of pink, white and purple tulips.[40] Beyond the yew hedge was a summerhouse, since demolished, framed in the painting by two large cherry trees in full pink bloom.

Next, in an unexpected burst of open space, comes the Great Lawn, unfocused so that all eyes turn naturally to the carefully relaxed elevations of Prentice's garden front. A long line of castellated yew (*62*) closes in the far side of the Lawn to the south and there is an exedral-shaped Pergola on concrete posts on the edge of the Lawn to the east. Completely hidden away behind the Yew Hedge is the Orchard, which is cut off from a modern secret garden with a lily pool by another solid yew hedge. Close to the service area of the main house on this south face is a new Herb Garden and this gives onto another Rose Garden at the south-east corner of the house where the stone paving and general design may well have been devised by Parsons.

It may not be a great garden; it has no dramatic advantages of site, no steep slopes to excuse a terrace, but it is eventful, it offers at least three surprise vistas, and it is comfortably human in scale. Only the Lawn is mildly pretentious and perhaps a shade too large. Thinking over Parsons' life after a visit, it is remarkable that a man who had travelled widely in Europe, visiting France, Italy and Greece, also America, and who most notably spent a year in Japan in 1892, should have allowed so little reference to foreign garden styling in his own grounds. He was clearly most contentedly English,

62 *The long castellated yew hedge lining the east lawn of Luggers Hill suggests that Parsons had been absorbing motifs from other Worcestershire gardens like Rous Lench*

and absolutely, therefore, a man of his times. Anyone who is charmed by his work should visit the Wiltshire garden he planned between 1908 and 1912 at Great Chalfield for Robert Fuller.[41] He was working in partnership with Captain Partridge and a financial backer, Charles Tudway. It may be a little disloyal to admit the truth, but the garden he devised on the long slope below the little church and Manor House is his masterpiece, a place of rare enchantment, better than any of his Worcestershire gardens unless, as seems very possible, he had a hand in Rous Lench, of which more in the next chapter.

10

Edwardian gardens and the influence of The Souls

As the previous chapter made clear, Worcestershire had its own highly individual and enthusiastic response to the mid-nineteenth-century Gardenesque, one far stronger than parallel ventures in neighbouring Gloucestershire. So it will come as no surprise to find that the county's gardens designed in that subsequent style, loosely described as 'Edwardian', come across as hesitant and generally uncharacteristic. It seems that the county's nouveau riche landowners, often wealthy Black Country industrialists, were understandably reluctant to adopt the self-conscious, poseur airs of an established aristocracy. They must have felt, therefore, little or no drive to surround their houses with faux Elizabethan-Jacobean gardens of manicured lawns and clipped yew hedge garden rooms, or to build authentic-looking stone pavilions of late sixteenth-century styling in which to conduct romantic trysts and refined adulterous liaisons.

It would be foolishly sensational to suppose that all the English aristocracy of that 1890-1914 period were confirmed adulterers dedicated to the planting of gardens where thick yew hedges offered sexual privacy. But there was an influential group of that disposition, gathered vaguely around Arthur Balfour, Margot Asquith, Lord Curzon and the Duchess of Rutland. They were high profile society and political figures of wide influence outside their immediate charmed circle of wit, art and elitist weekend parties. Their style and their intricate relationships have been admirably described in Jane Abdy and Charlotte Gere's book *The Souls*, published in 1984; and the houses which they frequented for their meetings did tend to favour that style of architectural and nationalistic gardening proposed in Sir Reginald Blomfield's trenchant polemic, *The Formal Garden in England* of 1892. At that time Britain was riding a tremendous tide of wealth and influence, the House of Lords was still an institution of real power, and it was beginning to seem natural to turn away from Italian, Dutch or French models of garden layouts and to follow instead English designs of a time when England, with the defeat of the Spanish Armada and the first successful settlements in Virginia, was on its way to becoming a first ranking European power. Souls' gardens, whether designed for adultery or simply for historic references were, therefore, the patriotic fashion.

Of Worcestershire's three leading aristocratic families: the Coventrys of Croome, the Lygons of Madresfield and the Windsor-Clives of Hewell Grange, the Coventrys had a long commitment to open, eighteenth-century parkscapes, so Croome was out of the Souls' garden stakes. That left Madresfield and Hewell to give the county a lead in Elizabethan and Jacobean revivalry, and here curiously were two families – the Lygons and the Windsor-Clives – ideally suited to Souls status. Yet while Abdy and Gere devote a whole revealing chapter to 'The Windsors' and the delicate melancholy of Alberta 'Gay' Paget, who married Lord Windsor in 1883, becoming Countess of Plymouth when the earldom was revived in 1905, there is not a mention of the Lygons in their otherwise cheerfully scurrilous accounts of bedding and flirting. Yet the seventh Earl Beauchamp and his wife Lettice, a sister of the Duke of Westminster, were perfect candidates for Soul status. He was politically powerful, the Leader of the Liberals in the Lords and devoted to the Arts and Crafts movement. Her wedding present to him was the decoration of Madresfield's chapel in a style of delicate, flower-like brilliance. Madresfield itself was a vision from one of Grimm's happier fairy stories.

So why did Abdy and Gere ignore them and their Souls-friendly additions to Madresfield's gardens? The answer must be the usual English one: we can cope with, even revel in, normal sexual improprieties, but when gay sex rears its head an embarrassed silence results. William, the seventh Earl Beauchamp, known as 'Boom' to his children, for obvious reasons, was bisexual. He fathered a delightful family of three sons and four daughters, but all to no avail when rumours of substance emerged of liaisons with men.[1] Even today accounts of his role in the family history are guarded, though everyone knows that his venomous Westminster brother-in-law harried him into exile. Instead of relating the facts, accounts of Madresfield's furnishings dwell on the statue which he carved of a young Australian golfer, caught naked in full swing: 'a difficult pose', as Clive Aslet blandly remarks,[2] and an unusual one for a Governor of New South Wales, as the seventh Earl was from 1899 to 1902, to set himself.

Madresfield's guidebook and Aslet's three scholarly *Country Life* articles on the house and its grounds are all irritatingly vague on the designers and the precise dates of the post-Gardenesque work in that strategic area east of the house, between the inner and outer moats, but overlooked by the family's intimate courtyard rose garden.[3] All that is known is that Thomas Mawson was approached by the Beauchamps in 1903, and it is stated without reference that the grounds in that area had, by 1909, been reconstructed.[4] Mawson's yew hedges (*63*), if they are of his planting, are clipped low to a simple geometric pattern and set around a small lily basin with a classical fountain. The parterres which once set off the yew enclosures were labour intensive and have been grassed over, but the two bold yew arches lend authority to an otherwise open site. However, the real interest lies in the immediately adjoining Lawn of the Twelve Caesars (*64*). This was laid out on the old Bowling Green. All the written accounts imply, without actually committing themselves, that this was also Mawson's work, but he was by training a town planner and not much

63 *Most of the grand and various gardens at Madresfield are Gardenesque in adventurous styling, but with these low geometric hedges, probably by Thomas Mawson of 1903, the restrained historicism of the Edwardians is setting in*

64 *Untypical of Mawson's garden designs, but suggestive of the seventh Earl Beauchamp's refined and sophisticated taste, this Lawn of the Twelve Caesars is sited impressively across the inner moat from the family's private garden at Madresfield*

given to such richly allusive historic gestures. The white marble busts of the Caesars are inset within the bold sweep of a yew hedge that is topped with domed extensions and they recall those equally romantic terms of the 12 months that look out from the contemporary gardens of Barrow Court, just south of Bristol, where the layout was by Francis Inigo Thomas.[5] The town planner Mawson seems an unlikely garden designer to have been selected by the fastidious seventh Earl. Nevertheless the Caesar's Lawn is one of Madresfield's, and the county's, best Edwardian gardens: sheltered, simple and serene; the busts are of the highest quality, and the fact that Vitellius looks outstandingly depraved while young Caligula is attractive does hint at the seventh Earl's personal preferences. The family archives would no doubt supply a date for their commissioning.

The Edwardian additions around Hewell Grange are much more ambitious. The Lygons could trace their ancestry back to 1260, but the Windsor-Clives, or at least the Windsor half of them, could trace their line back to a pre-Conquest Viking chieftain, surnamed after the Conquest, Fitzother. This explains the prevalence of Other and Ivo as favoured Christian names for eighteenth- and nineteenth-century earls of Plymouth. The Windsor name came from one of the family being appointed Constable of Windsor Castle in the reign of King Stephen. They were originally a Middlesex family, but Henry VIII arbitrarily replanted them in Worcestershire because he wanted their Middlesex property. Such a record must have made even the Lygons seem newcomers, and the Windsor-Clives were much richer than the Lygons. Their males had a habit of marrying rich heiresses, but then dying young, leaving their heirs as minors for long periods of financial consolidation. They had large land holdings in Glamorgan and Shropshire as well as their Worcestershire acres.

It may seem surprising that Robert Windsor-Clive and his lovely, melancholy wife Gay never produced quite the ideal Souls garden because they were, Gay in particular, the ideal Souls couple. But he was a scholarly enthusiast for the Italian Renaissance and that interest never allowed him to focus precisely upon the English Elizabethan. His ideal garden centrepiece was a replica of an Italian fountain, the remains of one still lie at the heart of the 'French' Garden, while a superb but inappropriate Italian Hall lies similarly at the heart of the monstrous Jacobethan house.

Gay had been the daughter of a diplomat, Sir Augustus Paget, and her mother, Walburga, was a friend of the Princess Royal, Vicky, who became briefly, by her marriage, Empress of Germany. Added to such connections Lady Gay Windsor was blessed with a sad, lovely face, she rarely smiled, and a crown of rich copper-gold hair. That made her a perfect subject for Edward Burne-Jones who produced one of his rare society portraits of her, with eyes downcast, her dress the essence of tasteful simplicity.[6] One of The Souls' standard adulterous males, Wilfrid Scawen Blunt, attempted a seduction and laid on a special vegetarian meal for her at a London restaurant. Characteristically she never turned up, though she had given him hopes when he was camping out in his Arab tent in the grounds of St Fagan's Castle, another of the Windsor-Clives' many homes.

The photograph of the French Garden at Hewell, illustrated in the excellent Parklands Survey, is of 1893 by Bernard Lemere and shows the four quarters of garden

65 *By the time this 1903 photograph was taken the low parterres of Hewell Grange's French Garden had been coaxed by chains and trellises into a head-high jungle of flowers and bushes.* Country Life *Picture Library*

laid out around the 'Perugia' fountain in ground hugging parterres.[7] Yet by the time of the *Country Life* photographs of 1903[8] a transformation has taken place (*65*), and the *Gardeners' Chronicle* of 1904 confirms this. Souls' gardens were meant to afford shade and private nooks for flirtations so it is possible that Lady Gay had done her best. Where there had been trim, ankle-high beds in 1893, by 1903 what can only be described as an enthusiastic head-high tangle of clipped hedges and chains festooned with roses and clematis had grown up. As the *Gardeners' Chronicle* reported: 'From the ground level it is not possible to obtain a view of the plan of this garden for the arches and festoons, but we had the opportunity to see it from the upper windows of the mansion, whence it may be clearly viewed in its completeness'.[9]

There may have been a note of disapproval here because confusion was not, in 1904, what a lordly garden was meant to convey, and, frankly, the *Country Life* photographs record an overgrown mess. Anyone visiting Hewell today and expecting to be overwhelmed by festoons will be surprised and pleased. The prison authorities have reduced the French Garden to its bare, green bones (*66*). Even the statues of the Four Seasons have been concealed, imprisoned even, within evergreen domes, where each

66 *Bodley & Garner's Jacobethan Hewell Grange commands its French Garden, now stripped down to its bare green bones by the prison authorities*

woman has to be visited individually. It is much more a Souls garden now than it ever was back in 1903. As if conscious that they had horticulturally sinned against fashion, the Windsor-Clives embarked on a series of massive garden simplicities around their garish French Garden. Between 1900 and 1903 18 giant stride grass terraces (67) were cut out from the hillside on an axis leading from a Rhenish-style water tower,[10] across Earl Robert's yew half-circle, right down to a landing stage on the lake. To one side of the steps, where the American Garden had been planted, an equally ambitious Maze of hornbeam hedges, gravelled with white granite chips, was laid out. Today it survives though it is barely penetrable. Another Edwardian feature was the forecourt to the house with hollies and a Venetian well-head, very much to the Italian taste of Earl Robert.[11]

Those 18 stepped grass terraces introduce what is Worcestershire's most frustrating problem of garden dating: one which concerns a garden that the *VCH* has described, with good reason, as 'an almost unique example of topiary art'.[12] The terraces are said to have been cut out as a tribute to the existing hillside gardens at Rous Lench, 10 miles away to the south but, like Hewell Grange, on the extreme eastern edge of the county.

Depending on one's point of view and a scholarly appraisal of the evidence, Rous Lench (*colour plate 18*) could be the most important garden, as opposed to park, in the entire county: a topiary treasure rather than an Arcadian landscape, and a place

67 *The 18 giant grass steps at Hewell Grange are only one section of an impressive vista from the Rhenish-style water tower down to a landing stage on the lake*

of rare and memorable atmosphere. The only other garden of the same multiple hedged construction which rivals it in age, variety and ambition is that in Wiltshire at Hazelbury Manor, on the hill above Box, near Bath.[13] The important difference between Hazelbury and Rous Lench lies in their dating. Hazelbury is definitely Edwardian, revamped imaginatively in the late twentieth century; Rous Lench is, arguably, of the same date – the sixteenth and seventeenth century – as its floridly half-timbered parent house, Rous Lench Court, in which case it should have been discussed in an earlier chapter of this book. The only excuse for placing it here is a hunch, unproven and instinctive, that the great topiary constructs of Rous Lench owe more to the Revd. Dr Chafy-Chafy, who bought the Court in 1875, than to any Jacobean owner of the house. If I am ever proved wrong, no one will be the more delighted. It would be most satisfying to give Worcestershire, England's greatest and earliest topiary garden. Judgement must now pass to readers, who will want to walk those shadowed terraces of castellated yew on one of the days when they are open to the public: an experience which they will be sharing, if folk lore is accurate, with Oliver Cromwell, to name but one.

The facts are that an Ordnance Survey map of 1884 shows the gardens very much as they are today: 7 acres steeply climbing the hill behind the Court and flanking the lane up out of the village.[14] The detail of the map shows three alleys climbing up, crossed by five level alleys with what appear to be indications of four terraced steps. That would seem to put the yew lines, if they were mature, comfortably earlier than Blomfield's polemic. But Blomfield was arguing for architectural gardens and Rous Lench has, apart from the late, ugly water tower at the top of the hill, little in the way of garden structures, only a brick and stone retaining wall at middle terrace level and a cosy little enclosed Secret Garden well to one side and disconnected by its Fernery, a typical Gardenesque feature, from the spreading topiary network of yews.

Rous Lench can be dated back somewhat earlier than the 1884 OS map. The sale particulars for 6 July 1875,[15] drawn up when Dr Chafy Chafy actually bought the place, included a useful map of the site (*68*) and described the grounds as 'Beautifully laid out and ornamented with Shrubs and quaintly shaped Yew Trees'. Yews grow slowly, but already, at the time of the sale, Rous Lench's yews were 'quaintly shaped', which could put them at least a century old. But 1775 is not a likely date for lavish topiary work. Addison and Pope were making fun of such quaintness in the first decade of the eighteenth century. This suggests, though does not prove, that the seventeenth century is the likeliest time for the yew planting and that the garden at Rous Lench is really a rare and distinguished survivor.

The broadest middle cross-alley and terrace has one enormous yew tree, which is traditionally known as 'Cromwell's'. The iron Puritan did sleep here in 1651, on the

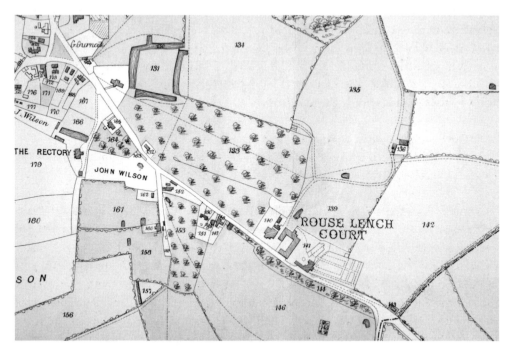

68 This map of 1875, drawn when the Revd. Dr Chafy-Chafy bought Rous Lench Court, proves that the geometric layout of the yew hedges was substantially in place before he got to work remodelling the Court and its grounds

night before the Battle of Worcester when Sir Thomas Rous owned the estate,[16] but it is unlikely that he spent any time planting a ceremonial yew to mark the occasion. Perhaps the mere absence of wrought iron gates in the usual, lordly Edwardian manner and the fact that there is not a single quaint stone pavilion for trysts is an indication of Rous Lench's age and authenticity. It is, however, easy to understand why the grounds are usually dated to the 1890s, because the first impact of the place, driving in on the very short drive from a lane lined with Scots pines, is lushly Edwardian. This is largely thanks to the dedicated hard work of the present owner, Brian Thorp, and his co-worker Graham Banner. In its Chafy-Chafy heyday the hedges are said to have required the work of five gardeners, clipping and trimming from 1 August to 5 November to keep them in order. We have a debt of gratitude to owners like Brian Thorp for shouldering these horticultural burdens with such obvious pleasure and enthusiasm.

Standing in the forecourt of the house we are on the lower edge of the great yew-hedged slope. To the west, downhill, is the reflecting lake which Brian Thorp has dug, seeing shrewdly that bright glimpses of its waters would enliven all the western views from the dark yew alleys. Beyond the lake, in mature woodland, lies the site of old Rous Lench, abandoned after the Black Death, but still encircled with a typical broad, Worcestershire defending moat. The house itself is impossibly picturesque in its black-and-white ranges that amble along two sides of the forecourt. An entrance archway from the road has been blocked up to create an extra room and give the place a sense of enclosure, but inscribed above it on the roadside a carving reads: 'Welcome ye Coming/ Speede ye Parting Guest', which immediately raises doubts as to dates. The Edwardians could rarely resist a whimsical or poetic inscription. It was a trick they had picked up from William Morris, who loved to include lines of his own or Chaucer's poetry with whatever he was building, viewing or printing. Madresfield was over-written again and again by the seventh Earl, with sentiments like:

> Shadows fly: life like a dome of many coloured glass stains the white radiance of eternity until death tramples it to fragments. The one remains, the many change and pass: Heaven's light for ever shines.[17]

It is easy to imagine the lines being boomed out by the Earl while his seven children exchanged knowing glances. As will be seen later in this chapter, the Field House at Clent has similar aspirant inscriptions. But here at Rous Lench they do suggest major works and a typically late Victorian mind behind them. The English Heritage Register of Historic Parks and Gardens dates the south range to the early sixteenth century and the east to 1840, but Dr Chafy-Chafy rebuilt the house after 1875 and then, after 1993, the architect Peter White restored it again, so little of the sixteenth century remains. However, the inscription was certainly in place when the house was sold in 1875 as it is quoted in the sale particulars. The courtyard looks Edwardian in its treatment. In the centre of a turning for carriages and cars is a tilted millstone with an ugly spiked agave. One of a pair of Mercury statues (*colour plate 19*) is poised on the terrace below,[18] the lawns are immaculate and tremendous specimen trees make a towering silhouette to frame the higgledy-piggledy, whimsical house. To the right a Ten Commandments-looking hedge seems to breathe the words 'Alfred Parsons', but the *Country Life* writer of 1899 reports a date of 1480 for this hedge, with no supporting evidence. Geraniums and splashes of red and white flowers all unite to raise the suspicions that this is quite a recent, though very impressive, garden.

Then comes the climb, the yews close in, and the atmosphere changes completely. It is difficult to convey the scale and complexity of these hedges; a web made by crossing three stepped and uphill double lines of yew averaging 15ft in height by five double, cross-alley ways. The beds of lavender and roses near the house give way to plain enclosed lawns between the billowing, vaguely battlemented and domed hedges (*69*). Rous Lench is not a peacock garden, its clipping theme is castle walls. The Italian garden is the first major cross-terrace, not notably Italianate, but it has the second Mercury statue. Then the climb leads into Oliver Cromwell's Walk, the second major cross-terrace. There are laurels and steps, Chafy-Chafy in feeling, and one isolated, full-grown yew tree that looks at least three centuries old. But it is the Top Yew Terrace, the third cross-alley that suggests a date for the layout. It is large enough for two Bowling Greens, side by side, which were not uncommon in the gardens of major seventeenth-

69 It is not easy for photography to convey the extent and dream-like variety of the steep mesh of yew alleyways on the hill above Rous Lench Court

century houses, when bowls leagues seem to have flourished rather as football does today. Next to them is a giant arbour or house composed of six yews, making a substantial green dome. The slope above it is supported by a manifestly old, stone and brick wall, while the hedge behind it is dramatically battlemented.

By this time a visitor has been walking and climbing for at least ten minutes, the house is rarely visible, but the maze of hedges offers occasional enchanting glimpses of the lake's blue waters. That domed yew arbour was a favourite garden device of Alfred Parsons. Did he plant this one for Chafy-Chafy or did Parsons pick up the idea of planting them from a visit to Rous Lench?[19] Now, as the ground levels out, the gardens widen, with a dog-leg reach on the right to the Scots pines of the lane and two battlemented arches on the left. These once led into the Kitchen Garden and that tall viewing tower which is Victorian in date, like that at Hewell Grange. This section of the grounds has been sold off and contains a private house. A little lower down on the same left-hand side is the entrance to the Secret Garden; the brick Cloister Court is post-1993, by Peter White.

The Secret Garden was conceived as a Fernery with crooked paviour paths, a shallow rectangular water trough, statues of nude girls and long-legged cranes. The tiny pools are ringed with iron and flanked by serpentine ways. There is a snarling gryphon, beds of roses and a brick garden house. In design terms it is a different world, but it comes across as fussy and feminine after the plain, dark certainties of the topiary garden. Lower down and much further out to the left, or to the right now the visitor is descending, is a thickly wooded Wilderness where an ironwork Regency seat circling a tree has been half devoured by the tree it rings. Below the Wilderness convention sets in with a line of columnar cypresses leading up to a Temple with lion masks, Edwardian again. The pleasure grounds play themselves out in an open field with pony stables; and a green way leads back to the specimen trees and the garden of the first Mercury below the forecourt. After several months of consulting the records and speculating[20] I have frankly to admit that, though there are few seventeenth-century elements to the grounds at Rous Lench, I am still ready to leave them in this late nineteenth-century chapter. Wherever they belong, they are most memorable and most inwardly turned, and I would strongly urge a visit.

It is difficult to decide where to go next to find the typical Edwardian garden because, for some obscure social reason, the county does not have one. However, Spetchley Park has the closest approximation to a formal Edwardian design, but one laid out in the grounds of a Regency neo-classical house rather than a medieval moated grange or an Arts and Crafts timber-framed hall.

Spetchley's grounds are not easy either to assess or to date; the years 1891 to 2000 probably span their creation. For a start they have no natural advantages. The site is level and the closest to the house of the two lakes seems more like a reservoir because there has been none of the tree planting on its banks which is so essential to frame water and which works so impressively around the many lakes of Kyre Park. Then it has to be said that John Tasker's house of 1811, on a bad, new site, away from the moats of the old house, is a Greek Revival structure of neither charm nor conventional classical vibrations.

Given a dim house on a dull site, with most of the intense flower planting hidden behind high brick walls, the gardeners of Spetchley have had their work cut out.

Much has been done. Whether it was tactful to site a nude statue of the Apollo Belvedere, the Sun god, in the shade of yew trees at the head of a straight, stagnant, moat-canal is questionable. But a Regency ironwork bridge vaults vigorously over one stretch of water; there is a Conservatory of restrained elegance of the same date – two Gardenesque features – and a charming Root House, a rare survival. Certainly Spetchley has much to offer plant enthusiasts and those solid yew hedges in the squares about the Fountain Garden, attributed to Ellen Willmott, the sister of Mrs Rose Berkeley, present the Edwardian experience better than any other garden in the county. Easily the most moving feature of these grounds is the Doric Temple (*70*) mentioned by H. Avray Tipping in his *Country Life* article of 1916,[21] which faces down the long axis to the fountain. With its *Rubaiyat of Omar Khayyam* quotation on the frieze: 'The Moon of Heav'n is rising once again: How oft hereafter rising shall she look through this same Garden after me in vain!', it was a memorial to Rose Berkeley, a devoted gardener, from her husband, and breathes the essence of elegant Edwardian melancholy.

In all the previous books of this series the Edwardian gardens, being conceived as settings for rather superior and very aspirant aristocratic houses, tended to be

70 *The Doric Temple on the Fountain Garden axis at Spetchley Park, laid out by Rose Berkeley in collaboration with Ellen Willmott, with the lead figures of Adam and Eve in the foreground*

immaculately well kept. This is certainly true of Spetchley's grounds, but it has been a pleasant embarrassment to find some in Worcestershire gently dilapidated and often discordant, even in their original conception. With that reservation it is a pleasure to end this chapter with the disorderly trio of Field House, Clent, Holland House, Cropthorne, and Holt Castle, all gardens of real character, but confused design.

Sir Edwin Lutyens laid out most of his gardens in the southern counties so Holland House, Cropthorne, which has a reasonably sound claim to at least a small Lutyens garden, deserves to come first, Lutyens being the ablest practitioner of the effortlessly aristocratic Edwardian manner. Holland House was originally three separate cottages that were linked to form a farmhouse around 1810. Mr H.H. Avery, a Birmingham industrialist, bought it, and in his chronological list of Lutyens' work, Butler notes for 1900: 'Garden at the Den, Pershore, for Mr Avery',[22] the Den and Holland House being two different names for the same building. Margaret Richardson also reports that Mr Avery wrote to *Country Life* requesting the name of an architect to 'do a garden sloping down to a river'.[23] If Lutyens did the work, he was probably assisted by Charles Frederick Butt, an Edgbaston architect who inscribed as a joke 'Drinkwater Butt' on one of the windowsills in the house.[24] So this is unlikely ever to have been one of Lutyens' serious compositions. Jane Brown only visited the house after she had finished her Lutyens and Jekyll book,[25] so her failure to include it is not significant.

One of the two timber-framed façades to the house faces directly onto Cropthorne's main street, but both are attractively bogus, full of gables, nooks and olde worlde inventions. The gardens have the same air of hit-or-miss improvisation, but their original charm has been seriously damaged by the insertion of a sharply-angled accommodation block of quite aggressive ugliness. As a Worcester Diocese Retreat and Refuge House such bedroom provision was necessary, but not at such a price. Immediately outside the garden door is the possible Lutyens contribution to the grounds, the Sunken Garden of herbs (*71*), with a central sundial naming 'none but the sunny hours'. This is reached down any of four diagonally-sited flights of golden limestone steps; Lutyens was never one for half measures or vague gestures. Between this and the ugly new block is a walnut tree which will set any amateur detective in gardens of the period looking for a mulberry to accompany it. Walnuts and mulberries are true Arts and Crafts plantings: useful as well as attractive, very William Morris. Sure enough, down to the left beside a cluster of pretty, vernacular staff cottages and in the Kitchen Garden a large mulberry tree sprawls its enormous fat limbs along the ground and, on my visit, showered the path with falling fruit.

Between the house and its Kitchen Garden is a yew-enclosed Rose Garden which must have given Lutyens some pain if, in his time, it had been clipped and hacked as barbarously as it has been now. But again the planning of its features is diagonal, so it may have been to his design, only the porthole windows and alcoves now cut into it are the work of an enthusiastic amateur with a power tool. The central axis of the garden drops very steeply down by terraced steps to the River Avon, but before the collapse there is a broad lawn with a grand cedar and an ill-sited Scots pine. A haphazard cluster

71 *The four diagonal paths, slightly overstressed geometry and the sundial's inscription mark this one section of the grounds at Holland House, Cropthorne, as a rare Edwin Lutyens venture into Worcestershire*

of clipped holly and yew bushes diversify a pleasant cottagey chaos, again with evidence of an overused power tool. It is the kind of garden which Ernest Gimson would have approved as the staircase balustrade in the house has his signature facetted carving and a gardener appears to have followed his lead working on the bushes.

The gardens of Holt Castle are an altogether more serious proposition as they enclose, on another steeply terraced site, one overlooking not the Avon but the Severn, an authentic medieval tilting ground; Holt's garden is private and I am grateful to Steve Worrallo for being allowed to take in an historic and atmospheric site at my own pace. It is a garden that can leap five centuries in the course of a few yards and it needs to be taken in thoughtfully. John Doharty junior was clearly charmed by it and illustrated the Castle in 1745 with the suggestion of a few feathery towers on a range of gables, also the indication of an 'Engine House', an 'Ash Bed', two avenues of trees to the north and a double avenue to the east, 'Gardens' and a terrace, which was, in fact, the tiltyard.[26]

A mature cedar dwarfs the lawned forecourt, but up above it on the north side is the crumbling sandstone wall of the medieval pleasance. Autumn crocuses were flowering on my visit and there was, of course, no mark of the original planting, just little birch trees and Japanese peonies. The formal Edwardian garden is set back from the brambled and wooded cliff edge, sheltered from any hint of a view of the Severn below by a high wall of pale green yew. There is paving around a lily pond and unclipped piers of topiary work, small Irish yews and all the signs of what happens when one gardener leaves before his successor has moved in. Between this yew wall and the cliff runs the long, broad terrace which is now known as Queen Adelaide's Walk. At its southern end there is a forlorn eighteenth-century brick garden house backed by holly bushes, it has a fireplace with a table and chairs. To the side there is a ruined greenhouse and an impressive tunnel of hornbeam leading back to the Castle. Sometimes a garden seems to be pausing for breath between the initiatives of its owners and gardeners, and that is how Holt Castle's grounds seem at present. They have fine bones but little flesh upon them, and the late twentieth-century pavilion at the top of a flight of steps on the northern boundary of that original pleasance lacks architectural invention. Originally the Castle must have been built to command a western prospect but now, at least from its gardens, it shrinks from that view, giving a strong impression of introversion and reserve. It could have had a confident Edwardian garden that metaphorically played Gothic trumpets; it was laid out for ceremony, but the fanfares are not sounding.

The gardens of Field House, Clent, are equally individual and odd, as is the Field House itself. It is a building so successfully brash and amateur in its styling, with Baroque giant pilasters and Venetian windows spread across two floors, that it comes as no surprise to find the garden equally quirky and memorable. That classical façade had canted bays in the Rococo style of the 1750s added to it, but in 1921 by Forbes & Tait for an owner whose initials 'E V' are on rainwater heads, and there are surprises around every corner, most of them apparently planted by the 1920s owner who had the instincts of a joker-manipulator.

A long, bumpy drive leads to the isolated 'Field' House and drops a visitor into an entrance front garden beset with lumpy balls of golden yew, scattered in no particular order. Behind this topiary ball game is a gleaming hedge of holly, but illogically in front of the yew balls is a brick-lined ha-ha, the apparent relic of a quite different layout. It will be recalled from an earlier chapter that the Field House commands, or is commanded by, a large Gothick folly, once rendered a staring white, in the grounds of the neighbouring Clent Grove. So was the original Field House, as its name implies, designed to sit in Capability Brownian isolation, divided from the natural fieldscape only by the ha-ha? Are all its garden features the work of 'E V' in the 1920s and planned as a protest against that Brownian simplicity? That seems to be the solution.

The two ponds illustrated on the 1860 sale particulars plan are lost now in nettled woodland and unrelated to the house.[27] But then even the Best Garden (72), described as 'Italian' yet clearly Japanese and seemingly designed in 1914 by the formidable Gertrude Jekyll herself,[28] is largely hidden from windows of the house because yews and magnolias have been allowed to grow up between garden and house. This Italian-Japanese Garden does, however, have great contradictory charm. The Jekyll Japanese pool is rectangular and crossed by submerged stepping-stones. On the pool's far side a tangle of willow and reeds rises in bold asymmetry from the water. Overlooking it and, from a style angle, completely contradicting its orientalism, is a two-storey brick

72 *Only one oddity among several in the unpredictable gardens of the Field House, Clent, this Best Garden is Japanese in its pool features, but is described as 'Italian' and attributed to Gertrude Jekyll*

summerhouse with those long, melancholy windows characteristic of the late Carolean or William and Mary period. This now serves as an inhabited house, but it still features strongly in the confused gardenscape. On the other side of the pool, hardly visible for the bushy growth of wisterias, is an almost crinkle-crankle wall, supported at frequent intervals by buttresses with boldly rounded angles. As a last contradictory feature the pool has a fountain with triple dolphins.

Photographs in a 1948 sale particulars[29] show this garden in perfect condition and clearly visible from the ground floor windows of the house. The stepping-stones in the pool were not then submerged and there was no suggestion that the garden was Japanese, only Italian. One clue to the charmingly perverse nature of 'E V' are his inscriptions carved on stone panels, conceived in that pushy Edwardian whimsicality. Here one admonition reads:

Ye also must share its joyous rayes
If ye would prolong life's happie dayes

while another, overlooking the Italian Garden, claims:

Here I mark ye sun's golden houres
Giving sweet fragrance to all garden flowers

The owner's quirky humour manifests itself again on the left of that ha-ha on the entrance front. Curved yew hedges offer tempting entry to a dark passageway, but to enter is merely to pop out on the other side of the yew roundel at almost the point of entry. Obviously 'E V' is the key to the Field House garden and, by that reading, it should be included in the last or modern chapter; but it is as if an Arts and Crafts enthusiast of the 1890s had lived on longer than might be expected and laid out a garden in 1921, 20 years too late. A sense of humour does not naturally spice up an Edwardian garden, but here a visitor gets a lively sense of being played with from 'the other side'. Gardens should play more often, and the abiding impression given by this chapter is that Worcestershire's average gardening landowners did not take the aristocratic solemnities and inventions of the age of Lutyens as seriously as they had taken the technical ventures of the Gardenesque.

11

The conservative modernism of a yeoman-bourgeois county

Worcestershire's distinctive and individual pattern of garden design has continued into the twentieth century. As the county responded enthusiastically to the garden technologies of the nineteenth-century's Gardenesque, but with reserve to the elitist historicism of the Edwardian, so its twentieth-century outpourings, while rich and often ambitious, have been generally traditional. Gertrude Jekyll has lived on in Worcestershire: herbaceous colour symphonies and coy lead statues are still trendy. Quirky Shenstonian individualism still flourishes, and if a big name is brought in to design a garden, sometimes several big names in sequence to the same garden, their contributions tend towards the ornamental and acceptable. This has not prevented the owners of Kyre Park from creating a grotto-tower building of ingenious originality or Stone House Cottage Garden and Nursery from becoming the most inventive and beautiful folly garden of the entire twentieth century. Readers will sometimes find it problematic to follow a pattern of design, but that will be because Worcestershire's modern gardeners have been prodigious in their expenditure. As the English Heritage Register of Historic Parks and Gardens admitted, in one of its usually exact and confident accounts at Spetchley Park, 'Disentangling the development of the gardens between 1891 and 1934 is difficult'. But then at Spetchley even the Edwardian statues of Adam and Eve are dressed in eighteenth-century French costumes. Worcestershire's gardeners have inclined to enjoy the kitsch without middle class inhibitions. That warm Black Country accent has found responses in the mood of new Worcestershire gardens.

One geographical generalisation needs to be mentioned. The further north and the nearer to Birmingham the more individual and Shenstonian the county's gardens tend to be. To the south and the Gloucestershire border a certain aristocratic reserve sets in. Technically, Overbury Court and Conderton Manor are in Worcestershire, but anyone dropped blindfolded into those villages in the lee of Bredon Hill would be excused for thinking they were in Cotswold Gloucestershire, the topographical aesthetic is so much that of golden oolitic limestone. The villages have been picture-postcarded by caring and seriously wealthy landowners; hence the grounds of Overbury and Conderton. Overbury was originally created for the Holland-Martin banking family, Conderton was bought by them in 1953 from the Atwood family. The Holland-Martins have never been short of money and have also been able to bring into Overbury entire sections of ornate stone carving whenever a redundant bank branch has been demolished.

At Overbury little Arts and Crafts touches of caring beauty are evident on either side of the stream that runs through the village: there are carefully carved mouldings on any village extensions and also on the lychgate, which is a war memorial designed by Sir Herbert Baker. Its massive oak timbers are etched with two miniatures, one of Christ crucified, one of Christ risen, and a moving inscription is inscribed on the coffin resting block. The church itself is intimately grouped in with Overbury Court and garden, its tower the deliberate focus of several vistas in the grounds.

If the garden of the Court has a fault it lies in its richness and variety. Like the houses of the village it has had almost too much money spent upon it. No fewer than six well-known designers have worked on the landscaping over the last 150 years: Geoffrey Jellicoe was the most inspired, Brenda Colvin, Guy Dawber, Russell Page, Aubrey Waterfield and Peter Coats also contributed; while the imposing façades of the house have, besides their original 1735 designer, been worked upon by Richard Norman Shaw (1897-1900), Ernest Newton in 1909 and 1911, and by Victor Heal in 1959. At the time of my visit a richly detailed new courtyard garden of polychromatic stone paving was being laid out between the house and the perfectly proportioned early eighteenth-century service range in a rustic darker stone. It would be wrong to describe Overbury's gardens as well designed like those of Conderton Manor. One single designer, Brenda Colvin, laid out Conderton; the six designers of Overbury have between them created a rewarding confusion of assorted, often disconnected parts, a delight to explore and a puzzle to attribute.

The long, broad south lawn of the Court's garden front is typical of the challenging stylistic mix of the grounds. Its perfect turf ends abruptly in a yew hedge of cup-shaped features that hangs literally inches above the village street, the hedge acting like an above-ground ha-ha to conceal the public way, which runs subserviently low. Disturbingly a big, vivid blue swimming pool has taken the place of an Edwardian sunken lily pond, but two rows of pyramidal Irish yews largely succeed in reasserting aristocratic order between the flashy pool and the genteel Croquet Lawn alongside it. In the left-hand corner a diagonally planned Gazebo angles itself above a double flight of steps and the stone paved seating nook at the end of Peter Coats' scalloped-edged gold and silver border of flowering herbs (73). The blues of catmint and lavender are slowly overcoming the intended dual colouring, but the effect is still refreshingly un-Jekyll. The Gazebo is of 1923,[1] but pure Edwardian in feeling, part of the nostalgia for a poetic past that suffuses house, garden and village. Honeysuckle, wisteria and *Clematis tanguitica* twine around the Gazebo walls while steps dive down under golden green leaves to give a secret exit to the village street. This is a thoughtful detail to balance and undercut the stately wrought ironwork and stone piers of the normal 1887 entrance gates to the courtyard and the front door.

73 *The diagonally planned Gazebo at one corner of Overbury Court's south garden was built on Edwardian lines as late as 1923. It commands both the village street and also Peter Coats' scalloped-edged gold and silver border*

Most of the urns and statues, which fronted the terrace overlooking this formal garden, have been stolen. The plinth of one has the inscription: 'Modelled by G B Amendola from the picture of Sir Frederic Leighton' which suggests the quality of what we have now lost to antique thieves. Bell's Castle just up the hill has also suffered from these night-time wreckers. That terrace ends at the west in a *scola* or exedral seat for thoughtful reflection, very Lawrence Alma-Tadema, and a recent Holland-Martin MP has littered it with Gothic fragments from restorations of the Palace of Westminster. Below this, and continuing the western axis, stretches a recent Italian Garden where a fountain plays in a forest of Corinthian columns rescued from a Liverpool bank, presumably a Martin's branch before the amalgamation. Running down south from the *scola* along the Croquet Lawn is a Rose Garden.

A towering yew hedge, sculpted into bays and buttresses, cuts off all this complex frontal area from the great lawn which leads to Overbury's most original and memorable feature. This is a very simple Water Garden (*74*) of sinuously curved reflecting pools inset within unadorned grass under vast plane trees and yews: a magical area of running waters where little cascades are studded with stones to create white-water effects, exactly like those at Kyre Park. This may originally have been an eighteenth-century feature as part of the water system is shown on an engraving of the 1780s, but it was almost certainly remodelled in the 1920s and is a composition which has all the hallmarks of Geoffrey Jellicoe's inspired invention. Above these tree-shadowed waters the long, easy slopes of Bredon Hill rise up with no apparent summit. On a grassy bank before the sheep walk begins there is a leat leading back to the watchful house and a superb mulberry tree drips fruit. Small dams widen the leat at intervals until it enters a Rock Garden, an intriguingly gloomy area of rough limestone boulders backed by yews. Ferns and broom crowd out the struggling flowers and narrow stepped paths lead to miniature ways among the rocks where water drips down a small cliff. This concludes

74 *The Water Garden is the most poetic feature of an impressive sequence of garden incidents at Overbury and is probably due to an inspired reshaping of an existing eighteenth-century water course by Geoffrey Jellicoe*

Overbury's multiple gardens. Above this concentration of pleasures lies a large upland park with a striking absence of the usual Worcestershire specimen trees.

Overbury's gardens were not laid out in a single year but over several decades, from 1923 to 1968, and the work is ongoing. The garden around Conderton Manor in the next village was planned by Brenda Colvin for a Mrs Maxwell in three campaigns, of 1932, 1934 and 1936.[2] These mark a decisive shift from relaxed design to the angularities of the Art Deco period, and produced a rare and interesting garden though not one that ever equals Overbury's romantic confusions. Entrance to the Manor is by a small exedra of yews; Colvin planned a narrower apsidal shape. On the other side of the Carolean-style house she has imposed her right angles on three existing terraces, each one gently profiled and leading out south along the hillside to give the fortunate owner perfectly composed views down the whole length of the north Cotswolds to Gloucester and beyond. Colvin laid out three vistas at right-angles to each other. One, a short one, went up rising ground to the left to a point where she had proposed two small garden buildings. Her central vista slices much further out to an exedra enclosing a pool with a cherub supported by swans. The third runs on the same axial line as the first down a long line of cider apple trees. Trees are the first love of Jane Carr, the present owner, who has been in possession for the last 35 years.

Brenda Colvin's plans (75), which are kept at the Manor, point out that the best vista from the garden front does not lie on any of her three formal lines but midway between the second and the third. Her three axial garden lines are a deliberate enrichment and distraction from the true vista which even includes Gloucester cathedral on a skyline. The initial Colvin planting was geometrically blocked for impact, not for Jekyll-type subtlety. On the top terrace, below what was then the Kitchen Garden, she proposed a long solid rectangle of dahlias; on the angle of the cider apple avenue there was a similar, massive rectangular bed of musk roses. Garden fashions change and today neither of these beds is planted out with her Art Deco crudity (76) and only a trellised Loggia stands where she had proposed the two garden pavilions. In the 1990s the Kitchen Garden was replanted with a lavish show of roses and hollyhocks to a cottage garden effect but on a grand scale. An early nineteenth-century Bark House survives from its Kitchen Garden days.

Further out east along that upper terrace is a Bog Garden of gunnera and cornus ending in one enormous, almost prone, willow tree, which sprawls like one of Tolkien's ents. Below the willow and hidden from the house is a swimming pool with a green-tiled pool house, its shutters pierced, Voysey-style, with hearts. This is not on the Colvin plans. Among the many rare trees planted by Jane Carr are a foxglove tree, several unusual acers and an oddball quince. The great cedar that dominates the grounds and the black mulberry at the start of the cider apple avenue are much older. With its wide, windy views and calm simplicities it is easy to enjoy Conderton's garden and intriguing to find that rarity, an Art Deco layout of the 1930s. But it has to be admitted that the block method of planting would have resulted in a brief blaze of one flower, the dahlias, and a short, intense perfume of the musk roses, with the rest of the year a green gap. It is only the intelligent and sensitive Carr modifications that have made the garden work.

75 *Brenda Colvin's 1932-6 designs for the gardens of Conderton Manor are a valuable record of the angularity of her flower beds and the conscious alignment of elements of her plan on contrived vistas out into the wider landscape.* By kind permission of Jane Carr

So chronologically crowded together and multiple authored are these twentieth-century gardens that it seems good sense to proceed geographically after Overbury and Conderton and move, first up the steep lane from Overbury to Bell's Castle and then down to Kemerton Court, as all four houses in this eminently liveable area lie within a mile of each other with Kemerton Priory half way between the last two. The smallest garden, less than half an acre, below Bell's Castle, is the most characterful and easily recalled of the group: a concentration of enchanting eccentricities tucked away on three narrow terraces under the Gothick windows of a seventeenth-century look-out tower which Admiral Bell Gothicised early in the nineteenth century. The Castle gives the impression, from its interiors as well as it gardens, of having been enjoyed by retired naval officers ever since.

At the top of the beech tree lined lane above Kemerton Priory the little Castle leans so heavily into the track on the left that sturdy buttresses have had to support its wall. The top door leads into a tiny front garden where the central path ends in an apse which has been cut into a drystone wall to house a cherub, the first of the Castle's wealth of garden statuary. But it is the scenery not the cherub that takes the eye. At the garden's far edge a steep valley pitches headlong down into a deep, half-wooded

76 *Colvin's plans for Conderton are a salutary reminder of the impracticality of blockish, Art Deco planting in a flower garden with one bed for one flower. The bones of her layout survive, but they have been enhanced by more practical and varied post-Jekyll planting*

combe of Bredon Hill, making it quite impossible to pass from the front garden to the back without going through the house or returning to the lane to take a lower gateway, which is guarded by a sculpted lion on its outer face and by a ramping unicorn on its pediment. That way drops a visitor into a cross between a terraced garden and a sophisticated antique shop; surely the most incident-packed hillside in the county.

On its far side, and the whole garden is only a few yards across, is a wall of mature woodland growing on the almost cliff-like slope. A semicircular Doric columned Garden House has been built here, on whose rear wall is a window with only one function: to look down into the wood when the snowdrops are out, as that is the only view. The top of this garden is bounded by the Castle, with a three-storey, diagonally set, tower dignifying its otherwise playful façade. A terracotta Michelangelo David occupies a niche. Blocking the garden from the lane is a range of vernacular cottage buildings where a stair has been upgraded with an ironwork balustrade inset with a triton. Half way down its three terraces a swimming pool has been squeezed in and at the last terrace's apparent conclusion is a stone balustrade where Italianate Flora negresses of limestone, expertly carved, hold fruit and flowers and a centrally placed gentleman lies forlorn and shattered due to recent vandals (77). The statues are flanked by obelisks balanced on the back of elephants, and they look back to a tufa rock Grotto with a triton boy inset within one of the terrace breaks. That should be enough, but on the wood-side of their terrace a serendipitously unexpected flight of steps curls down to yet another, fourth, terrace where another semicircular Grotto has been cut back into the wall. And still there is more. Down steep tufa rock banked steps is the Scout Hut, dank and deserted, but with fabulous views out over Severnside.

The ultimate treasure up on the top terrace of this most intense of gardens is a rotating wooden Garden Seat with a pyramidal roof. Its slatted sides are painted a silvery green and it moves to the slightest push, enabling us to share the enjoyment of all those lost eighteenth-century 'Windsor Seats' for lazy viewing. Visually drunk with unimagined garden experience I made my way back to the lane and, in three minutes, had driven down to an entirely different, yet equally valid, garden experience at Kemerton Priory.

This garden, on the same though more gradual hillside, lies well within the village, not raunchily isolated like the Admiral's Castle. It was dreamed up in the long tedium of a German Prisoner of War camp by Peter Healing as he brooded over William Robinson's *English Flower Garden* of 1892, which had, improbably, found its way into the Camp library. Released at the War's end, he returned with his garden plans drawn in Indian ink on parchment, and together with his wife bought the Priory house with a substantial ruin of the medieval priory on a terrace beside it. He then proceeded to

77 *Beautiful Italianate statues of the goddess Flora as a negress stand on the apparent last terrace of the deceiving South Garden at Bell's Castle. Vandals have tried to steal them*

trump in colour subtleties and rare species of flowers, like campanulas from the Azores, anything that Gertrude Jekyll had ever planted.[3]

I have never concealed my preference for 'hard' landscaping and gardening and my unease at the ephemeral and ever varying garden that depends upon flowers, their colour symphonies, frail architectural profiles of shrubs and scents. This is such a garden and obviously, even years after Peter Healing's death, remains delicately rich in colours, but it also has form and hard bones. The house wall, grey rather than golden, was radiant with a pale blue creeper and, pulled in tightly below it, was the stony little sun-trap garden (*78*) with two jewel like geometries of paving slabs, two square lily ponds and box hedges around miniature lawns, all next to a grotto-like well that once served as a carding house for Bredon's sheep flocks; an old crab apple tree leans heavily over it. The priory ruin and a big dark yew house created another incident, otherwise the garden is an ambling uneven lawn with border after border of flowers chiming around and above it, climbing past punctuating columnar cypresses to a sudden surprise pergola walk of black grapes and a tremendous double border, Healing's set-piece, divided narrowly by stepping-stones which the flowers overflow. There is no other shape apart from a stream garden to one side with arum lilies, hart's tongue ferns, candelabra primulas and mercifully underplayed gunnera. A few of the borders are subtly pale with white phlox and gypsophila, but for the most part Healing, an ex-interior decorator, went for savage, hot splashes of colour with plants such as Achillea 'Golden Plate', helenium, antholza and *Lobelia cardinalis*.

78 *Among the overwhelmingly rich grounds of Kemerton Priory, planned out when Peter Healing was a prisoner of war, his hard, geometrical sun-trap garden by the carding well stands out with reassuring clarity of form*

Passing downhill to level ground at last, by high walls and tall trees, the visitor will see a sudden side glimpse of the front porch of Kemerton Court inset between picturesque Cotswold elevations and apparently almost gardenless on this east side. At the Court, contrary to this first impression, the garden issues are those of open landscape, not flowery borders or crowding statuary. There is a spacious Walled Garden, admirably kept, to the north and then, beyond a deep, wet ha-ha boundary, lies the question mark of where to plant new trees and how to deal with an existing right-of-way. This westward-facing garden front of the Court is provincial Baroque in character and it could be argued that such a house demands attention with quite subtle garden symmetries around its skirts. This would, of course, be an excessively high maintenance solution to the present bland setting and Adrian and Meriel Darby, aided by their son Matt, who is a landscape consultant, have sensibly opted for a Capability Brown-style opening out of the landscape with an arc of trees which will lead the eye to the Malverns and then frame the hills.[4]

The intention is to use traditional native tree species in the wider parkland to compliment the more exotic American specimens that have been planted close to the house in recent years to produce, as Matt describes it, a Poussinesque recession so that the eye is encouraged to move around the landscape in carefully contrived vistas. This ambitious scheme has been partially funded by DEFRA with three fields being taken out of arable use and laid to pasture, thereby enlarging considerably the original eighteenth-century park. No attempt will be made to conceal the lane which runs from Kemerton to Kinsham across the mid-ground of this arc of trees. It will be left as a public amenity for the visual enjoyment of the house by travellers and to provide what Humphry Repton would have termed 'animation' in the landscape from the drawing room windows of the Court.

The garden at Bell's Castle resulted from an obsession with garden rooms and statuary, Kemerton Priory's garden is the sum total of one man's obsession with imprisonment and expressionist flower colour, but both gardens were restrained and disciplined to some extent by their creator's middle class awareness of propriety and establishment aesthetics. What happens when an ebullient, artisan gardener breaks through the class barriers and gardens uninhibitedly, armed with technical know-how, a sense of humour and untrammelled by aesthetic limits? Worcestershire, by its proximity to the Black Country, is a county where there is more than one answer to that question, and the most resounding is the garden of Astley Towne House, south of Stourport. This must be the most engaging and successful Pooteresque garden in Britain. To come across it in sunshine, while its big Tree House was still in construction and its projector, local builder Tim Smith, was in cheerful, extrovert good form, would restore anyone's faith in human nature. Tim and his wife, Lesley, have created a defiantly brilliant garden from scratch by observing the garden competition and then matching it.

The way to the Towne House is down a very narrow, high hedged, lane and the half-timbered yeoman cottage is tucked away at right-angles to the lane. What catches one's attention is not the quaint house, but a towering Gothick column[5] with clustered shafts rearing up above the trees behind it, and a life-size statue of Hercules perched on the top (79). Smith stuck the whole column up, piece by piece, in one day, then

*79 Rearing up with defiant
impudence behind the Towne House,
Astley, is this statue of Hercules
poised on a Gothick column salvaged
from a redundant local church*

dropped Hercules down quickly using a crane, in order to stabilize its uncertainty. That
was the first visual impression, but the path around the Towne House begins through
a 'hot' flower and shrub area of exotics that rivals, up here in the frosty Midlands, any
of Cornwall's sub-tropical recreations. This sandy-loam frost pocket has been coaxed
by some rough horticultural magic into a chemical coloured life, with banana plants,
garish tree dahlias, livid chard leaves, a huge cornus, bamboos, canna lilies, a false caster
oil plant, a prunus with the loveliest pink and brown bark, one rotting tree fern and
one flourishing tree fern, a huge-leafed *Tetrapanax*, which the horse chestnut tree above
was bombing cruelly with spiky grenades, lobelias and *Geranium maturensis*, all crammed
into one brief, steep, climbing border.

Then, in supreme impudence, comes a steal from Prince Charles' Highgrove
with a battered Stumpery and a wooden Doric Temple (*colour plate 20*) its pediment
authentically stuffed with crooked branches. Inside it the night sky of stars has been
copied in luminous paint: one up on royalty. A whole grove of tree ferns, healthy this
time, was growing next to it. In mocking contrast, at the edge of the slope behind the
house, two existing dark yew trees have been clamped together around a Gothick door
with a window of stained glass flowers salvaged from some demolished church. On

the left-hand yew a large wooden owl broods balefully down. Turning out, back from these shadows, into the sunlight, there is a revolving Summerhouse, its wide open doors inviting visitors into a comfortable interior where a clock ticks on the mantleshelf and cane chairs are set next to a table for tea. All around its sharp, painted pediment the borders of the paths are brightly herbaceous and the yew bushes are lemon yellow: no colour symphonies here.

The next transition in mood and space requires a climb up steep wooden steps through a leafy bush into a high, spacious Tree House, not yet completed on my visit (autumn 2005) but neighboured by Hercules, who seems to stand even higher on that column. Down below, at the end of a short lavender-lined path, is a Chinese Pavilion similar to one at Biddulph Grange in Staffordshire, and set to face the garden door of the house. I congratulated the delightful couple who have created it all and who are still creating, then left to digest the message of a classless, positive society where anyone can, in garden terms, do anything; and, I believe, should.

If the Towne House is too much to absorb it is worth trying another essay in the same individual style, but one more Shenstonian and sentimental, or would meditative be a fairer description? This is the garden of the White House at Dunley, a colour-washed roadside house with its gardens rising steeply behind it. On my visit the owner, Tony Tidmarsh, disappeared back into the house for several minutes to turn on the garden machinery. As a result, when we stepped outside, the Cascade (*80*), all of 10 yards long and easy to step over, was babbling busily but ending mysterious at its own foot as recycled waters dived down into one of several lavatory cisterns which Tony has buried under this 'Italian Garden'. The Shenstone borrowings are apparent in the ironwork loggia arches. Each one celebrates the marriage or partnership of one of Tony's children, an alliance in one case between the USA and Britain; each one is dated. Everything in the White House garden lies closely together. A *Clematis tanguitica* and wisteria tunnel leads down to a lower garden which can be glimpsed from the upper lawn through a strange terracotta arch, salvaged from the girl's entrance to Tipton Board School. Here too a fountain plays and an antique head is framed by the arch. Down that creeper tunnel to the back door there are stone beasts' heads, a peacock plaque and a toy Tree House. Back up again (for there is no defined circuit) there is an orchard lawn with three lily pools and a raw brick arch commemorating the marriage of another daughter. Uneaten fruit lies thickly on the grass and the lawn undulates away into low trees and a rising hillside. As at Shenstone's The Leasowes, this garden has been seen as a diary of significant emotions and a thanks-offering for various happinesses. It has also, one suspects, become itself a purpose for living.

Later last winter I visited Peter and Jean Reynolds, who own and garden Bannut Tree House, a long, low-lying, entirely unpredictable house that C.F.A. Voysey, most adventurous of all the Edwardians, designed in 1890 for R.H. Cazalet, and which the local builder, William Porter, built for £1,700 on Castlemorton Common in the eastern lee of the Malverns.[6] It is, like all Voysey houses, unique, and so the tending of its grounds is quite a responsibility. When I asked Peter how much time he spent on

80 *This active miniature Cascade in the front garden of the White House, Dunley, runs for 10 yards then vanishes at its foot into a concealed system of lavatory cisterns. The metal plaques record memorable events in the life of the Tidmarsh family*

his garden he thought for a moment and then admitted to spending several hours on it most days, when his wife was walking their dogs up on the hills. So a garden can easily be a life, not, as in the case of the Towne House, a ribald comment upon it, but a duty, as at Bannut Tree, to preserve the correct garden frame for a remarkable building, Voysey's only essay in the half-timbered manner.

As it lies today Bannut Tree's garden perfectly reflects the stylistic currents moving when the house was built. Big water butts and creepers punctuate the four-gabled garden front; the Arts and Crafts designers were great on chunky utility. To the east and overlooked by the kitchen is a quartered potager of Reynolds vintage in perfect harmony with the functional nature of the house. To the south a big lawn dotted with cherry and perry trees, fruits to be used, sweeps down to a yew enclosure laid out by Peter Reynolds, and ending in a little yew house: reminiscent of the more formal Edwardian garden. To the right is a triangular-shaped lawn (*colour plate 21*), alive in spring with a sweep of daffodils of a type which has never been available in the twentieth century, so it must be of the first planting of the 1890s. This is flanked by a walk lined with scalloped stone walls of the 1920s, and then Nature takes over in a deep dingle: a Wild Garden around a stream planted with oaks and yews. Voysey's other house, Perrycroft, a few yards outside

Worcestershire at Colwall on the west side of the Malverns, has just the same balance of garden: a steep lawn with a useful tree or two and then wild Nature with pools of water. Incidentally, 'Bannut' is Worcestershire dialect for 'walnut' and a walnut tree, useful again, is growing between the house (it was never a real farm, Voysey was essentially an architect for the suburban middle class) and its barn, which equals the house in unexpected angles, batters, buttresses and perverse ironwork.

Mention of formal clipped yew hedges at Bannut Tree House is a reminder of how much of that Edwardian formalism, largely unrepresented in the actual Edwardian years, has continued to be laid out in Worcestershire's supposedly modern twentieth-century gardens. A detailed description of the county's most successful, if sentimentally compromised, modern gardens was given, right out of its correct chronology, in the first chapter of this study. That was because Veronica Adams had laid out her quick-step geometry of beds, complete with lead shepherds and shepherdesses, within the warm brick walls of Birtsmorton Court's sixteenth-century Walled Garden. If we refer back to its quartering and feminine charm, enlivened by Mike Roberts' inspired ironwork (*colour plate 22*), we will recognise the Adams signature in another 'Millennium' garden which she designed in the 1990s and laid out for the Berkeley family; again within a walled garden and again a walled enclosure surrounded by dazzling herbaceous borders, at Spetchley Park. She deploys there the same quartering of beds with low geometrical hedges enclosing themed flower-beds as at Birtsmorton, responding to the firm enclosing walls. Mr R.J. Berkeley's informed guidebook to the grounds dwells lovingly on the many plant riches in the borders outside the Kitchen Garden walls: the Judas trees around the murky Horse Pool, the double-flowered pomegranate, *Punica granatum* 'Flore-Pleno' between the greenhouses and the scented *Osmaronia cerasiformis* at the end of the West Border. What is a little surprising is the appearance on the axis of the Fountain Garden of her favourite lead statues, a shepherd and a shepherdess in eighteenth-century costume, curiously named Adam and Eve. Perhaps she was conscious that Spetchley developed under the influence of Ellen Willmott in the Edwardian period and felt that the eighteenth-century-style figures would be in keeping.[7]

Another and very superior cluster of late, very late, post-1983 Edwardian-style yew geometry is gathered together in the gardens of Little Malvern Court in the lee of Little Malvern Priory (*81*); but here the clipping has an abstract Mondrian quality that qualifies it as modern rather than *fin de siècle*. The garden plan at the Court was designed for Tim and Alexandra Berington by Arabella Lennox-Boyd and Michael Balston in 1982-3; it was continued and developed under Michael Balston's supervision after 1988. To sit among these ruthlessly chunky blocks with roses in the remote background against the walls of the house and that patriarchal lime tree focusing every vista of the grounds around it, is one of the county's most satisfying garden experiences. The entire garden of the Court unfolds from that tree via a yew exedra and its flanking Tower Garden down steps to the Lower Terrace and then to the chain of five monastic fish ponds with a wisteria-twined wooden bridge across the middle water. It is a garden soon absorbed, but gloriously flattered by its close relationship with the Herefordshire Beacon, which heaves up above it as massively as some 3000ft mountain in the Grampians. Such is the visual pull of the Malverns that this garden barely relates to its own priory church even though its roses lap up to the stone walls.

Worcester may not have a moral, ecological garden like Dorset's Sticky Wicket at Buckland Newton,[8] but it does have a garden of architectural salvage, which is equally moral and visually just as satisfying. This is at Huddington Court, a haunted house of almost ferocious, angular character, a half-timbered abstract sculpture, gaunt and redolent of the Gunpowder Plot's horrid aftermath, of plotters betrayed, pursued, hunted down and tortured. My own memories of Huddington, however, are mild and warm: a cup of china tea taken in a kitchen parlour as angular within as the house is without, but a room alive with old cats and affectionate dogs. My host, Professor Hugh Edmondson, the active and positive owner of this concentration of violent history, is the grandson of Dunstan Edmondson, the man who bought and rescued the house from the earls of Shrewsbury, and the son of Hubert Henry Edmondson, who brought in most of the garden features and buildings that are now sited within Huddington's double moats, the inner wide, deep and lilied, the outer almost dry. Hubert Henry saved much of the county's garden heritage when it was under threat of demolition and destruction. Very little of Huddington's garden really belongs to the house but, when making a circuit of those moats, it is impossible to walk more than a few yards without stumbling over riches preserved from some

81 *Few modern gardens can equal the dedicated Mondrian-like abstract quality of the clipped yews in the Tower Garden and on the lawns flanking the Rose Garden close up against Little Malvern Court*

otherwise lost Worcestershire garden. Huddington is the county's true garden museum, one still working, relaxed and un-labelled, as a real garden should be.

The Court lies low among trees at the end of a short lime tree avenue, planted by Hubert Henry 40 years ago. This brings a visitor immediately into an enchanting sequence of lawns and unconnected garden structures, all gathered around that romantic moat. At no point in the sequence is a visitor unaware of the multiple, elegant yet threatening timbered façades of the Court, presiding over everything. That first lawn on the right runs up to one of two Pigeon Houses, black-and-white against the autumn foliage of Feckenham Forest which closes in upon the Court and its chapel-church. A second timbered Pigeon House lies away on the far side of the moat garden. Together with an original black-and-white Privy, which leans functionally over the carp-filled water, and a small but exquisitely angled cruck Cottage across the lane, the five buildings could be seen as Worcestershire's timbered heartland, a demonstration piece. There is also the Coach House with its clock tower, rescued like so much of the garden's balustrading and statuary (*82*), from Strensham Court's demolition in the early 1960s; under its red-tiled roof this is also black-and-white half-timbered, and the clock is original, weight driven.

Working clockwise from the east side of the house with its soaring brick shaft of a chimneystack there is, within the inner moat at its narrowest, a small stone-paved

82 *A statue of the goddess Ceres at Huddington Court, one of several rescued by Hubert Henry Edmondson from the 1960s demolition of Strensham Court*

pleasance of low box hedges, a pampas clump and the first scatter of more than 20 stone urns (Hubert Henry's hobby) which erratically punctuate the grounds. There is also the first of eight flights of steps down to the water. This is a most accessible, fishable moat, no dark forbidding water, though deep and very cold from springs that rise at its north-east corner. It is alive with carp, hence the steps for fishermen. A lovely arched bridge, of brick but stone balustraded, the first of three in these prodigiously crowded grounds, crosses the moat to the unexpected elegance of a timbered front porch with very early, 1584, Ionic columns. But our route will keep between the twin moats.

Next comes a little lawn with a sundial, a stone seat and ironwork gates leading down to the towerless Norman church. The second Pigeon House stands by the statue of a boy, more urns, a stone trough and low yew hedges in an attractive huddle. Now, unexpectedly in this homely crush, comes a stately balustraded terrace with a four-columned Doric Orangery (*colour plate 23*) reassembled in the 1960s from Strensham Court; in Strensham it served as a folly pavilion. On the balustrade there are statues, from Strensham again, one of a shivering January, an Italian favourite copied from a Medici villa outside Florence. This area works as a viewing terrace, but its views are dark and limited. It should be noted that my visit was on a misty autumn afternoon, perfect for the brooding Huddington aura. Across the inner moat from this terrace walk is that wildly picturesque Privy.

Features crowd in confusingly on this sector. Visible down the western reach of the moat is an inappropriately elegant, white ironwork bridge (*83*) that Hubert Henry rescued from Erdiston; it is stamped '1827 Stourport Iron Works'. Luckily it was an exact fit for the moat, but it is entirely non-functional, just a rescued ornament. Behind us across the outer moat, leading into the dark remnants of Feckenham Forest, is Lady Winter's Walk, said to be haunted by the eviscerated ghost of her plotter husband. A Gothic font stands on a small balustraded terrace overlooking a big rectangular pool which serves as a combined reservoir and fish resource. Here the water that keeps the moat living and healthy steps down to a corner ornamented with stone plaques brought in 1964 from Crofton Hall in Lancashire, another rescue operation; a man with a flail features on the carving. A pretty little stone Gazebo from the Strensham sale, one of the five pavilions by my count that are scattered between the moats, overlooks nothing more than the outer moat, but it has a second plaque of that man with a flail. Now come three big conventional topiary peacocks and the other Pigeon House. The main bridge to the house has tall gatepiers topped with horse heads; there is a white seat around a plane tree, yet another collection of urns, a statue of a boy pulling a thorn from his foot and the circuit of the moats has been completed.

The fifth of November conspirators got back here on the sixth and, on the morning of the seventh, heard Mass in the upstairs chapel, then fled, pursued by the Sheriff's men to their admonitory deaths. This is probably the most historic site in Worcestershire and, to me, the county's most interesting, as opposed to great or beautiful, garden; one where three generations of Yorkshire medics, the Edmondsons, in between healing bodies, have healed a garden.

That only leaves two garden achievements to celebrate, the Rapunzel Folly Tower at Kyre Park and the eight matchless folly towers at Stone House Cottage Garden, both

83 *In the wonderful confusion of garden salvage crammed in between the twin moats of Huddington Court, this 1827 Stourport Iron Works former road bridge has a startling elegance*

very recent and most encouraging signs of our national garden directions. In future years the last half of the twentieth century is likely to be seen as a golden age of English gardening. In one sense the Rapunzel Tower at Kyre (*84*) is a second-hand achievement as there was a folly tunnel on the site before, though it had fallen in. The aim of the tunnel was to give any visitors making a clockwise circuit of the lakes a sudden surprise view out over the Lily Pond to the cedar and up to the house. But in their imaginative and costly restoration the 1990s owners went much further. A tunnel still leads from the leafy recesses of the park through darkness to that surprise view, but the darkness is now interrupted, or perhaps it originally was, by a well of light where the head of a Medusa is carved in the floor and there is a grotto-recess of dimly discerned stone skulls. Above this rises the bizarre, half-Gothick, half-classical Rapunzel Tower with its viewing gallery and winding stepped access. Given a softening coat of render and some ivy it should weather down into a most acceptable feature, an oddity in an odd landscape.

Stone House Cottage Garden and Nursery is very different. When writing about it I have to restrain my language of praise because in my personal assessment it is far and away the most poetic and important folly garden of the twentieth century, and few eighteenth-century folly gardens can equal its tightly integrated charm. Travellers driving in to Kidderminster along the A448 from Bromsgrove may notice across the fields on their right, as they approach the village of Stone, a cluster of pale brick towers on the skyline like some modest Carolean Camelot, eight towers and each one of them topped

84 *The Rapunzel Tower on the lowest lake at Kyre Park has been added boldly to top an existing but much decayed Grotto and tunnel to a surprise view, a daring 1990s addition to a most unusual garden circuit*

differently to any of the others. Curiosity might and should induce the driver to turn right up a steep, bumpy drive under evergreen trees and branch right again off this, before ending up at Stone House. This will bring a visitor to James and Louisa Arbuthnott's Stone House Cottage Garden and Nursery, a strictly commercial enterprise for the sale of an unusually choice selection of plants, all growing within an amazingly various circuit of walls, towers and Stone Cottage itself. It is not in any sense a garden for visitors to pay to enter, only to enter to buy. The bonus is the circuit of towers, every one a folly and the work, almost single-handedly, of James Arbuthnott, England's unsung folly king. What is difficult to convey to someone used to single folly towers rising up starkly to command landscape, is the way Arbuthnott's towers compose. If we think, on the one hand, of the Great Wall of China, on the other of the multiple garden buildings at Stowe Landscape Gardens in Buckinghamshire, then the vision is still inadequate. But they do line a wall and they are cheerfully intimate, buildings of pleasure, though one, the octagonal Waterloo Tower, contains, as it name suggests, visitors' lavatories.

The best way to think of James Arbuthnott's vision and, possibly, his inspiration, is to imagine what Christopher Wren, working on a tight budget – no marble, very little stone and largely salvaged, but mellow, bricks – could have achieved in his relaxed old age, not that he ever did retire. A lilting quality of the poetic absurd possesses each structure. The first which a car will pass on the way to the visitors' car-park is a single-storey railway station, multi-arched and, of course, of brick. Then a whole line of three or four towers opens up, but before they can be taken in the car has to swing in next to the Waterloo Tower and a tall eucalyptus and there, overlooking a sales area of plants, vaguely contained in a cloister, are all eight towers and a glimpse of the Arbuthnotts' house, which is every bit as inventive as the towers themselves.

There is no standard height to the towers (*colour plate 24*), each one is an individual invention, together they are far more of an achievement, and the comparison is being made deliberately to emphasis their importance, than Sir John Vanbrugh's Romano-medieval folly wall at Castle Howard. But the idea behind both constructs seems to have been the same: a city wall with a varied profile. One tower ends with a pyramidal roof and a weathervane, another has a Romanesque crown of four round arches dramatised by grey bricks, a third, the Pigeon House Tower, is topped by the wooden cote and by four Goetheian spheres, one at each corner. Another is a bell tower with the bell seen in outline on a bar; one, the Albert Hall, has a Flemish-style curved gable. There is no end to the trimmings; around one corner are two little alcove seats, in a second there is a devotional niche; one loggia leading into the garden is five-sided, for there is a garden.

James built the towers, his wife Louisa planted the garden, and they are an amazing duo. Louisa Arbuthnott, who was my guide around the Nursery and up the Pigeon House Tower, still seems surprised at what her husband has created around the business which helps keep them and their four children. Looking down from the Pigeon House

85 James Arbuthnott's marvellous wall of eight folly towers, each one distinct, different yet harmoniously Carloean in feeling, encircles Louisa Arbuthnott's rampageous flower garden at Stone House Cottage Garden and Nursery

Tower (*85*) the beauty of their joint concept becomes apparent. A long double yew-lined path leads axially, but not in any precise direction, across the densely planted inner ground and a cross-axial yew path strikes it, but again not at any calculated geometrical point. While the architecture is vaguely Carolean vernacular and, therefore, classical, the mood and the planning are creatively chaotic. Every inch of the ground brims with plants, most of them for sale. Louisa explained that one quite short range of wall had eight distinct climbers and that she planted according to several micro-climates in the garden. I saw the garden at its November and January flowerless worst and it was still a green pleasure ground of leaves broad, feathery, lanceolate and various. The Arbuthnotts' house, with four children to accommodate, had to expand. The mid-Georgian-style canted bay in its centre, which completely took me in, is another Arbuthnott invention, and to the right of it the wing allows a little balconied courtyard alive with climbers. Walking towards a sally-port the house shows another face with a big, multi-windowed garden room, and the archway leads to an area for ericaceous plants. One peril on the many narrow paths is the dog traps which are designed to stop the obsequiously affectionate Welsh sheep dogs from racing into areas where there are delicate plants. I avoided most of them and came away awed and delighted that two people could achieve so much and remain modestly unaware of the stature of their creation.

In retrospect Stone House Cottage Garden and Nursery seems essentially Worcestershire. Like its neighbour Staffordshire, the county has an unpretentious but highly inventive earthiness. Every town and every village is distinct and surprising; the stone, the brick, the half-timbering, come and go in architectural unpredictability. This is the centre of England, working class, yeoman and hard-working. Kidderminster, so close to Stone, is an actively unlikeable town. Whenever I try to drive around its multiple expressionist roundabouts I think of Nikolaus Pevsner who had to go there often on business for Gordon Russell and hated the place. What would he have thought of the Camelot that has arisen at Stone? Give him his due, he had little feeling for bland classicism and a real liking for, and understanding of, the English genius for garden architecture and garden design generally. As it was published in 1968, the eight towers of Stone are not mentioned in the Worcestershire volume of Pevsner's *Buildings of England* series. In the future, when the book is revised and up-dated, they will merit a long entry, and I look forward to the day when they will feature on a dust-jacket. At the end of this chapter it is a pleasure to record that the English genius for garden improvisation and innovation has not deserted us and that from an unexpected quarter, those often mocked garden centres like the Arbuthnotts, the Webbs of Wychbold, which has laid out a chain of themed gardens: Scented, Spectrum, New Wave, English Rose along the banks of the fast flowing Salwarpe, and the Burford Nurseries, this last just across the border into Shropshire, invention and inspiration is being dispensed as it was in the eighteenth century from the great country houses. It is heartening to end on such an optimistic note.

Notes

Introduction: a county of elusive character

1 *Worcestershire Record Office* (hereafter WRO), 974/1.
2 Valentine Green, *The History and Antiquities of the City and Suburbs of Worcester*, 2 vols., 1796, 2, Appendix, pp.xxxvii-xlvii: 'Royal Visits extruded out of the Chamber Order Book...for the year 1575, pp.122-8'. Quotation given here on p.xxxix of Green's study.
3 Ibid.

1 An inland county curiously obsessed by water

1 *Victoria County History of Worcestershire* (hereafter VCH), vol.4, pp.426-31.
2 David Wilson, *Moated Sites*, Princes Risborough, 1985, p.29.
3 See Arthur Oswald, 'Holt Castle – 1, Worcestershire', *Country Life*, 20 July 1940.
4 WRO, 974/1.
5 Bodleian Library, Oxford, Gough Maps 33, f.73v.
6 See *Country Life*, 3 May 1902 for a history of the ownership of the Nanfans and contemporary photographs which show how little it has changed since then.
7 According to F.W.B. & Mary Charles in their *Conservation of Timber Buildings*, 1984, p.104, it is structurally unwise to infill any timber-framed building with anything except wattle-and-daub, bricks being far too heavy. One wonders if they had considered the life span of wattle-and-daub in a range overhanging water.
8 John Harvey, *Mediaeval Gardens*, 1981, has a scholarly and satisfying chapter 7 on early vegetable introduction.
9 Harvey, *Mediaeval Gardens*, Appendix, p.166 has a very interesting but inconclusive discussion on this vegetable.
10 Ibid., p.16.
11 Ibid., p.17.
12 Ibid.
13 As the *VCH* calls them.
14 This is, however, anecdotal. Sir William Russell had been the Royalist Governor of Worcester. See T.R. Nash, *Collections for the History of Worcestershire*, 2 vols., second ed., 1799, 2, Appendix, p.civ.
15 For Bindon see Timothy Mowl, *Historic Gardens of Dorset*, Stroud, 2003, pp.15-25.
16 A site plan is given in *VCH*, 4, p.432.

17 Thomas Habington, 'A Survey of Worcestershire', *Worcestershire Historical Society*, 2 vols., Oxford, 1895, 2, 7, quoting the Worcestershire 'Red Booke'.
18 Ibid.
19 Harvey, *Mediaeval Gardens*, p.58; p.17.
20 Ibid., p.103.
21 Ibid., p.84.
22 Ibid., plan on p.85.
23 Ibid., p.13.
24 Recent archaeological investigation of medieval sites has proved that the traditional art historical approach to the period where gardens are interpreted as small, enclosed spaces, such as those depicted in contemporary paintings, is too narrow. There is much field evidence to suggest that medieval designed landscapes broke out into the surrounding countryside and were consciously contrived to command views. See Chris Currie, *Garden Archaeology: A Handbook*, CBA, York, 2005, pp.9-10; also A.E. Brown (ed.), *Garden Archaeology*, CBA Research Report 78, 1991, and Paul Everson, 'Medieval gardens and designed landscapes' in Robert Wilson-North (ed.), *The lie of the land. Aspects of the archaeology and history of the designed landscape in the South West of England*, Exeter, 2003, pp.24-33.
25 David Robertson (ed.), 'Diary of Francis Evans, Secretary to Bishop Lloyd', *Worcestershire Historical Society*, Oxford, 1903, p.6.
26 Ibid., p.146.
27 There is a 1789 view of the Castle illustrated in James Lees-Milne's first *Country Life* article on Hartlebury which shows the three-sided moat clearly (16 September 1971); see 23 September 1971 for the second article.
28 For the early history of the house see Clive Aslet, 'Madresfield Court', Worcestershire – 1', *Country Life*, 16 October 1980.
29 For Huddington prior to the influx of garden refugees, see *Country Life*, 1 August 1936.
30 *VCH*, 3, p.419; pp.420-22.
31 *Worcestershire Transactions*, vol.26, p.495.
32 I am most grateful to Elizabeth Atkins for sharing her knowledge of Feckenham Forest and for showing me the John Doharty the Younger 1744 map of the area, a copy of a survey carried out in 1591.
33 Both these houses are shown surrounded by their moats on the Doharty copy-map. So too is 'North Grove Hall' (now Norgrove Court) at Webheath, whose moat has disappeared.
34 Habington, *Worcestershire Historical Society*, 1, pp.543-4.
35 Richard Lockett, *A Survey of Historic Parks and Gardens in Worcestershire* (Hereford and Worcester Gardens Trust, 1997), p.121.

2 The lure of dazzling example – the aftershock of Westwood Park

1 Timothy Mowl, *Historic Gardens of Cornwall*, Stroud, 2005, pp.35-40 and pp.147-52 respectively.
2 Mowl, *Dorset*, pp.28-33.
3 Timothy Mowl, *Historic Gardens of Wiltshire*, Stroud, 2004, chapters 2 & 3.
4 Ibid., p.50-3.
5 See Brian S. Smith, 'The Dougharty Family of Worcester, Estate Surveyors and Mapmakers', *Worcestershire Historical Society*, New Series, vol.5: Miscellany II, pp.138-77.
6 WRO, cb 009:1, BA 5403/10: 'An Exact Map of The Manor of Clains, Survey'd and Map'd by John Doharty junior in 1751, 1752, 1753'.
7 Sensitively restored after the fire of 1896 by the Worcester architect, Lewis Sheppard; see James Lees-Milne, 'Severn End, Worcestershire – 1 & 2', *Country Life*, 24 & 31 July 1975. For earlier illustrations of the grounds see *Country Life*, 14 October 1899.
8 *Country Life*, 31 July 1975.

9   Ibid.

10 WRO, 6134/44.

11 See Christopher Hussey, 'Westwood Park, Worcestershire – 1 & 2', *Country Life*, 14 & 21 July 1928.

12 *Country Life*, 14 July 1928.

13 After being created a baronet. His father was, therefore, the second Baronet.

14 Created Baron Coventry of Aylesborough in 1628, one of his grandsons, John, became the first Earl of Coventry in 1697.

15 See *Country Life*, 21 July 1928.

16 See Timothy Mowl, 'Antiquaries, Theatre and Early Mediaevalism' in Christopher Ridgway and Robert Williams (eds.) *Sir John Vanburgh and Landscape Architecture 1690– 1730*, Stroud, 2000, pp.71-92.

17 A term used contemporaneously by Horace Walpole.

18 These houses were first brought to my attention in the early 1980s by Roger White. They all have details borrowed from Batty *Langley's Antient Architecture Restored and Improved* of 1741-2 (re-issued as *Gothic Architecture* in 1747), hence the common use of the descriptive term 'Gothick'. Church House, Belbroughton and Tudor House at Chaddesley Corbett are others of this regional type.

19 WRO, 7335/155.

20 For the restoration see Jeffrey Haworth & Gervase Jackson-Stops, *Hanbury Hall, Worcestershire*, National Trust, 2005, pp.30-5.

21 George London's plan for this feature is annotated with vistas to the Malverns, Berrow Hill, Woodberry Hill, Abberley, the Brown Clee, Titterstone Clee, Kinver Edge, the Clents, the Lickeys and several church steeples.

22 See Catherine Gordon, *The Coventrys of Croome*, Chichester, 2000, to which I am much indebted for the biographical information on the family.

23 Illustrated in Gordon, *The Coventrys*, fig.36 on p.76.

24 Ibid., p.77, citing Antony Archives, CVA/AA/3.

25 This view, unsigned and undated, is in the Croome Estate Office. I am most grateful to the Croome Trustees and to their archivist, Jill Tovey, for allowing me access to the Croome archives. The view is illustrated in Gordon, *The Coventrys*, plate 14 on p. 43.

26 Gordon, *The Coventrys*, p.77, citing Antony Archives, CVE/Z/10.

27 Ibid., p.77, citing Antony Archives, CVE/Z/10.

28 Ibid.

29 Gordon, *The Coventrys*, p.78. The plan is preserved in the Croome Estate Office. It is thought to be by John Doharty Junior and of the early 1750s.

30 Gordon, *The Coventrys*, p.78, citing Antony Archives, CVA/II3/22 & 27.

31 A design for the stables was submitted by Francis Smith of Warwick: Gordon, *The Coventrys*, p.78.

3 The earl, the landscaper and a morass

1   From the Trust's current promotional leaflet.

2   Pirton is shown on Mark Pierce's 1623 survey at Croome Estate Office; the map is illustrated in Gordon, *The Coventrys*, colour plate IX.

3   Gordon, *The Coventrys*, p.103.

4   Ibid., colour plate XI.

5   See Timothy Mowl, 'Rococo and later landscaping at Longleat', *Garden History*, vol.23, part 1 (Summer, 1995), pp.56-66.

6   Preserved in the Croome Estate Office and illustrated in Gordon, *The Coventrys*, plate 68 on p.121.

7 First mentioned to me by Jill Tovey.

8 W.S. Lewis (ed.), *The Yale Edition of Horace Walpole's Correspondence*, 48 vols., New Haven & London (1937-83), 9, p.237.

9 Gordon, *The Coventrys*, p.104.

10 Ibid., p.104. The Bridge was illustrated in Halfpenny's *Improvements in Architecture and Carpentry* of 1754.

11 John Broome's survey of Croome drawn in 1763 shows that Brown clumped not only the drive, but also Pirton park with exact geometrical circles of trees; see Gordon, *The Coventrys*, plate 67 on p.120.

12 Gordon, *The Coventrys*, p.95, quoting from a Horace Walpole letter to Horace Mann of 27 July 1752.

13 Ibid., p.124.

14 Ibid., plates 72-3 & 74.

15 The stucco of the interior was modelled by Francesco Vassalli in 1761.

16 Wyatt's drawing for a 'Saxon Hexagon Tower' is in the Croome Estate Office; it owes something to an engraving of the keep at Orford Castle, Suffolk, in William King's *Observations on Ancient Castles* of 1783.

17 For the Wilson painting see Gordon, *The Coventrys*, colour plate XIX.

18 See Mark Laird, *The Flowering of the Landscape Garden 1720-1800* (University of Pennsylvania Press, Phildelphia, 1999).

19 Gordon, *The Coventrys*, plates 77-78.

20 The Countess Barbara seems to have taken the Grotto into her particular care. She ordered the 'Specimens of Petrifactions' from Derbyshire in 1783, and helped to install them (Gordon, *The Coventrys*, p.99).

21 There is a 1796 drawing for this by Wyatt in the Croome Estate Office.

22 The Adam design for this at the Croome Estate Office dates from 1766, though the building was not completed until 1772.

23 An Adam letter of 19 September 1765 refers to a 'Drawing of the Ruin for a visto' from the house; the Castle was built between 1766 and 1767 (Gordon, *The Coventrys*, p.121).

4 William Shenstone – bad poet, great gardener

1 See particularly Christopher Gallagher, 'The Leasowes: A History of the Landscape', *Garden History*, vol.24, part 2 (Winter, 1996), pp.201-20, John Reily, 'Shenstone's Walks: The Genesis of The Leasowes', *Apollo*, September 1979, pp.202-9 and the *New Arcadian Journal*, vol.53/54 (2002): 'Arcadian Greens Rural – The Leasowes, Hagley, Enville, Little Sparta'. For Thomas Jefferson's debt to The Leasowes in the planning of his landscape at Monticello, see Paul Underwood, 'Monticello, The Ferme Ornée', HND in Landscape Design and Construction, University of Glamorgan, March 2005.

2 Marjorie Williams (ed.), *The Letters of William Shenstone* (Oxford, 1939), pp.401-2. The letter sounds disenchanted: 'I am given to understand that I may exepct a visit this summer from the Bishop of Worcester; from Lord Ward, Lord Coventry, and Lord Guernsey. – it may be so; but honours of *this sort*, which would formerly have affected me, perhaps *too* deeply, have now lost much of their wonted poignancy....an hour or two's interview with you or Mr. Graves outweighs the arrival of the whole British Peerage'.

3 Williams, *Shenstone*, p.197: Shenstone to Lady Luxborough, 3 June 1749.

4 Ibid: 'What do you think, Madam, of my publishing verses once a week upon my Skreens or Garden-Seats, for ye Amusement of my good Friends ye Vulgar? The Verses for ye present week are publish'd in Virgil's Grove, Rue de Virgile'.

5 Williams, *Shenstone*, p.159, Shenstone to Lady Luxborough: 'I am going to procure a Convex Glass to see Landskips with, & to have it fitted up by a Joiner in my Neighbourhood'.

6 Ibid., p.159: 'Some Means of excluding ye Light seems obviously requisite. A Coach *may* be darken'd & so it may be us'd upon ye Road'.

7 See Patrick Eyres, 'An Overview of Ian Hamilton Finlay's Little Sparta', *New Arcadian Journal*, vol.53/54 (2002), pp.110–14; also Yves Abrioux & Stephen Bann, *Ian Hamilton Finlay: A visual primer*, 1992.

8 Williams, *Shenstone*, p.559.

9 Ibid., p,563: Shenstone to Thomas Percy, 1 October 1760.

10 Ibid., p.193: Shenstone to Lady Luxborough, 14 May 1749. Her husband had put her away on a modest allowance supposedly for her relations with the writer, John Dalton, tutor to Lord Beauchamp.

11 Ibid., p.199: Shenstone to Lady Luxborough, 6 June 1749.

12 Ibid., p.187: Shenstone to Lady Luxborough, 7 April 1749.

13 Ibid., p.197: Shenstone to Lady Luxborough, 3 June 1749.

14 Ibid., p.156.

15 Ibid., p.112: Shenstone to unknown correspondent, 20 September 1747.

16 J. Dodsley, *The Works in Verse and Prose of William Shenstone Esq.*, 2 vols., third ed., 1768, 2, pp.287–316: 'A Description of the Leasowes'.

17 Ibid., 2, p.311.

18 Ibid., 2, p.295.

19 Ibid., pp.295–6.

20 His obituary is given in the *Gentleman's Magazine* for 19 July 1742.

21 Williams, *Shenstone*, p.56: Shenstone to Richard Jago, July 1742.

22 Dodsley, *The Works*, 2, p.294.

23 Ibid., p.293.

24 Ibid., 2, p.314.

25 Williams, *Shenstone*, p.106: Shenstone to Richard Graves, 1746.

26 Ibid.

27 Dodsley, *The Works*, 2, pp.315–6.

28 Ibid., 2, p.312.

29 Ibid.

30 Ibid., 2, p.317.

31 Ibid., 2, p.307.

32 Ibid., 2, p.298.

33 Ibid., 2, pp.298–9.

34 Ibid., 2, p.297.

35 Quoted in Harry Gilonis, 'Emblematical and Expressive: the gardenist modes of William Shenstone and Ian Hamilton Finlay', *New Arcadian Journal*, vol.53/54 (2002), pp.86–106; pp.91–2.

36 Ibid., p.11 with an illustration.

37 Quoted by Reily, *Apollo*, September 1979, p.203.

5 Lyttelton's Hagley and the 'true rust of the Barons' wars'

1 Williams, *Shenstone*, p.215: 'The poor Summer-House was, as it were ye Scape-Goat, which suffer'd for all the Blunders I had committed else-where. I believe yr Ladyship is my witness that I thought it bad, & talk'd of pulling it down long ago – but many things may be said in behalf of *me* tho' not of it. I built it merely as a *Study*, without regarding it as an *object*.

2 Ibid., p.244.

3 Lewis, *Correspondence*, 35, p.148: Walpole to Richard Bentley, September 1753. My thanks also to Joyce Purnell for organising access to the park.

4 J. Cartwright (ed.), *The Travels through England of Dr Richard Pococke 1750-57*, 2 vols. (Camden Society, 1888-9), vol.1, pp.223-30 & vol.2, pp.233-5.

5 For a rudimentary but quite useful map of the park see Michael Cousins, 'William Shesntone: Jealous of Hagley', *New Arcadian Journal*, vol.53/54 (2002), pp.60-73; p.71.

6 See J. Mordaunt Crook, *The Greek Revival: Neo-Classical Attitudes in British Architecture 1760-1870*, 1995 edition, pp.96-7 & plate 48; see also David Watkin, *Athenian Stuart: Pioneer of the Greek Revival*, 1982, pp.23-5 who cites a letter from Lyttelton to Mrs Elizabeth Montagu of October 1758: '[Stuart] is going to embellish one of the Hills with a true Attick building, a Portico of six pillars, which will make a fine effect to my new house, and command a most beautiful view of the country' (p.97).

7 See Michael Cousins, 'Athenian Stuart's Doric Porticoes', *Georgian Group Journal*, vol.xiv (2004), pp.48-54. I am grateful to Michael Cousins for bringing this to my attention.

8 Pope's Urn originally stood here.

9 Shenstone records in a letter to Lady Luxborough of 16 June 1748 that 'Mr Lyttelton has near finish'd one side of his Castle. It consists of one entire Tow'r, & three Stumps of Towers, with a ruin'd Wall betwixt them': Williams, *Shenstone*, p.147.

10 Lilian Dickins & Mary Stanton (eds.), *An Eighteenth-Century Correspondence*, 1910, p.135.

11 The tallest tower originally had a reception room on the top storey and the remainder was used as a lodge by the keeper. The listing of two tables in the 'Slaughterhouse' suggests that the keeper slaughtered and dressed deer here. Information from Jennifer Meir.

12 See Timothy Mowl & Philip White, 'A folly from the brush of a folly builder', *Follies*, no.5 (Winter, 2005), pp.1-4; see also Michael Cousins, 'The Sham Ruin, Hagley, Hereford & Worcester', *Follies*, no.10:1 (Summer, 1998), pp.3-4.

13 Cartwright, *Pococke*, 1, p.225.

14 Williams, *Shenstone*, p.114: Shenstone to Richard Jago, 17 September 1747: 'They are going to build a Rotund to terminate ye visto at Hagley'.

15 In addition to the letter books at Hagley, there are some le tters between Lyttelton and Sanderson Miller in the Warwickshire County Record Office, CR125B/348: Lyttelton to Miller, 1 June 1749. I owe this reference to Dianne Barre. This, and other Miller letters, are printed in an abridged form in Dickins & Stanton, *Correspondence*.

16 Ibid., CR125B/350: Lyttelton to Miller, 18 July 1749: 'I forget now how many Chairs are wanting for the Castle; but how can I bespeak them without the model you drew for them? You know they are not to be common chairs, but of a Gothick form.... There is no manner of need of my seeing the Painted Glass, you have been so good to send for the Castle, before it is putt up'. I owe this reference to Dianne Barre.

17 Ibid.

18 Ibid.

19 From George Lyttelton's letter books at Hagley Hall. I owe this reference to Dianne Barre.

20 Subsequent quotations come from Cartwright, *Pococke*, 1, pp.223-30.

21 Lewis, *Correspondence*, 35, p.148-9: Walpole to Richard Bentley, September 1753.

6 Hermit-hollowed, Gothick-castled, Brownian grand

1 Cartwright, *Pococke*.

2 See Paul Stamper, *Historic Parks & Gardens of Shropshire*, Shrewsbury, 1996, pp.51-3; also David Watkin, *The English Vision: The Picturesque in Architecture, Landscape and Garden Design*, 1982, pp.73-5.

3 Richard Lockett, *A Survey of Historic Parks and Gardens in Worcestershire* (Hereford and Worcester Gardens Trust, 1997).

4 For these buildings see Ray Desmond, *The History of the Royal Botanic Gardens Kew*, 1995, pp.13–18.

5 *VCH*, 4, p.158.

6 See OS Landranger, Sheet 150. Lockett, *Survey* records a medieval deer park at Wadborough; there is still a 'Deerfold Wood' to the south-east of Wadborough Manor.

7 Bodleian Library, Oxford, Gough Maps 33, fol.70r. Stukeley published an engraving taken from the sketch in his *Itinerarium Curiosum* of 1724, vol.1, plates 13 & 14.

8 Bodleian Library, Oxford, Gough Maps 33, fol.68v. The engraving was later published in Nash's *Worcestershire*.

9 Habington, *Worcestershire Historical Society*, 2, p.17.

10 Ibid.

11 *VCH*, 4, p.231.

12 Nash, *Worcestershire*, 2, p.48.

13 Bodleian Library, Oxford, Gough Maps 33, fol.70v.

14 WRO, 705:550/5723.

15 Information taken from a pamphlet in the church written by Andrew Wehner.

16 It was green when I inspected it in the early 1980s; the house has now changed hands and I have not seen it since.

17 WRO, 1947/2. The plan also shows a 'pool' up to the north above the stables. This no longer exists.

18 *VCH*, 3, p.34. If it was not Hellier, then the next likely owner to have remodelled the house was Thomas Burne junior, in residence in 1786.

19 Pevsner, *Worcestershire*, p.113.

20 WRO, 5403/10. See also Nicholas Kingsley, 'The Work of Anthony Keck', *Country Life*, 20 & 27 October 1988.

21 I am most grateful to Mike Pengelly for allowing me access to the grounds, and to John Comins for guiding me around with the Windsor-Clive family members and for sharing with me his knowledge of the estate. I am also indebted to the meticulously researched conservation plan prepared by Parklands Consortium Limited, 2001.

22 The earldom of Plymouth had become extinct in 1843. Lord Windsor came of age, inheriting enormous wealth, in 1878.

23 See Michael Hall, 'Hewell Grange, Worcestershire', *Country Life*, 7 October 1993.

24 WRO, 970:51. 128, BA 11301 (1), Photocopy of the Red Book, f.3.

25 Ibid., plate XIX.

26 Ibid., f.9.

27 Ibid., f.2.

28 Ibid., plate III; see Uvedale Price, *An Essay on the Picturesque*, 1794, p.28.

29 WRO, Red Book, f.3.

30 The facing sandstone was brought by canal from Cheshire.

31 Plate V.

32 See Andor Gomme, *Smith of Warwick: Francis Smith, Architect and Master Builder* (Stamford, 2000), p.532.

33 WRO, Red Book, f.9. One of Brown's followers, Nathaniel Richmond, was employed at Hewell in 1770, but most likely for the design of a new hot house rather than any major landscaping activity. See David Brown, 'Nathaniel Richmond (1724–1784), "Gentleman Improver"', PhD thesis, University of East Anglia, 2000, p.119.

34 Brown was paid £700 in that period. See the Parklands Consortium Survey which cites the Plymouth Estate Rentals and General Accounts in the Glamorgan Record Office and Lewis Windsor's bank account at Hoare's Bank (vol.1, pp.10–13). I am

grateful to John Comins for making this available for study.

35 Williams, *Shenstone*, p.384: Shenstone to Lady Luxborough, 11 November 1753.
36 Ibid., p.392: Shenstone to Richard Jago, 29 January 1754.
37 Ibid.
38 Parklands Survey, 1, pp.11–12.
39 Although Repton does not mention the dam in his Red Book, the planting is in his spirit.
40 See H. Avray Tipping, *Country Life*, 17 & 24 March 1917.
41 The deer park was created by grant of 1275. Its main feature is Kyre Pool, a 500m-long piece of water in the northern sector.
42 From a letter of June 1784 in Hereford Record Office; information supplied by David Whitehead for the Register of Historic Parks and Gardens in Worcestershire and quoted therein.
43 Stamper, *Shropshire*, p.57.

7 Bonaparte, Mountnorris and gardens on the cusp

1 Richard Varden, together with J. Varden, perhaps his brother, exhibited designs for Arley Castle at the Royal Academy in 1843.
2 Napoleon dropped the 'u' in 'Buonaparte' in order to claim the ancestry of a noble Tuscan family spelt Bonaparte. For biographical details on Lucien see Lucien Bonaparte, *Memoirs of the Private and Political Life of Lucien Bonaparte, Prince of Canino*, 2 vols., 1818.
3 Ibid., 1, p.165.
4 Ibid. The *Memoirs* read at times like a script for the *Godfather* films.
5 'Retire miserable wretch!', Napoleon told him, 'go to your living, and there await the effects of my just wrath': Bonaparte, *Memoirs*, 1, p.174.
6 *Charlemagne: ou l'église deliverée.* The mere title had infuriated his elder brother.
7 WRO, Prattinton microfilm, I.xi; cited in Lockett, *Survey*, p.247.
8 Bonaparte, *Memoirs*, 2, p.65.
9 Ibid., 2, p.72, footnote.
10 Colvin, *Dictionary*, p.1009.
11 I am most grateful to Dick Hickton for providing a copy of the lithograph of Thorngrove drawn by Varden and produced by G. Hullmandells. Dick and June Hickton have been resident for 12 years and are responsible for the immaculate condition of the house and grounds. The view and plan must date from post-1835 when Varden purchased the practice of a retiring Worcester architect; see Colvin, *Dictionary*, p.1009.
12 Viscount Valentia published his three volume *Travels* in 1809.
13 Nigel Goodman, *The Gardens of Arley* (First magazine, 2003), p.3.
14 For extracts of these letters see Goodman, *Gardens of Arley*, p.27.
15 I am most grateful to Nigel Goodman for guiding me around this private area of the estate.
16 Robert Woodward junior's 'Hortus Arleyensis' of 1907 lists 111 specimen trees in Naboth's Vineyard; information from Goodman, *Gardens of Arley*, p.16. See also *Arley Arboretum, Worcestershire* (privately printed, 1999).
17 I am grateful to Michael Darvill for guiding me expertly around the Arboretum.

8 Great trees and artificial stones – the county's Gardenesque

1 Colvin, *Dictionary*, pp.1031–2: 'By 1805 his practice as a landscape-gardener was reported to be "all over England"'.

2 The Marchioness had originally commissioned John Nash who, between 1807 and 1808, produced watercolours, preserved at the house, for the new Court, gardens, park and the entrance lodge on the Worcester road. Due to pressure of work in London, Nash had to decline the commission. For an illustration of one of the Nash proposals see Arthur Oswald, 'Ombersley Court, Worcestershire – III', *Country Life*, 16 January 1953.

3 Information from a memorandum on the house and garden by the present Lord Sandys. I am most grateful to Lord Sandys for a personally conducted tour of the estate.

4 WRO, 1294: *c.*1810 Parish Map, and WRO, 8217/5: 1801 rough plan.

5 Webb's alterations are also shown on a survey by 'Mr Wardmore' of 1811 preserved at the house.

6 See Timothy Mowl, 'The Williamane – Architecture for the Sailor King', *Georgian Group Symposium: Late Georgian Classicism*, 1987, pp.92-106.

7 'Hadsor, Droitwich, The Seat of Lady Hindlip', *Country Life*, 17 August 1901. I am much indebted to Jane Bradney's researches on Hadzor, which inform this section.

8 Birmingham City Record Office, MS 3102/C/D/10/55/41. Information from Jane Bradney.

9 For Shrubland Park see Tom Williamson, *Suffolk's Gardens & Parks: Designed Landscapes from the Tudors to the Victorians* (Bollington, Macclesfield, 2000), pp.122-29.

10 Royal Institute of British Architects, Drawings Collection, VOS/100/125.

11 See particularly Robinson's *Designs for Ornamental Villas, and Wetten's Designs for Villas in the Italian Style of Architecture* of 1830.

12 *Country Life*, 17 August 1901.

13 I am indebted to John Comins for information on the Old Rectory.

14 Pevsner, *Worcestershire*, p.150.

15 WRO, 5064/15: 1827 Survey of Evesham by Nathaniel Izod.

16 The house is now Bredon School.

17 Pevsner, *Worcestershire*, p.174.

18 For the architectural development of the house and its gardens see the admirable English Heritage guidebook: *Witley Court and Gardens*, 2003. See also Shirley Evans, *Nesfield's Monster Work: The Gardens of Witley Court* (Great Witley, 1994).

19 See Evans, *Nesfield's Monster Work* for an informed introduction to the man and his activity. Mrs Evans has almost completed (Spring 2006) a PhD thesis on Nesfield (Falmouth College of Art).

20 For illustrative coverage of Nesfield's parterres see the English Heritage guidebook, pp.14-16.

21 Ibid., p.11.

22 There was, however, a Kitchen Garden on this side before 1793; see Lockett, *Survey*, p.267.

23 Ibid., p.13.

24 The Lodge is illustrated in the Witley Court guidebook, p.20. William Shenstone saw it in November 1762: Williams, *Shenstone*, p.643: Shenstone to Richard Dodsley, 20 November 1762: 'About a Week ago, I paid a Visit of two or three Days, which I had long promised to Lord Foley...The two Things at present remarkable are, his *Lodge* and his *Chapel*. The Portico of the former, (designed by *FLEETCROFT*) affords three different and striking Prospects.

25 WRO, 4600/160 ii; cited by Lockett, *Survey*, p.1.

26 Quoted in the Historic Gardens Register.

27 Early postcards show the original planting to have been much more sedate with few flowers.

28 See John de la Cour, *Madresfield* (guidebook, no date), p.34. For the history of the house and grounds see Clive Aslet, 'Madresfield Court, Worcestershire – I, II & III', *Country Life*, 16, 23 & 30 October 1980.

29 I am indebted to Peter Hughes for arranging a private visit to Madresfield and to Lady Morrison for allowing me access. Tim West was helpful in identifying the more obscure specimen trees in the ground

30 See Edward Hubbard, *The Work of John Douglas*, 1991.

31 WRO, BA 11, 301 (VI): *The General History of Hewell Grange 1857-1932* containing extracts from the writings of Robert George Windsor-Clive, first Earl of Plymouth in the new creation (1905), privately printed.

32 Quoted in the Parklands Survey, 1, p.19.

33 Ibid., 1, p.17.

9 Alfred the Uncertain and the American invasion of Broadway

1 Writing an essay for the catalogue of a late Parsons exhibition in 1891 the American novelist, Henry James, actually suggested that love of old gardens might fill the spiritual vacuum post-Darwin. See Anne Helmreich, *The English Garden & National Identity*, Cambridge, 2002, p.32.

2 For a convincing account of this mood and its consequences see Mark Girouard, *The Return to Camelot: Chivalry and the English Gentleman*, New Haven & London, 1981.

3 I am much indebted to Marion Mako's thorough and extremely informative dissertation on Parsons (1847-1920): 'Painting in Three Dimensions: Alfred Parsons at Broadway 1885-1920', MA, University of Bristol, September 2004 for the biographical material here. Marion kindly effected introductions to the owners in Broadway and accompanied me on visits to their gardens. See also Nicole Milette, 'Landscape Painter as Landscape Gardener, the Case of Alfred Parsons RA', University of York, Institute of Advanced Architectural Studies, 1997, and Alan Crawford, 'New Life for an Artist's Village: Broadway, Worcestershire - 1', *Country Life*, 24 January 1980.

4 In his *The English Flower Garden* of 1883 Robinson praised Parsons along with Corot, Turner and Crome as artists whom gardeners should copy.

5 Mako, 'Painting in Three Dimensions', p.8. footnote 23, quoting E.V. Lucas, *Edwin Austin Abbey, Royal Academician, The Record of his Life and Work*, 2 vols., 1921.

6 Ibid., plate 35, from Worcestershire Record Office, x705:1235,11302 (lxi).

7 'Our Artists in England', *Harper's Magazine*, 1889, p.58.

8 Ibid.

9 *Notes on Japan*, with illustrations by the author, 1896.

10 See Gordon, *The Coventrys*, p.131.

11 For Blomfield and Robinson see David Ottewill, *The Edwardian Garden*, 1989, particularly chapters 1 & 4, and Helmreich, *English Garden*, chapters 2 & 5. See also Richard A. Fellows, *Sir Reginald Blomfield: An Edwardian Architect*, 1985.

12 See Nicholas Alfrey, Stephen Daniels & Martin Postle (eds.), *Art of the Garden: The Garden in British Art, 1800 to the Present Day*, Tate exhibition catalogue, 2004, catalogue entry 75.

13 William Robinson, *The Wild Garden*, fourth edition, Oxford, 1894 (Scolar Press facsimile, Ilkley, 1977), plate opposite p.134.

14 Ibid., pp.2-3.

15 Ibid., p.210.

16 Ibid., p.211.

17 Ibid., p.271.

18 Ibid., plates opposite p.258, 268 & 262 respectively.

19 Ibid., p.184.

20 Ibid., p.115, p.100 & headpiece on p.12 respectively.

21 Ibid., p.234.

22 Ibid., p.45 & p.257 respectively.

23 Ibid., p.137.

24 Ibid., p.131.

25 The second, posthumous edition appeared in 1892 to coincide with Blomfield's book.

26 John D. Sedding, *Garden-Craft Old and New*, 1892, pp.162-3.

27 See Mowl, *Cornwall*, pp.120-22.

28 Pictures of the garden in its prime appeared in *Country Life*, 14 January 1911.

29 I am most grateful to Lord Birdwood for allowing me access to the garden.

30 'Orange Lilies' was the Diploma painting that Parsons submitted to the Royal Academy in 1911 when he was made a full Academician. See Alfrey, *Art of the Garden*, catalogue entry 82.

31 Quoted in Mako, 'Painting in Three Dimensions', from Lucas, *Edwin Austin Abbey*, 1, p.158.

32 Arthur Quiller Couch, *The Warwickshire Avon*, 1892, p.28.

33 Ibid., p.53.

34 Mako, 'Painting in Three Dimensions', plate 20.

35 Quiller Couch, *Warwickshire Avon*, pp.88-9.

36 I am most grateful to Michael and Jill de Navarro for their kind hospitality at Court Farm.

37 Mary Anderson, *A Few More Memories*, 1936, p.256, quoted in Mako, 'Painting in Three Dimensions', p.54.

38 Ibid., p.255, quoted in Mako, 'Painting in Three Dimensions', p.57.

39 I am most grateful to Kay Haslem for allowing me access to the garden at Luggers Hill (now renamed Luggers Hall).

40 Mako, 'Painting in Three Dimensions', plate 93.

41 See Mowl, *Wiltshire*, pp.150-2. Interestingly Parsons made no attempt there to create enclosed garden rooms, though he did plant a massive yew house, much like one at Rous Lench.

10 Edwardian gardens and the influence of The Souls

1 See Clive Aslet's three articles on Madresfield in *Country Life*, 16, 23 & 30 October 1980.

2 *Country Life*, 30 October 1980.

3 Whilst I am most grateful to Lady Morrison for allowing me to walk the grounds, she did not give me access to the family archives.

4 Register of Historic Parks & Gardens, citing R. Sidwell, *West Midlands Gardens*, 1981.

5 See David Ottewill, *The Edwardian Garden*, 1989, pp.15-17.

6 Jane Abdy & Charlotte Gere, *The Souls*, 1984, opposite pages 117 (contemporary photograph) & 123 (Burne-Jones painting).

7 Laid out in 1888 by the Head Gardener, Edward Ward: WRO, BA 11488 705: 1242, parcel 13 (xi) 7. Parklands Survey, fig.23.

8 Parklands Survey, fig.24.

9 Quoted in the Parklands Survey, 1, p.21.

10 Designed by Bodley & Garner and built in 1891.

11 Much of this information on the late nineteenth-century work in the gardens is taken from Alberta, Lady Plymouth, *Robert, Earl of Plymouth 1857-1923* (privately printed, 1923).

12 *VCH: Worcestershire*, 3, p.498.

13 See Timothy Mowl, *Historic Gardens of Wiltshire*, Stroud, 2004, pp.153-6.

14 1884 OS map, 25 miles to the inch.

15 WRO, b 705:300, 1751/8, 1775.

16 *Country Life*, 16 September 1899.

17 Carved on the Staircase Hall cornice and quoted by Aslet in *Country Life*, 30 October 1980.
18 The Mercury statues do not feature in the 1899 *Country Life* article.
19 In 1782 Nash mentioned a 'summer-house at the top of the garden', probably within this yew structure (2, p.84).
20 Like everyone else, Lockett hedges his bets on garden dating, but quotes the *VCH* as claiming that the Revd. Dr Chafy-Chafy laid it all out, without giving any documentary evidence to support the assertion (p.222).
21 *Country Life*, 15 July 1916.
22 I am grateful to Peter Middlemiss, Warden of Holland House, for information on the building and the grounds. I did not meet him on site, but a follow-up visit was made by Marion Mako, who undertook some further research on the house and gardens.
23 Letter to Mrs R.E. Ducie from Margaret Richardson, Deputy Curator of the RIBA Drawings Collection, 26 June 1979 (RIBA MS collection); information from Marion Mako via Peter Middlemiss.
24 The inscription is recorded in Christine Collins, *Building Piece by Peace* (privately printed), available at Holland House.
25 Jane Brown, *Gardens of a Golden Afternoon*, 1985.
26 WRO, S 705:114, BA 974/1: 'An Exact Map of the Castle and Manor of Holt', by John Doharty junior of 1745.
27 WRO, 4000/853.
28 Lockett, *Survey*, p.61. A record of her relations with 'E V' would be most revealing.
29 WRO, b 705:1041.

11 The conservative modernism of a yeoman-bourgeois county

1 The Gazebo is a copy of one at Westall Hill Manor, Fulbrook, just north of Burford in Oxfordshire.
2 Brenda Colvin's Notebook records the Conderton commission (no.199) that she was given through the influence of a Miss Kennedy. Interestingly she also records her Overbury commission (no.201), of December 1933, as having been acquired through Sir Herbert and Mrs Maxwell of Conderton. Information from Trish Gibson.
3 See Arthur Hellyer, 'Colour Harmonies and Rarities: Garden of The Priory, Kemerton, Worcestershire', *Country Life*, 4 September 1986.
4 I am indebted to Matt Darby for showing me his model of the proposed landscape plan and to his father, Adrian, for making available a report of a public enquiry on a right-of-way at Kemerton.
5 The column is a refugee from St Michael's church, Stourport.
6 See 'Walnut-Tree Farm, Castlemorten', *Country Life*, 28 October 1899.
7 The lead figures do not feature in H. Avray Tipping's entry on Spetchley in his *English Gardens*, 1925, pp.325-30, based on his 1916 article for *Country Life*, and the guidebook does not offer a date for them, so I assume they are of recent introduction.
8 See Mowl, *Dorset*, p.166-7.

Gazetteer

The following is a list of gardens of significant historic importance, which are covered in this book and are open to the public.

Abbreviations

NT	National Trust
EH	English Heritage
P	Privately owned but regularly open
NGS	Privately owned but open occasionally as part of the National Gardens Scheme
H/CC	Hotel/Conference Centre
LA	Local Authority
GC/N	Garden Centre/Nursery
M	Museum

Arley Castle Arboretum (P)
Astley Towne House (NGS)
Birtsmorton Court (NGS)
Chateau Impney, Droitwich (H)
Croome Landscape Gardens (NT)
Hagley Hall (P)
Hanbury Hall (NT)
Hartlebury Castle (M)
Harvington Hall (P)
Kyre Park (P)
Kemerton Priory (NGS)

Little Malvern Court (P)
Luggers Hall, Broadway (NGS)
Madresfield Court (P)
Spetchley Park (P)
Stone House Cottage Garden & Nursery (GC/N)
The Leasowes (LA)
Overbury Court (NGS)
Webbs of Wychbold (GC/N)
White House, Dunley (NGS)
Witley Court (EH)

Index

Page numbers in **bold** refer to illustrations and captions